Human Rights and U.S. Foreign Policy

☆

THE MANNING J. DAUER

PRIZE WINNER 1987

☆

Human Rights
and U.S. Foreign Policy
Congress Reconsidered

☆

David P. Forsythe

UNIVERSITY PRESSES OF FLORIDA

University of Florida Press / Gainesville

Second printing, 1989

Material in chapter 3 has appeared in David P. Forsythe, "Congress and Human Rights in U.S. Foreign Policy: The Fate of General Legislation," *Human Rights Quarterly* (August 1987).

Library of Congress Cataloging in Publication Data

Forsythe, David P., 1941–
    Human rights and U.S. foreign policy: Congress reconsidered /
David P. Forsythe.
      p.   cm.
    Bibliography: p.
    Includes index.
    ISBN 0-8130-0885-9 (alk. paper)
    1. Human rights. 2. United States—Foreign relations—1981–
3. Legislative power—United States. 4. Executive power—United
States. I. Title II. Title: Human rights and US foreign policy.
K3240.4.F68   1988
342'.085—dc19   87-21909
[342.285]   CIP

UNIVERSITY PRESSES OF FLORIDA is the central agency for scholarly publishing of the State of Florida's university system, producing books selected for publication by the faculty editorial committees of Florida's nine public universities: Florida A&M University (Tallahassee), Florida Atlantic University (Boca Raton), Florida International University (Miami), Florida State University (Tallahassee), University of Central Florida (Orlando), University of Florida (Gainesville), University of North Florida (Jacksonville), University of South Florida (Tampa), University of West Florida (Pensacola).

ORDERS for books published by all member presses should be addressed to University Presses of Florida, 15 NW 15th Street, Gainesville, FL 32603.

Printed in the U.S.A. on acid-free paper. ∞

For Annette

Contents

The role of Congress is another question. There is no doubt that congressional concerns and pressures have played a very positive role in giving impetus and backing to our efforts to influence other governments' behavior. This congressional pressure can strengthen the hand of the executive branch in its efforts of diplomacy. At the same time, there can be complications if the legislative instrument is too inflexible or heavy-handed, or, even more, if Congress attempts to take on the administrative responsibility for executing policy.

—Secretary of State George Shultz, "Human Rights and the Moral Dimension of U.S. Foreign Policy," in *Current Policy No. 551,* February 22, 1984.

Preface

International human rights can be studied from many different perspectives. The prevalent approach in the United States has been the legal one. Professors of law have been prominent in the study of human rights, and courses dealing with human rights issues are found primarily in law schools. While many legal scholars are active in the political process and understand it well, many studies overemphasize legal obligations, rules, theories, and structure while undervaluing considerations of power and policy. The first objective of this book is to correct that imbalance. The place of human rights in U.S. foreign policy depends mainly on considerations of power and policy and only tangentially on law. In the interplay of politics and law, politics is the more determinative factor. Little is ever done merely because a legal rule requires action, and almost never is anything done merely because a court orders it.

Moreover, many studies of human rights that attempted to place the issues in their proper political context have focused either on international developments (e.g., the United Nations and regional organizations) or on foreign policy as conducted by the executive (e.g., Carter's policy, Reagan's policy). Yet it was Congress, not the Carter administration, that put international human rights back on the foreign policy agenda of the United States. And it was primarily Congress that prevented the Reagan administration from taking the subject off the foreign policy agenda in 1981, as it evidently wished to do. But Congress has been little studied in connection with human rights in U.S. foreign policy. The second objective of this book is to correct that imbalance also.

The third objective of this book is to summarize what Congress has done on human rights in foreign policy from 1973, when a House subcommittee began to put the subject on the contemporary foreign policy agenda, to 1984 and the end of the first Reagan administration. (Events from 1984 to the time of writing in mid-1987 are referred to in passing.) This objective, having to do with descriptive information, is new in two ways. The few published works that track congressional activity are basically legal rather than political—lists of statutes and nothing more (e.g., House Committee on Foreign Affairs, *Human Rights Documents*, Part I, Washington, 1983). In this study, I seek to place the statutes in their political context. Furthermore, I present congressional activity in a policy framework by organizing the analysis of human rights legislation into hortatory, general, country-specific, and function-specific categories.

The fourth objective of this book is to analyze congressional human rights actions in terms of their impact on the executive and on world politics. The two concluding chapters deal with the nature of the congressional process, asking whether congressional concern with human rights is systematic, institutionalized, and predictable. There I propose an answer to the question of whether congressional activity has had an impact on the executive's conduct of diplomacy and, if so, which types of legislation and in what ways. Finally, I broach the question of whether Congress has been wise in its legislation and its actions defensible or commendable and, if so, according to what standards or criteria.

Two aspects of congressional activity on human rights are not analyzed here. No attempt is made to analyze the letters and phone calls by individual members of Congress on human rights matters. There are a great many such efforts in Washington, but there is no way to chart the volume, for no one keeps track of them, or to analyze their impact. When asked about such activity, senators and representatives, with few exceptions, say they have no idea whether their demarches achieve results in most cases.

Nor does this study analyze congressional action on human rights in direct relationship to international human rights treaties, an important and worthwhile subject. Why the Senate finally gave its advice and consent for ratification of the Genocide Convention but failed to do so for the United Nations Covenant on Civil and Political Rights and the United Nations Covenant on Social, Economic, and Cultural Rights is clearly important, and why the Congress has, contrarily, shown so little interest in other international treaties is likewise important. But since there are other studies on these subjects and there is much to analyze on congressional legislative actions involving international human rights, I have directed this study to the latter subject only.

Several grants from the Nebraska Foundation Fund for Research on the U.S. Congress made this study possible by facilitating both some early consideration of the subject and several trips to Washington for interviews. A summer faculty fellowship from the Research Council of the University of Nebraska allowed the preparation of a complete draft during the summer of 1986. Another grant from the Research Council helped with technical preparations.

The director of the Foundation Fund, John Hibbing, a specialist on Congress and associate professor of political science, was most helpful in my work, as was Susan Welch, Regents professor of political science at the University of Nebraska. In particular, chapter 2 on human rights voting in Congress could not have been done as it was without her considerable skills with the computer. See further Forsythe and Welch, "Human Rights Voting in Congress" (full facts of publication appear in the bibliography). William P. Avery, another faculty member at the University of Nebraska, was helpful at an earlier stage of chapter 2, which can be seen in Avery and Forsythe, "Human Rights, National Security, and the U.S. Senate: Who Votes for What, and Why."

In addition to documentary evidence and secondary works, this study is based on interviews in Washington between 1979 and 1986, with some earlier ones dating from the period 1972–74. Three Washingtonians were especially helpful without bearing any responsibility for my statements of fact or interpretation: Margaret "Peggy" Galey, a staff member of the House Foreign Affairs Committee; Mark Tavlarides, staff director of the House Subcommittee on Human Rights and International Organizations; and Frank Sieverts, deputy assistant secretary of state for human rights and humanitarian affairs during the Carter administration. The manuscript, in part or in whole, was read by them and by Cynthia Sprunger, minority staff consultant, House Subcommittee on Human Rights; George Lister, senior policy advisor assigned to the Human Rights Bureau during the Reagan administration; Marilyn Zak and later Travis Horel, coordinators for human rights, U.S. Agency for International Development; Lars Schoultz, professor of political science at the University of North Carolina; Holly Burkehalter, then on the staff of Americas Watch; and Howard Tolley, professor of political science at the University of Cincinnati.

Interviews were not for attribution. In the Department of State they were held with Patricia Derian, John Salzburg, Stephen B. Cohen, Charles Runyon, Roberta Cohen, Gary Mathews, Roger Pilon, James Michael, Ken Peoples, Alan van Edmond, Frank Marlkey, Fred Ashley, and James Montgomery. Both Elliott Abrams and Richard Schifter declined to be interviewed. In the Congress, interviews were held with various staff members of the Senate Foreign Relations Committee and the House Foreign Affairs Committee, including subcommittees. Additional interviews were held in the offices of Senators Lugar, Percy, Zorinsky, Packwood, Wallop, Dodd, Sarbanes, Chiles, McGovern, Stewart, Church, Harkin; and Congressmen Bereuter, Wilson (Texas), Patterson, Fraser, Bonker, Yatron, and Leach. Further interviews were held with officials of private organizations that tracked Congress and human rights, such as Amnesty International, Americas Watch, Washington Office on Latin America, Washington Office on Africa, Americans for Democratic Action, Friends Committee on National Legislation, United Church of Christ, and International Human Rights Law Group.

Most of the processing of the manuscript was done by Debra Dean under the direction of Helen Sexton. They put up with enough technical glitches in the computers and printers of the University of Nebraska Political Science Department to last a lifetime.

The author accepts full responsibility for the contents of the pages that follow.

Chapter 1

Congress and Human Rights Legislation: An Overview

No single prescription can be written to give force to a policy of deeper concern for human rights. . . . The most obvious option is to let the offending country know that human rights violations will cost them something in their relationship with the United States. . . . the steps taken by the United States should apply steadily increasing pressure until the message about human rights gets through to the other government.
The U.S. response in the past has been modest and largely ineffective.
—Donald M. Fraser,
"Freedom and Foreign Policy," 146–47

In the early 1970s, some members of Congress began to feel that American foreign policy under the Nixon-Kissinger team had become divorced from traditional American values. Some said the policy was too Machiavellian and amoral, overly concerned with an impersonal balance of power. Some claimed U.S. policies were too brutal in Southeast Asia or too indifferent to torturers in Latin America. In 1973, these and other critical views converged in a series of hearings held by the usually obscure Subcommittee on International Organizations and Movements (later renamed the Subcommittee on Human Rights and International Organizations) of the House Committee on Foreign Affairs. The Democratic chair of that subcommittee, Minnesota's Donald M. Fraser, was not hesitant to criticize Republican policy, and he chose to frame his criticism in the language of human rights.[1] His efforts gained considerable support.

This concern for the place of human rights in U.S. foreign policy was only part of a growing assertiveness by Congress about many aspects of foreign policy. From 1970 to 1975, Congress ended U.S. involvement in the Vietnam War, passed the War Powers Act over the president's veto, blocked CIA involvement in Angola, instigated an arms embargo against Turkey for its policies in Cyprus, established some control over intelligence activities, and moved in other ways to legislate foreign policy in opposition to an unwilling president. The Watergate scandal further emboldened the legislature. It has been said that the Constitution invites a struggle between the political branches for control of foreign policy; after largely deferring to the executive branch for two decades, Congress accepted that invitation. Human rights lay at the center of its renewed concern,[2] a more durable and troublesome concern than many anticipated.

In the mid-1970s, a shifting and erratic bipartisan majority in both houses of Congress cared little that Kissinger increasingly used the rhetoric of human rights, even of morality, to defend the Republican record.[3] It was equally indifferent when Jimmy Carter later tried to appropriate the language of human rights for his administration.[4] Still later the Reagan administration confronted a Congress insisting on attention to human rights in places like El Salvador and Guatemala, South Africa and Chile, Romania and the Philippines. Between 1973, when Fraser's series of systematic hearings and concluding report drew attention to the issue,[5] and the end of the first Reagan administration in 1984, Congress placed numerous human rights statements on the books. Beyond resolutions in favor of goodness, Congress adopted six potentially important general statutes on human rights. At one time or another it adopted country-specific legislation pertaining to about twenty nations. Periodically it passed specific rules requiring the president to pay detailed attention to a series of functional human rights matters, hoping thereby to ensure that its mandate would be carried out. For more than a decade after the human rights issue resurfaced in American foreign policy, Congress apparently tried to make human rights a major concern of the United States in its international affairs.

It may surprise some to learn that the boundaries of this subject are not clear, that it is not easy to specify precisely the scope of congressional actions on human rights. The United States has taken an essentially unilateral stance on the subject of human rights. It has not ratified the major international treaties on human rights, such as the United Nations Covenant on Civil and Political Rights, the United Nations Covenant on Social, Economic, and Cultural Rights, and the Organization of American States Convention on Human Rights. Therefore one cannot identify legislation pursuant to these major human rights treaties and say simply that this is the corpus of U.S. human rights legislation. Where the United States is a full party to a human rights treaty, as it is to the International Protocol on Refugees, one can do so. Otherwise one must look for U.S. legislation that refers to "internationally recognized human rights" or to specific international instruments (such as the 1948 Universal Declaration of Human Rights) or that encompasses a subject like emigration (which can be inferred to fall clearly within the scope of the international instruments on human rights).[6] This latter guideline allows considerable room for debate as to what constitutes human rights legislation.

For example, a congressional report about human rights lists a number of acts having to do with global hunger and food policy.[7] A close reading of this list, however, coupled with a broader understanding of American approaches to these socioeconomic subjects, leads to the conclusion that Congress has dealt with food policy out of moral concern or for the sake of U.S. political expediency. It has not approached the subject of hunger from the perspective that people have a right to be free from hunger just as they have a right to be free from torture. Congress has endorsed the latter right but never, specifically, the former.

When Congress passed the International Security and Development Cooperation Act of 1981, for example, thus devoting its attention to shortages of food, fuel, and water as well as to sickness and overpopulation, it said:

> The Congress finds that the Nation's understanding of global and national security must be broad enough to include the problems cited in this section, and that adequate protection of the security of the United States requires effective action on these global problems, and in particular on the problems of hunger, disease, and extreme poverty. . . .
>
> The Congress, affirming the value of human life, finds and declares that the elimination of hunger and its causes is of fundamental moral significance and, further, that it is in the political, economic, and security interests of the United States. Therefore, the Congress declares that the elimination of hunger and its causes shall be a primary objective of United States relations with the developing countries.[8]

Nowhere in these or any other statutes does Congress declare that freedom from hunger or malnutrition is an internationally recognized human right.

It may be that Congress does not need to recognize the category of socioeconomic rights in order to take pragmatic steps to alleviate hunger and other economic and social deficiencies. Congress has certainly shown an interest in "basic human needs," in helping to meet at least some of the requirements of "needy people," and in doing something about a number of socioeconomic problems—illiteracy, for example.

It remains incorrect, however, to attribute to Congress a real endorsement of socioeconomic rights, which would smack of socialism, creeping or otherwise. As an aide to a Republican member of Congress said in a 1984 interview, "It is the type of issue that sends moderate Republicans scrambling to the corridors to avoid a vote."

One general phrase in "soft" legislation that seems to endorse the concept of socioeconomic human rights has never led to any follow-up. At one point Congress did adopt—without vote—the following language:

> The Congress declares that the individual liberties, economic prosperity and security of the people of the United States are best sustained and enhanced in a community of nations which respect individual civil and *economic rights*. . . . [emphasis added]
>
> United States development cooperation policy should emphasize four principal goals: . . .
>> (3) the encouragement of development processes in which individual civil and *economic rights* are respected and enhanced. . . . [emphasis added][9]

These references may be intended to refer to a popular American definition of "economic rights"—namely, the right to own private property. The legislative history on this point is unclear.

It is true that the Carter administration, in a general statement of policy that had little bearing on day-to-day activities, endorsed the concept of socioeconomic rights and actually listed them as more important than general political rights.[10] That administration also signed and sent to the Senate the United Nations Covenant on Social, Economic, and Cultural Rights.

But Congress has indicated repeatedly that the phrase "internationally recognized human rights" includes freedom from "torture or cruel, inhumane, or degrading treatment or punishment, prolonged detention without charges and trial, causing the disappearance of persons by the abduction and clandestine detention of those persons, and other flagrant denial of the right to life, liberty, or the security of person." [11]

In another statute, Congress defined the rights at issue as those violated by "a consistent pattern of gross violations of internationally recognized human rights, such as torture or cruel, inhumane, or degrading treatment or punishment, prolonged detention without charges, or other flagrant denial to life, liberty, and the security of person." [12] Congress has never tried to reach an exhaustive definition of "internationally recognized human rights," but its examples of rights covered by that phrase have all been from the civil-political realm.

It is certainly reasonable to consider basic human needs as the political equivalent of fundamental socioeconomic human rights. Yet it is important to note that Congress has chosen to emphasize socioeconomic needs rather than rights, as has the Reagan administration. Indeed, even the Carter administration's *practice* fit the dominant American pattern. [13] Therefore, in the analysis that follows, food policy is not treated as a human rights subject because the dominant American approach (symbolic gestures from the Carter administration notwithstanding) deals with socioeconomic subjects by discretionary, not obligatory, policy responses.

Reasonable observers can also debate whether a statute should be considered human rights legislation when it covers discrimination against American nationals at home or abroad who contract to provide defense items. [14] (I hold that it should not be so considered.) Human rights in American foreign policy is understood in this study to pertain to the rights of foreign nationals and their connection with U.S. policies.

To understand human rights legislation from a political rather than a legal perspective, it is useful to organize it into three broad categories, the last having two subgroups (see table 1.1). By taking the year 1984, we gather a true sample of the congressional process, though some of the legislation has since been changed.

1. *Hortatory statements.* Some congressional statements provide no rationale either for a presidential decision or for subsequent congressional action. In short, these statements become dead letters, typically for a long time. Such congressional statements may be law in the technical sense or they may be nonbinding sense-of-the-Congress reso-

Table 1.1. Types of legislation on human rights (a policy framework, 1984)

1. Hortatory statements

Endorsement and reaffirmation of international human rights in U.S. foreign policy, including economic rights.

No assistance to regimes suppressing rights listed in the Universal Declaration of Human Rights.

United States to disengage from regimes practicing genocide (sense of Congress).

No assistance to go to regimes holding political prisoners (sense of Congress).

2. General norms

No security assistance to regimes displaying a consistent pattern of gross violations of internationally recognized human rights, unless president certifies extraordinary circumstances so required; applies to military training, to transfer of crime control equipment, and to economic support funds.

No economic assistance to regimes displaying a consistent pattern of gross violations of internationally recognized human rights, unless assistance will directly benefit needy people; applies to OPIC insurance and to PL 480 and transfer of agricultural commodities.

U.S. delegations to international financial institutions to use their voice and vote to advance the cause of human rights and to develop standards about meeting basic human needs.

U.S. executive agencies authorized to grant refugee status to persons with a well-founded fear of persecution and not to return refugees to a situation of persecution.

Regimes with nonmarket economies to be denied most-favored-nation trade status and trade credits when they unduly restrict emigration.

U.S. Export-Import Bank to take human rights considerations into account in its policies when such action clearly advances U.S. interests.

3. Specific rules

A. Country-specific

El Salvador	Uganda
Guatemala	Pakistan
Nicaragua	Mexico
Haiti	South Korea
Argentina	
Chile	

Table 1.1—Continued

Soviet Union
Cuba
Laos
Cambodia

B. Function-specific

Creation of Bureau of Human Rights and Humanitarian Affairs in Department of State.

Require Department of State to compile country reports on human rights situation for all members of the United Nations.

Require various executive agencies to report to Congress about their decisions related to human rights.

Creation of Commission on Security and Cooperation in Europe.

Endorsement of interagency coordination of human rights within Department of State (sense of Congress).

Prohibition of U.S. funds for police training, prisons, and internal surveillance and intelligence in foreign countries.

Designation of a minimum amount in Agency for International Development budget for programs to promote civil and political rights.

Special appropriation for the International Committee of the Red Cross and its program for "political" detainees.

Establishment of National Endowment for Democracy.

Link part of U.S. contribution for the Organization of American States to its Human Rights Commission.

Special South African Fund for education and human rights.

Link U.S. participation in UNESCO to free flow of information according to Article 19 of Universal Declaration of Human Rights (sense of Congress) and bar funds to UNESCO if journalists licensed or restricted.

Seek accountability regarding MIAs in Southeast Asia.

NOTE: All references are to laws, unless designated sense of Congress. Dates not given for legislation because amendments changed form at different times.

lutions; politically, they are simply forgotten, as the mentioned endorsement of economic rights has been. Not a single congressional aide interviewed in 1984 was familiar with it.

In 1982, Congress adopted the Foreign Assistance and Related Programs Appropriations Act. Section 511 of the act reads: "Funds appropriated by this Act may not be obligated or expended to provide assistance to any country for the purpose of aiding the efforts of the government of such country to repress the legitimate rights of the population of such country contrary to the Universal Declaration of Human Rights." [15] As of late 1987, no one at either end of Pennsylvania Avenue has paid attention to this section.

In the Bretton Woods Agreement Act, Section 5(b) reads: "It is the sense of the Congress that the Government of the United States should take steps to disassociate itself from any foreign government which engages in the international crime of genocide." [16] Neither Congress nor the executive branch has tried to name such a government, much less disengage from it; in fact, neither branch has paid any attention to this provision of the act.

Section 32 of the Foreign Assistance Act of 1973, one of the first congressional declarations on human rights, stated, "It is the sense of Congress that the President should deny any economic or military assistance to the government of any foreign country which practices the internment or imprisonment of that country's citizens for political purposes." [17] But the Nixon administration did not have the same "sense" as Congress. International law contained no definition of political imprisonment, and to follow congressional guidelines would have terminated virtually all U.S. economic and military assistance programs. Even Amnesty International preferred to use the term "prisoner of conscience" to try to define "political prisoner." [18] For these and perhaps other reasons, this sense-of-the-Congress resolution died an early and generally unlamented death.

One can see, then, that certain congressional statements about human rights evaporate into the political atmosphere. The product of transitory sentiments in the Congress, they fail to influence public policy, although the ones in statutory form are "on the books" for enterprising politicians, bureaucrats, activists, and lawyers to use. [19]

2. *General legislation.* Some congressional statements are noted carefully by executive branch officials or members of Congress. Invariably they are laws, or, at some point, they take that form. Because they are general and generate some degree of continuing congressional interest, Congress subsequently strives to oversee executive interpretations (or evasions) of them. Three, perhaps four, such general laws lay at the core of the human rights debate in Washington politics from 1973

to 1984, and several more tangential ones fit into this second category as well.

In 1974, following the Fraser hearings, Congress expressed its belief that U.S. security assistance should be linked to human rights concerns. As in its early statement about political prisoners, Congress did not bind the president legally but sent a political signal that more attention should be given to human rights in regimes receiving U.S. security assistance. Given the reluctance of Secretary of State Kissinger to acknowledge congressional signals on this subject, and despite the election of Jimmy Carter, Congress made this linkage legally binding in 1978 by revising the long and complex section of the Foreign Assistance Act of 1961 (as amended) known as Section 502B. One key part of this law states: "No security assistance may be provided to any country the government of which engages in a consistent pattern of gross violations of internationally recognized human rights."[20] Another part states that the president may certify in a report to Congress that "extraordinary circumstances exist warranting provision of such assistance." This law, among other things, extends the ban beyond strict military assistance to include law enforcement assistance, domestic intelligence assistance, transfer of crime control equipment, military training (IMET, or international military education and training), and economic support funds (ESF). The basic motivation behind this law is stated in the law itself: "The President is directed to formulate and conduct international security assistance programs of the United States in a manner which will promote and advance human rights and avoid identification of the United States, through such programs, with governments which deny to their people internationally recognized human rights." Section 502B has been one of the primary congressional statements about human rights and American foreign policy, even though by 1984 no administration and no Congress had publicly and formally identified a regime that showed a consistent pattern of gross violations, nor had the executive branch certified an exception for reasons of extraordinary circumstances.

The 1974 Congress also directed its human rights concern toward development assistance. Unlike security assistance, the provision on developmental economic assistance was made legally binding from the start. Its primary sponsor, Congressman Tom Harkin (D., Iowa), submitted a strong, if general, amendment on the floor of the House, which picked up support not only from persons interested in human rights but also from those interested in reducing foreign aid. What became known as the Harkin amendment, or Section 116 of the Foreign Assistance Act of 1961 (as amended), reads (as of 1984) in part:

> No assistance may be provided under this part to the government of any country which engages in a consistent pattern of gross violations of internationally recognized human rights, including torture or cruel, inhuman, or degrading treatment or punishment, prolonged detention without charges, causing the disappearance of persons by the abduction and clandestine detention of those persons, or other flagrant denial of the right of life, liberty, and the security of persons unless such assistance will directly benefit the needy people in such country.[21]

This Harkin amendment became so well known to persons involved with human rights in Washington that it became a generic term. Members of Congress proposed or threatened to propose various "Harkin amendments" as a way of linking human rights to international financial institutions, American bilateral financial dealings, government-sponsored insurance for American exporters and investors, and so forth. Later legislation made Section 116 applicable also to the transfer of agricultural products under the "food for peace program (PL 480)[22] and to U.S. insurance (via the Overseas Private Investment Corporation, or OPIC) for American investors abroad.[23] The amendment as revised over the years became long and complex, but its intent was clear. Where there was a consistent pattern of gross violations of human rights, the United States should not encourage or reinforce such violations by economic assistance promoting general economic growth that would benefit the repressive regime. Assistance that would directly benefit the needy section of the population, however, could continue. As we will see, this legislation did affect the deliberations of the executive branch, and the U.S. Agency for International Development, in particular, did on occasion differentiate developmental aid from assistance to the most needy.

With the election of Jimmy Carter in 1976, one might have thought that the Democrat-controlled Congress would withdraw from its human rights activism since the new president had promised to give attention to human rights as a central part of his foreign policy. Some

Democrats like Fraser did so for a time but only in part. Not only was Section 502B revised in 1978 to put more pressure on the president to link human rights to security assistance, but also a third general human rights statute was put on the books in 1977 after much wrangling and over initial opposition from the new administration. In the International Financial Assistance Act of 1977, Congress stipulated in subsection (a):

> The United States Government, in connection with its voice and vote in the [international financial institutions], shall advance the cause of human rights, including by seeking to channel assistance toward countries other than those whose governments engage in—
>
> (1) a consistent pattern of gross violations of internationally recognized human rights, such as torture or cruel, inhumane, or degrading treatment or punishment, prolonged detention without charges, or other flagrant denial to life, liberty, and the security of person; or
>
> (2) provide refuge to individuals committing acts of international terrorism by hijacking aircraft.[24]

In a key section of this act Congress said, "The United States Executive Directors of the institutions listed in subsection (a) are authorized and instructed to oppose any loan, any extension of financial assistance, or any technical assistance to any country described in subsection (a) (1) or (2), unless such assistance is directed specifically to programs which serve the basic human needs of the citizens of such country." The Carter administration did not want this language adopted since it restricted executive branch actions in foreign policy, and both the Department of the Treasury and international financial institutions such as the World Bank argued that "political" considerations such as human rights should not intrude on the "purely" economic functions of international financial institutions. Congress, unpersuaded by these arguments, passed the act and periodically examined whether its intent was being carried out by various administrations.

In 1980 Congress revised U.S. law pertaining to refugees, in part to make American legislation consistent with the international treaty on the subject. In 1968 the United States had acceded to the 1967 protocol (or additional treaty) on refugees. Yet U.S. practice had continued to display a strong cold war bias in its handling of refugee matters; persons fleeing communist regimes were given preferential status as refugees, while those fleeing persecution from noncommunist regimes might or might not be given refugee status and then political asylum.

For this and other reasons Congress enacted a new law that in effect incorporated language from the International Convention Relating to the Status of Refugees, to which the United States had never become a party even though it had acceded to the subsequent protocol. Legalities aside, Congress authorized the president in 1980 to consider as a refugee a person who "owing to a well-founded fear of being persecuted for reasons of race, religion, nationality, membership of a particular social group or political opinion, is outside the country of his nationality and is unable or, owing to such fear, is unwilling to avail himself of the protection of that country."[25] Subsequently, sectors of Congress gave considerable attention to the question of whether the Reagan administration was giving preferential treatment to refugees from communist countries like Poland, while considering fugitives from Central American countries like El Salvador and Haiti as "economic migrants" rather than refugees with a right not to be sent back to situations of persecution.

In 1974, at perhaps the peak of congressional assertiveness in foreign policy, Congress passed what is generally referred to as the Jackson-Vanik amendment to the Trade Act. Directed at "any non-market economy country," this provision was designed to deny most-favored-nation status and credit or credit guarantees to any country that

(1) denies its citizens the right or opportunity to emigrate;
(2) imposes more than a nominal tax on emigration or on the visas or other documents required for emigration, for any purpose or cause whatsoever; or
(3) imposes more than a nominal tax, levy, fine, fee, or other charge on any citizen as a consequence of the desire of such citizen to emigrate to the country of his choice.[26]

This and other parts of the act were supposed to "assure the continued dedication of the United States to fundamental human rights." Passed despite the strong objections of Secretary of State Kissinger and the administrations he represented, this amendment and its application received considerable congressional attention. By the 1980s, some in

Congress were working closely with the Reagan administration in enforcing the act in Eastern Europe.

At least one other general provision on human rights has been adopted by Congress with some impact on policy—if only slight impact on human rights. In the amended Export-Import Bank Act of 1945, Congress passed some "soft law," stating, "It is further the policy of the United States that. . . ." There followed a long paragraph stating the general concerns that should be included in U.S. policy involving the Export-Import Bank—the public bank that extends credit to parties purchasing American goods and services. At the very end of the paragraph specifying congressional economic concerns, Congress authorized the president to "deny applications for credit for financial or noncommercial considerations" such as "international terrorism, nuclear proliferation, environmental protection and human rights," thus linking human rights to the Export-Import Bank. But the thrust of the legislation made it clear that "only in cases where the President determines that such action would be in the national interest, where such action would clearly and importantly advance United States policy" were the economic functions of the bank to be restricted. In some slight follow-up to this legislation, Congress has legislated other human rights concerns into the bank's transactions but not directly under this general wording.

Congress seized upon the Export-Import Bank Act of 1945, as amended, to write in the so-called Sullivan principles regarding integration of the labor force in the Republic of South Africa. The purpose of the principles, formulated by an American black minister active in international labor matters, was to deny Export-Import Bank credits to any party supporting apartheid in South Africa. In order for bank loans to be extended to firms purchasing American goods and services destined for that country, the secretary of state was required by law to certify that "the purchaser has endorsed and has proceeded toward the implementation" of the Sullivan principles.[27] At the time of writing no such credits had been extended, because the secretary had made no such certification.

In sum, one can see that through this second group of laws, Congress has tried to incorporate a broad human rights concern into U.S. bilateral and multilateral policies spanning security and developmental assistance, bilateral and multilateral financial and commercial transactions, and policies affecting refugees. Thus far, only the central but general parts of the statutes have been noted. Many of the statutes are long and detailed, and the specific mandates that some contain (reporting requirements, for example) are addressed in the third group of congressional acts pertaining to specific legislation. Indeed, as we will see in some detail, Congress has passed general legislation, but it has not stopped there. Because it has not trusted the president or approved of how he has implemented the general provisions enacted, Congress has adopted a rather large body of specific legislation on human rights.

3a. *Country-specific legislation.* As table 1.1 indicated, by 1984 country-specific provisions on human rights had been enacted. Some of these provisions were quite weak and of only temporary importance. A congressional act passed in 1978 expressed the sense of the Congress that, should the administration conduct negotiations with Cuba, that government's "disrespect for the human rights of individuals . . . must be taken into account in any such negotiations." [28] Another sense-of-the-Congress resolution passed in 1973 stated that "the president should request the Government of Chile to protect the human rights of all individuals." [29]

But some of the country-specific legislation came to occupy a position of profound saliency in debates over American foreign policy. The best example of this type of congressional law on human rights pertained to El Salvador. From 1981 to 1984, Congress repeatedly passed legislation requiring the president to make a "certification" every 180 days that progress was being made on specified human rights matters if economic and security assistance to that country were to continue. Extensive hearings and hours of debate on this subject—not to mention hours of action off the floors of both houses—preceded each controversial vote. In a series of actions of deepening complexity, President Reagan exercised the "pocket veto" over one version of the certification provision while Congress was in recess at the end of 1983; but a federal court later ruled that this was an unconstitutional act since the pocket veto could only be used at the end of a session of Congress, not during a recess. In the meantime, however, the Congress passed further legislation that tied U.S. assistance for El Salvador to human rights standards without the device of certification.

We will examine the case of human rights in El Salvador more thoroughly later. It is sufficient for now to note that Congress, including the Republican-controlled Senate, adopted very specific language regarding human rights in El Salvador. It provoked a full-blown debate over the importance of human rights, especially in comparison to the strategic issue, and over whether the president should be so limited in foreign affairs by the Congress.

El Salvador was not the only country targeted for country-specific legislation by Congress. When in the 1980s the Reagan administration asked Congress to repeal the ban on arms sales to authoritarian Chile, Congress consented after much acrimonious debate; but it again required the president to certify progress on specified human rights matters. In particular, Congress required the president to certify that Chile "has taken appropriate steps to cooperate to bring to justice . . . [persons] indicted . . . in connection with the murders" of persons in the United States.[30] As of mid-1987, the president had not done so; arms sales to the Pinochet regime remained effectively blocked for human rights reasons though the general ban had been removed. In addition to this legislation directed at Chile, Congress also voted for presidential certification of progress on specific human rights matters regarding Nicaragua and Haiti.[31]

While some country-specific human rights actions by Congress could be quickly forgotten, others were extensively debated. Indeed, interviews in the Department of State in 1984 indicated that specific legislation was the type of human rights action most dreaded by the executive branch. Such legislation frequently tied the president's hands and left the executive branch little room to maneuver in foreign affairs. Of course, some congressional actions could be function-specific rather than country-specific, and it is to that last type of human rights provisions that we now turn.

3b. *Function-specific legislation.* One can identify—generically or individually—about fifteen provisions emanating from Congress that mandate specific actions on human rights by the executive branch without regard to particular countries. Reporting requirements are generic; other kinds of requirements are individual.

One of the most important of these is the 1977 law creating the Bureau of Human Rights and Humanitarian Affairs in the Department of State.[32] This provision was coolly received in the department, especially by the career Foreign Service officers trained to put a high premium on stable and friendly relations with the states to which they were assigned. After all, raising the issue of human rights can be destabilizing if perceived as an unfriendly act. Moreover, some in the department thought it was a bad idea to restrict responsibility for human rights to a distinct bureau rather than to integrate human rights administratively into American diplomacy. But Congress held the opinion that it was important to give human rights an administrative base, an administrative territory. If policy sometimes evolved through struggles over such territory, and if a bureau in the department was responsible for the province of human rights, then the existence of a human rights bureau headed by an assistant secretary of state was conducive to promoting the cause of human rights in bureaucratic struggles. The cause would be advanced not only by substantive commitment but also by the bureaucratic imperative.

By 1984, the bureau had been headed by two assistant secretaries for human rights: Pat Derian under Jimmy Carter and Elliott Abrams under Ronald Reagan. An examination of their records will be presented in chapter 6, although much information about their activities is not available to the public. It is not easy to establish clearly how many battles they fought within the executive branch or how often they won. It seems that frequently, under both Democrats and Republicans, what the bureau wanted was opposed by a regional bureau more interested in stable security relations than in human rights, or perhaps by a Department of the Treasury more interested in "business as usual" than in "complicating" economic relations with human rights considerations, or perhaps by a Department of Commerce more interested in promoting sales than in combating repression by restricting them. Both assistant secretaries developed a reputation for assertiveness, although not along the same policy path. The prevailing view of the bureau was that on many issues during both administrations its goal of supporting human rights lost out to more traditional concerns for security and economic well-being represented by other parts of the Departments of State, Defense, the Treasury, and Commerce. Nevertheless, Congress seemed generally satisfied by the restructuring it had brought about, and no administration asked Congress to return to the status quo.

One of the tasks of the Bureau of Human Rights, mandated by Congress, was to compile a report on the human rights situation in every member state of the United Nations.[33] Congress had first required reports only on countries receiving U.S. security assistance, but this approach seemed unbalanced, especially to conservatives in Congress, who wanted attention to communist nations' violations even though they received no U.S. aid. So Congress made the scope of the reports nearly global. (Some observers have speculated that a number of conservatives wanted to kill the project by making the task so large as to be unmanageable.) The first reports compiled under Secretary of State Kissinger, thin in substance, were delayed in publication. Under the two following administrations there was progressively more compliance with congressional intent, either because the executive branch desired it or feared criticism from members of Congress aligned with private human rights groups. The annual country reports thus became a major statement on the condition of international human rights in the world.[34] No other reports attempted quite so much, although Freedom House, a private organization in New York, tried to analyze civil and political rights globally, and Amnesty International, headquartered in London, periodically published global reports on selected topics such as the extent and location of torture in the world.[35]

The State Department's annual human rights reports were deficient, however. Social, economic, and cultural rights were not treated as human rights or subjected to extensive analysis, and some claimed that a political bias could be found in the reports on several countries. But by 1984, critics of the administration in Congress were applauding Reagan's Bureau of Human Rights for the general objectivity of its reports. And a number of private human rights organizations were also saying that, whatever the particular biases, the reports remained important and useful tools for the analysis of human rights conditions.[36] The fundamental question, in principle, had become not so much the facts about civil and political rights but rather to what extent violations of these rights affected the conduct of American foreign policy. (Few policy makers anywhere in government showed much concern about socioeconomic rights.)

A generic congressional action, found in much legislation, is to require the executive agency involved to report to Congress on how it has taken human rights into account in its policies. This requirement has been attached to legislation affecting not only the Department of State and the Agency for International Development but also the Department of the Treasury, the Department of Commerce, the Overseas Private Investment Corporation, and the Export-Import Bank. It is obviously designed to keep Congress informed, and it can trigger congressional hearings if the Congress is dissatisfied with presidential performance. Congress can rely to some extent on private human rights groups to monitor executive actions, but increasingly it requires the executive branch to compile sometimes extensive and detailed reports on its implementation of legislation. Some reports become routine, but some become the focus of extensive debate, depending upon the politics of a follow-up, if any, in Congress.

Another function-specific law of some importance prohibited the United States from providing police training to foreign states.[37] This 1974 law, which replaced a similar one of the preceding year, grew out of congressional concern that the United States was directly participating in repression, including torture, especially in Latin America. Congress therefore blocked funds "to provide training or advice, or provide any financial support, for police, prisons, or other law enforcement forces for any foreign government or any program of internal intelligence or surveillance." It was a specific, sweeping ban, adopted at the height of congressional assertiveness (1974–78). While apparently no overt U.S. monies were expended on foreign police training from 1975 to 1984, it was not clear what might have been done covertly between the CIA and "internal intelligence or surveillance" agencies in foreign countries. But by 1984 the Reagan administration was finding this prohibition on police training onerous enough to seek its repeal. In the view of the administration, if the police were brutal in places like El Salvador and Uganda, then it was important to be able to provide them with remedial training. Some in Congress, however, were not convinced that such U.S. training in the past had proved ameliorative, and they fought to maintain the 1974 ban until 1985, when it was partially repealed.

Like the ban on police training, much U.S. human rights legislation is negative in the sense that it seeks to block some financial, monetary, military, or diplomatic transaction because of violations of human rights. Some general language is more positive, urging or requiring the United States to promote or encourage the protection of human rights. Several specific measures are also of this positive variety. In Section 116(e) of the Foreign Assistance Act, Congress "authorized and encouraged" the executive to use "not less than" a specified amount of economic assistance "for studies to identify, and for openly carrying out, programs and activities which will encourage or promote increased adherence to civil and political rights. . . . None of these funds may be used . . . to influence the outcome of any election in any country."[38] Under this legislation, the United States supported a number of organizations and programs for the positive advancement of human rights in countries eligible to receive U.S. developmental assistance.

One of the more controversial positive approaches to human rights development was Project Democracy. After much wrangling and many false starts, deletions of funding, revisions of intent, and the like, Congress approved in 1983 a program to promote democracy around the world. The Reagan administration had long criticized the Carter administration and others for failing to deal with human rights in a structural sense. A favorite way of dealing with this distinction was to note that one could seek either the release of political prisoners or the promotion of a democratic system in which no political prisoners were detained. The Reagan administration in particular showed a pronounced tendency to collapse "human rights" into "democracy" or "democratic freedoms" and to talk about, if not push for, structural change toward democracy. After the president made a speech to the British House of Commons calling for a crusade for democracy, his administration presented its ideas in legislative form to Congress, which finally approved a similar version.

A private corporation was created with public funding. The purpose of the project was to help build the infrastructure for democracy but not to support particular political parties or candidates and not to try to affect the outcome of any particular election. From the beginning some members of Congress had reservations about how the project would operate in practice. Not a few were concerned that the vision of democracy held by the Reagan administration might be narrowly conservative and that funds under the program would flow only to those with similar ideological orientations. Nevertheless, and despite the fact that some of these concerns proved to be justified, Project Democracy was finally authorized so that a bipartisan board, technically private in nature, dispensed funds to private groups in a supposedly public process. Project Democracy funds were administered separately from AID funds, which went for essentially the same cause under Section 116(e) of the Foreign Assistance Act.

Another positive and specific act of Congress was a special appropriation of money to the International Committee of the Red Cross, headquartered in Geneva, for its work with "'political' detainees." Yet another positive action tied part of the U.S. contribution to the Organization of American States specifically to the work of the Inter-American Commission on Human Rights. These exercises of the power of the purse did not prove controversial.

Function-specific requirements concerning human rights can be found in other legislation. In the International Financial Institutions Act of 1977, Congress instructed the secretary of the treasury to fashion policy in international financial institutions so as to take into account "the responsiveness of the governments [of Southeast Asia] in providing a more substantial accounting of Americans missing in action."

In 1983, Congress directed considerable attention to the United Nations Educational, Scientific, and Cultural Organization (UNESCO). Finding, among other things, that "Article 19 of the Universal Declaration of Human Rights provides for the right to freedom of expression and to 'seek, receive, and impart information and ideas through any media and regardless of frontiers'," Congress expressed its sense that UNESCO "should cease efforts to attempt to regulate news content and to formulate rules and regulations for the operation of the world press." But Congress, having expressed this nonbinding sense, then went on to bar funds for UNESCO "if that organization implements any policy or procedure the effect of which is to license journalists or their publications, to censor or otherwise restrict the free flow of information within or among countries, or to impose mandatory codes of journalistic practice or ethics."[39] This binding provision, qualified, to be sure, by an "if" condition, was superseded by the Reagan administration's decision to withdraw from UNESCO. The 1983 congressional wording was a signal to Reagan that he could proceed to "get tough" with UNESCO, which he did. As far as human rights was concerned, Congress had linked its power of the purse in part to the rights proclaimed twenty-five years earlier in the U.N. General Assembly resolution known as the Universal Declaration of Human Rights.

In other function-specific acts, Congress created in 1976 the Commission on Security and Cooperation in Europe to help monitor developments under the Helsinki Act of the preceding year. The commission, a two-branch agency, focused largely on human rights rather than on security or economic issues. It came to be called the Fascell Commission by some because of the dynamic role played in its proceedings by Congressman Dante Fascell (D., Florida), and it was active for much of its existence.

Congress also mandated several programs to promote human rights, broadly defined, in South Africa. There was an educational program to train nonwhite South Africans both within the republic and abroad. There was a separate program to promote an integrated South African society through upgrading the private infrastructure of democracy.

Finally, in 1981 Congress declared its sense that the coordination of human rights with economic assistance had worked well in the Carter administration and that the process should be strengthened and expanded in the future. This measure was intended as a signal to the Reagan administration not to de-emphasize the human rights issue. It was adopted in the context of swirling rumors that the new administration intended to do just that.

Classifying U.S. congressional actions on international human rights according to various schemes presented here highlights several points. Within general legislation one can cite this or that particular paragraph or combine several statements into one or more generic provisions. The scheme of classification presented here was adopted to highlight several points.

First, some congressional actions, even though they may produce law, are exceedingly "soft." The softest of these actions are the hortatory statements, whether legally binding or not. They are the sweepingly general statements by Congress that purportedly declare policy but that lead neither to executive action nor to congressional oversight.

A second type of congressional action on human rights declares general policy and elicits some subsequent interest by some part of the Congress. Because the language is general, the congressional statement is not self-enforcing. Whether the language of Congress actually becomes policy depends first on the good faith of the executive branch in implementing the provisions and second on the ability of Congress to compel compliance.

A third type of congressional action is more specific, whether pertaining to countries or functions. Some language may be almost self-enforcing—that is, the executive branch has so little room to maneuver under the legislation that it is difficult for an administration to do other than what is specified by Congress. This is relatively hard law. Some supposedly specific legislation, however, can still be circumvented by the executive branch if congressional interest and consensus are lacking. Congress may pass a law requiring the executive branch to certify progress on human rights in certain countries, but the subsequent political process determines how seriously that requirement is taken.

It bears stressing at this early point that congressional voting establishes both the legislative and the subsequent oversight framework. (Some human rights legislation has been approved without vote, in the sense that certain conference committee reports on the human rights provisions of a multipurpose bill were approved by consensus.) The specific dynamics of the vote creating legislation indicate support for an idea and hence the prospect for continuing interest by members. If, as was true, the Harkin amendment linking U.S. economic assistance to human rights was supported by members interested in either upholding human rights or cutting foreign aid, one might predict some splintering and continuing congressional division when overseeing the act in practice. If, as was true, liberals and conservatives, Democrats and Republicans, supported an economic embargo because of human rights violations in Idi Amin's Uganda, one might predict that the executive branch would be forced to give way to strong and unified congressional sentiment. Thus voting in Congress on human rights has been part of setting the legal framework for action, but at the same time it has been part of the oversight process in which Congress, at least sometimes, seeks to compel the executive branch to follow congressional mandates—though not always successfully.

As will become clear, I do not conceive of legislation and oversight as two separate processes. This study is basically about oversight, by which I mean the entire follow-up process to original legislation. If one wishes to know what has happened to a piece of human rights legislation, and why it was implemented or not, one has to look at executive action and its interplay with congressional communiqués (letters and telephone calls and conversations), hearings, *and subsequent legislation*. Thus, as I argue explicitly toward the end of this study, legislation, oversight, and subsequent legislation comprise a mostly seamless web in the policy process. Once there is original legislation, there may be congressional oversight, which may lead to legislation either to reword the original law or to exercise the power of the purse in relation to the executive's behavior under the law. Some choose to distinguish between legislation and hearings as forms of oversight. This seems artificial, and I choose to frame this study otherwise. To make a complicated subject simple, I conceive of oversight as follow-up.

We turn now to congressional voting on human rights to seek further understanding about how the policy framework came to be and about the prospects for effective oversight from a watchful and unified Congress. We do not expect the U.S. Congress often to be watchful and unified concerning international human rights, but its actions can be surprising.

Chapter 2

Congressional Voting on Human Rights Measures

There is no simple or enduring domestic consensus behind concern for human rights in U.S. foreign policy—by the executive branch, the Congress, or the American people.

—Sandra Vogelgesang,
American Dream, Global Nightmare, 111–12

That Congress is able to legislate on matters of human rights, a seemingly obvious point, appears remarkable as one probes specific congressional actions. Some legislation has been put on the books without a vote on its particular human rights language; such legislation can evolve from bargaining on elements of more general bills in such ways that neither the House nor the Senate ever votes formally on its specific human rights provisions.

But Congress also uses roll call votes on human rights provisions, and as we examine this process two striking points emerge. If one examines the roll call votes on human rights (or a representative sample of them), there seems to be pure randomness in Congress's actions. Almost no pattern emerges. One cannot predict who will vote for what type of legislation, and one cannot explain members' past votes. If, however, one breaks down these roll call votes into liberal and conservative proposals, one finds a clear partisan and ideological voting pattern. Both the apparent randomness and the clear split lie behind congressional action on human rights. The split especially affects congressional oversight of what it has already legislated, which will be covered later.

Although much human rights legislation has come about through roll call votes, details of this process have not been analyzed. A 1979 study used eight Senate votes during the period 1973–76 to conclude, primarily, that a senator's view of human rights legislation was strongly linked to the senator's position on national security issues.[1] Senators scoring high on the National Security Index (NSI) compiled by the private and conservative American Security Council were decidedly less likely to vote for the human rights legislation proposed during the Ninety-third and Ninety-fourth Congresses. Party affiliation, geographical region, and the security of one's seat were factors exerting weak but discernible influences on Senate votes.

The authors noted, however, that further study was necessary, given the limited number of human rights measures then available for analysis. Here I will examine congressional votes on selected human rights measures during the period 1977–84. I hypothesize that the conclusions from the 1979 study will explain more recent congressional behavior on human rights as well. That is, I posit initially that a constituency's influence on its member's vote will be weak and that what I call political factors—above all views concerning national security—will be more important. This approach means that the NSI ranking will manifest great explanatory and predictive ability.

An Overview of Human Rights Voting

The scope of human rights voting in Congress remains difficult to define. Because the United States has not become a party to most human rights treaties, one cannot simply look for legislation pursuant to such treaties. In addition to such treaty legislation, for example, the Refugee Act of 1980,[2] one must also look for legislation that refers to international human rights explicitly or that can be reasonably inferred to fall within the domain of internationally recognized human rights. The former indicator is obvious enough, because some congressional action does indeed make explicit reference to international instruments. The latter can give rise to problems of definition. Yet some legislation, for example the Jackson-Vanik amendment concerning emigration from nonmarket societies, clearly addresses subjects covered by international human rights (the Universal Declaration of Human Rights of 1948 and the United Nations Covenant on Civil and Political Rights of 1966 affirm the right to leave and return to one's country freely).

Even when a congressional action has been judged to fall within the issue area of human rights according to these guidelines, there is no concomitant argument that any member of Congress necessarily sees the issue as a purely human rights matter. A member may view it as a test of power between Congress and the president, or of national versus international jurisdiction, or of economic versus idealistic considerations, or of security versus morality, and so on. In short, what an observer may fairly and properly call a human rights vote may not be seen as a purely human rights vote by any given member of Congress. Just as a national security vote may be intertwined with institutional and political considerations, so a human rights vote may be bound up with other matters while maintaining its basic character.

With these considerations in mind (which also implicitly guided the 1979 study), I identified fifty-one roll call votes dealing with human rights on the floor of Congress during the Carter and first Reagan administrations. The rather large number of votes in this issue area is important in itself, indicating the salience of international human rights (however used) in Washington politics during this period. During the Carter administration, especially, there was much confusion in Congress about international human rights. Hence it is helpful to categorize these votes based on consensus and conflict, then to analyze them further.

Some roll call votes manifest overwhelming consensus and thus provide few insights into why members of Congress voted as they did. But not all consensus adoptions reflect the same political dynamics. One type of consensual congressional action has been dubbed "motherhood resolutions," nonbinding resolutions endorsing something favored by almost everyone in Washington, at least in principle. Such resolutions condemning the Soviet invasion of Afghanistan (which violates the first article in the two 1966 U.N. human rights covenants dealing with the collective right of national self-determination) and bemoaning the suppression of labor rights in Poland seem to have had no immediate or specific impact on subsequent decisions in Washington. Whatever signals these votes send to foreign capitals, most of these consensual human rights statements seem to disappear as far as concrete policymaking in Washington is concerned.

A second type of consensual congressional action is more important for subsequent policy. On rare occasions—two during the period under study—one or both houses of Congress will overwhelmingly criticize an executive policy concerning human rights. The rarity of the events may signify how difficult it is to obtain consensus criticism of an executive human rights policy once it is established. In 1979, the House of Representatives unanimously urged President Carter to restrict trade with Uganda, then under the murderous control of President Idi Amin. President Carter at that time resisted the interruption of business as usual; later the administration changed its position and instituted a trade embargo.

President Reagan endured severe congressional criticism during his first term when, in 1981, administration officials voted against nonbinding regulations of the World Health Organization that sought to regulate the marketing of infant formula in the Third World. The Senate, although controlled by the Republicans, voted 89−2 to express its disapproval of the administration's position. (A standing vote in the House registered a 301−100 margin critical of the president's policy.) The Senate vote revealed a pervasive belief in the rights of Third World infants and mothers to adequate health and nutrition (affirmed by the U.N. Covenant on Economic, Social, and Cultural Rights). The Reagan administration did not repeat its defense of totally free enterprise within the World Health Organization, especially since the main target of the organization's action, the Nestle Corporation, had accepted its guidelines.

Finally there is the type of consensual congressional action that reflects a preceding compromise on a contentious issue. Compromises frequently occur on omnibus or general bills. Both houses of Congress, for example, argued bitterly over the propriety of human rights provisions in legislation authorizing and appropriating economic and military assistance to El Salvador. But sometimes the final version of the human rights provision in the El Salvador bill was approved by consensus after various agreements had been made off the House floor. We can see this same type of final and general consensus vote on a measure dealing with funding programs for international refugees.

Many of the votes on human rights in Congress during the Carter and first Reagan administrations did not reflect consensus, a fact important in itself. There seem to have been several types of disagreements. First, a liberal-conservative split seemed to permeate congressional actions on human rights. Liberals were prone to target military regimes allied with the United States (Guatemala, Chile, the Philippines, South Korea), while conservatives targeted leftist regimes (Cuba, Angola, Vietnam, Ethiopia, Laos). Several general proposals, not linked to specific countries, also gave rise to liberal-conservative disagreements.

A second type of disagreement I label "smoke-screen votes," for on some occasions the human rights issue seemed clearly to be used in pursuit of other objectives. Though sometimes a judgment call, this classification can sometimes be appropriate. After various votes concerning the Panama Canal treaties during the Carter administration, for example, congressional opponents of the treaties tried to restrict the U.S. funding to Panama ordered by the treaties—the rationale for restriction being the alleged human rights deficiencies in Panama. Die-hard treaty opponents proposed the "human rights" amendments to legislation only after the treaties had been ratified by the Senate, but they did not long persist. When the treaties were no longer a salient issue, proposals for human rights in Panama receded. In this case and a few others, the "human rights issue" was clearly a smoke screen for some other primary concern. This type of vote and the first category of disagreement (liberal v. conservative over human rights) differ at least in degree. The liberal-conservative split on human rights is not the same as the disagreement over whether to use human rights as a means to some other objective, such as blocking the Panama Canal treaties after they had been ratified.

Finally, there seemed to be "special cases" of conflicting views on human rights. In 1980 Senator Adlai Stevenson, Jr. (D., Illinois) proposed a delay in providing economic assistance to Israel because of that government's settlement of Jews in the West Bank. Israel's policy violated the Fourth Geneva Convention of August 12, 1949, a treaty dealing with human rights in armed conflict which has provisions covering territory occupied through armed conflict. Senator Stevenson's proposal also sought to protect the collective human right of self-determination for Palestinians by preserving the possibility of the creation of a Palestinian entity in the West Bank. This measure thus constituted human rights legislation on two grounds. But it remained a special case. Matters involving Israel usually get sympathetic attention in the U.S. Senate, where Israel has many friends and where pro-Israel lobbies have been powerful. In any event, Senator Stevenson garnered only six votes for his proposal; many of the usual advocates of human rights in U.S. foreign policy voted against these human rights provisions.

To recapitulate: I have defined human rights legislation in relation to international legal instruments in human rights. I have found Congress acting through both consensus and conflict. Consensus statements have included motherhood resolutions, criticism of the president, and compromise votes masking previous conflicts. Actions arising from conflict have included a liberal-conservative division on what human rights legislation to adopt, a smoke-screen vote that was not primarily a human rights vote, and a special case involving Israel. Setting aside consensus actions for the moment (because a statistical analysis of such votes cannot possibly illuminate anything), I now turn to congressional conflict over human rights in foreign policy. This legislative conflict has seemed to influence, or potentially to affect, U.S. foreign policy on human rights.

Senate Conflict over Human Rights.—In the early 1970s, Senate liberals, followed by liberals in the House, most often raised the human rights issue. They were reacting to the foreign policy of the Nixon-Kissinger team, which they regarded as amoral or immoral and insufficiently sensitive to human rights. Hence, the early proposals on human rights assumed a liberal character: restricting aid to countries holding political prisoners, invoking the cloture rule to compel a vote to ratify the genocide convention, prohibiting military aid to the Chilean junta, and so forth.

Conservative senators, after resisting these moves, countered by proposing their own human rights measures, raising human rights issues when introducing bans on assistance to leftist countries. Sometimes they argued that acceptable human rights standards had been met, as in motions to lift sanctions against the white minority regime in Rhodesia. At other times, they emphasized human rights violations, as when trying to punish the regimes in Eastern Europe. Thus conservatives found that they too could play the game of human rights legislation.

As a result, one could no longer speak of being for or against more human rights legislation in U.S. foreign policy, as one could in the early 1970s, but rather for or against a particular type of human rights legislation. In the period under study, congressional activism on human rights peaked during the Carter administration. From the various and conflicting proposals that flooded Congress then, I have selected six representative liberal measures (see table 2.1).

In 1977 the Carter administration made it a top priority to roll back the Byrd amendment, which permitted the importation of Rhodesian

Table 2.1. Human rights roll call votes, 1977–84: Senate liberal proposals

Congress	CQ no.	Bill no.	Description	Type of pro– human rights vote
95th	59	174	Halt importation of Rhodesian chrome, to comply with U.N. sanctions for self-determination in Zimbabwe (*CQ*, March 19, 1977).	Yea
95th	197	HR5262	Require U.S. delegations to international financial institutions to vote against loans for gross violators of human rights, unless funds directly benefit basic human needs (June 18, 1977).	Yea
95th	243	S3075	Prohibit lifting of U.S. sanctions on Rhodesia until free and fair elections held with international observation (July 29, 1978).	Yea
97th	274	S1196	Require U.S. aid to El Salvador be linked with certified progress on human rights (September 26, 1981).	Yea
97th	321	S1196	Kill Helms amendment permitting military aid and sales to Chile (October 24, 1981).	Yea
97th	258	HR494	Require U.S. aid to El Salvador be linked with certified progress on specified human rights, including good faith efforts in search for killers of six Americans (July 31, 1983).	Yea

chromium and thus placed the United States in violation of United Nations mandatory economic sanctions on white minority rule in that former British colony. This liberal measure pertains, at its core, to self-determination and majority rule in what is now Zimbabwe. It is important to understand the context of this human rights vote. Other concerns had always been interwoven with the question of U.S. sanctions on Rhodesia in the name of human rights. The U.N. Security Council resolution approving sanctions was a rarity because it was legally binding and therefore called into question U.S. compliance with international law. Yet strategic concerns outweighed legal ones. Some argued that if the United States did not import Rhodesian chromium it might become dependent upon exports from the Soviet Union. Others worried that some American companies might suffer losses if the United States complied with the sanctions while other nations' firms violated them, with or without the knowledge of their governments. And there was the usual question of whether a senator should support the president's policy in foreign affairs, a question entangled in partisan and institutional loyalties. About the time of this vote, the Senate voted nine additional times on various Rhodesian alternatives. On balance, conservatives stressed strategic and economic priorities, liberals stressed human rights and compliance with international law. (That liberals rather than conservatives should prefer international law and order is an irony that need not detain us here.) Finally, another possible concern, not explicitly voted upon or voiced in debate, was racism (an affinity for whites, a skepticism of black capacity for democratic self-government). In sum, this first liberal Senate vote, apparently simple, was in fact complex. A yea vote was pro–human rights, indicating a desire to return to economic sanctions in support of human rights in Rhodesia.

Also in 1977 various liberal senators sought to push human rights considerations onto international financial institutions such as the World Bank. As noted, President Carter resisted this move (despite his rhetorical support for human rights), as did Robert McNamara, president of the World Bank. Some argued that such an effort politicized the multilateral banks by introducing noneconomic factors. Nevertheless, some liberal senators persisted, and the second vote in the study reflects the effort to add a "Harkin amendment" to the legislation authorizing funding for the banks. This second vote was on a proposal requiring U.S. delegations to international financial institutions to vote against loans to countries that were grossly violating human rights unless the loans would directly improve basic human needs in those countries. At the time of this Senate vote, there were seven other proposals before the Senate concerning international financial institutions. Some of these measures would have labeled certain leftist countries as ineligible to receive U.S. support (Cambodia, Cuba, Laos, and Vietnam). Others would have reduced funding in general, whether for human rights or other reasons. Again, while this debate centered on human rights, economic, strategic, partisan, and institutional interests obviously affected it. A yea vote was pro–human rights.

Throughout the late 1970s, the Senate entered further into the Rhodesian imbroglio. Conservatives tried repeatedly to force President Carter to lift U.S. economic sanctions. The third vote in the study reflects a liberal counterattack. In 1978, liberals proposed an amendment to the foreign military aid bill, specifying that no U.S. sanctions against Rhodesia could be lifted until free elections were held under international observation. All of the crosscutting issues found in the first vote were still at work. In addition, there was the question of whether the steps taken by the Rhodesian whites to alter the status quo warranted a change in U.S. policy. (This type of vote and issue resurfaced in the 1980s on the issue of white minority rule in South Africa.) Free elections to secure self-determination and majority rule remained the central issue. A yea vote was pro–human rights.

Few issues in the Senate were more controversial than the one in 1981 leading to the fourth vote in the study. With Ronald Reagan by then in the White House, liberals pushed the idea that U.S. assistance to the government of El Salvador should be made conditional upon a president's certifying that progress was being made in certain human rights matters. Supporters of this move claimed that U.S. assistance would not produce a stable government in that poor and conflict-ridden country unless human rights reforms accompanied it. It was feared that assistance without progress in human rights would lead to the same tyranny that had plagued the country before. Opponents argued several points: (1) that since the president was committed to human rights reforms, there was no need for a specific timetable based on periodic certification; (2) that in the context of admitted human rights problems, a lack of certification and hence a cutoff of U.S. assistance would lead to a "stop and go" foreign policy; (3) that a lack of certification and assistance would help the leftist rebels who would, if they came to power, compile an even worse human rights record. Other arguments on both sides focused on the president's credibility in pressing for human rights reforms, the wisdom of legislating foreign policy, the amount of progress that had been made on human rights, and the real need for security assistance. The fact that Democrats voted overwhelmingly for the proposal (37–7) while Republicans opposed it two to one (17–35) indicates that partisan views played some role. A yea vote was pro–human rights.

The fifth vote reflects long Senate involvement in foreign policy toward Chile. Since the overthrow of President Salvadore Allende in 1973, Chile had been watched closely by Senate liberals, primarily because of the harsh rule of the subsequent junta under President Augusto Pinochet. It had been one of the first countries designated by Senator Edward Kennedy (D., Massachusetts) and others for reduced or terminated U.S. assistance. Many conservatives in Congress had long disliked this emphasis on Chile, generally believing that Chilean violations of human rights should be overlooked in the name of security (it was rabidly anti-Communist) or economics (it was open to U.S. corporations under principles almost purely capitalistic). In 1981, Senator Jesse Helms (R., North Carolina) proposed that the president be authorized to resume military aid to Chile, arguing specifically that the 1976 ban on military sales and assistance was much harsher than anything the Senate had done to South Africa, Angola, Vietnam, or Cambodia. Liberals tried unsuccessfully to table the amendment. A vote to table was a pro–human rights vote. (Though the Helms amendment passed, later congressional action required the president to certify Chilean progress on certain human rights issues, including the intended extradition of the Chileans indicted by a U.S. grand jury for the murder of two persons on U.S. soil, a certification that could not be fudged by the executive branch. Thus, while Congress lifted the ban on military assistance with one action, the specific ban it imposed with its second action has effectively blocked military assistance to Chile. Helms won a battle but continued to lose the war.)

The sixth liberal proposal again involves presidential certification of progress on human rights, this time in El Salvador, as a condition for continued economic and security assistance. There are at least two reasons for including this 1983 measure on El Salvador, even though it closely resembled a 1981 vote. First, the case of El Salvador was one of the most salient issues in Congress during the early 1980s. Senators debated and wrangled over it, the president applied pressures because of it, and constituencies showed considerable interest in it. For all of these reasons, a senator probably considered carefully any vote on El Salvador. Second, the certification measure proposed was more precise than the others, indicating as one of the conditions for continued U.S. assistance the necessity of progress in the effort to bring to justice the killers of six Americans. It was a certification on human rights that the executive branch could not treat lightly. A yea vote was pro–human rights.

Though certain proposals on human rights came from conservatives, some of the liberal legislation discussed was proposed to countervail conservative measures. Three such conservative acts bear detailed analysis (table 2.2).

In 1977, in the context of a broad debate on U.S. policy on international financial institutions, Senator Robert Dole (R., Kansas) proposed that U.S. delegations to such institutions oppose loans to Vietnam, Laos, and Cambodia on human rights grounds. This suggestion substituted for an earlier proposal that had also included Cuba, and Dole made it after liberals had proposed a general measure, noted earlier, on gross violations of human rights. Dole wanted to ensure that these three communist countries were defined as gross violators. His measure passed but was dropped later from the bill reported out of conference committee. Liberal and conservative members, and the president, eventually accepted more general language that did not name specific countries. Though the Dole measure was conservative, a yea vote was pro–human rights.

Senator Helms proposed the second conservative measure after the House had voted to restrict foreign aid to Idi Amin's Uganda. When that 1978 House measure came before the Senate, Helms added to it three communist states (Vietnam, Cambodia, and Cuba). This Helms amendment succeeded in the Senate, with Democrats as well as Republicans voting for it overwhelmingly. A yea vote was pro–human rights.

The third conservative vote in the Senate concerns a 1983 measure involving U.S. policy toward the International Monetary Fund (IMF). Senator Gordon Humphrey (R., New Hampshire) proposed that the U.S. delegation to the IMF vote against drawing rights (or loans) for nations not having free elections and free emigration—basically, certain East European communist countries. When another Republican,

Table 2.2. Human rights roll call votes, 1977–84: Senate conservative proposals

Congress	CQ no.	Bill no.	Description	Type of pro–human rights vote
95th	202	HR5262	Instruct U.S. delegations to international financial institutions to vote against loans to Vietnam, Laos, and Cambodia (*CQ*, June 18, 1977).	Yea
95th	172	S3074	Prohibit any U.S. assistance to Vietnam, Cambodia, Cuba, and Uganda (July 1, 1978).	Yea
98th	121	S695	Motion to table amendment that would instruct U.S. delegation to IMF to oppose loans to nations not holding free elections and not allowing free emigration (June 11, 1983).	Nay

Senator John Heinz (Pennsylvania), moved to table this amendment, both Republicans and southern Democrats divided and the motion to table succeeded, thus defeating the substantive motion. A pro–human rights vote thus became a vote against tabling, but in this case a pro–human rights vote also promoted a conservative interpretation of human rights, one that directs human rights concerns only against communist regimes that are also strategic adversaries of the United States. (The People's Republic of China, for example, is not thought to restrict emigration unreasonably.)

House Conflict over Human Rights.—A number of proposals introduced in the House resembled those in the Senate, and in some cases the House inherited measures from the Senate. But in other instances,

Table 2.3. Human rights roll call votes, 1977–84: House liberal proposals

Congress	CQ no.	Bill no.	Description	Type of pro– human rights vote
95th	116	HR5262	Authorize funding for international financial institutions, including requirement that United States vote against loans to nations with a consistent pattern of gross violations of human rights (*CQ*, April 9, 1977).	Yea
95th	253	HR6884	Delete $700,000 in military aid for Argentina and prohibit military sales because of human rights violations (May 28, 1977).	Yea
95th	325	HR5262	Instruct House delegation to conference committee to insist on international financial institution language restricting loans to gross violators of human rights (June 17, 1977).	Yea

representatives introduced proposals different from those already voted on in the Senate. I ended up with House votes from the Carter administration only. Human rights votes peaked in the House then, and thus they greatly outnumbered votes during the first Reagan administration. Also, the votes from the Carter period were roll call votes on clearer human rights measures. I would have preferred to add some "clean" roll call votes from later years but was unable to find any (table 2.3).[3]

The first bill concerns the familiar vote on whether the U.S. delegation to international financial institutions such as the World Bank should vote against loans to countries with consistent and gross violations of human rights unless such loans would aid the most needy people. It was the generic "Harkin amendment," which, in its original House form, required a negative U.S. vote in the international financial institutions and which was therefore different from the final adoption requiring that the United States vote to promote human rights through these institutions. The Harkin amendment thus passed but was altered through conference committee bargaining with the Senate.

The second item involves an effort led by Congressman Gerry Studds (D., Massachusetts) that failed by thirteen votes (187–200) to delete $700,000 in military assistance to Argentina and ban military sales there. This human rights proposal first passed on a small standing vote but was reversed on a roll call. As with similar legislation, it is not clear to what extent representatives rushing onto the floor for a roll call were familiar with the arguments on either side of this conflict. Republicans voted overwhelmingly against it, despite the opportunity to grab the initiative in making foreign policy during a Democratic administration.

The third vote—again about the question of human rights and indirect assistance—was a follow-up to the first vote. It instructs House members of the conference committee on international financial institution authorization to maintain the House-approved language on human rights. It is, thus, a vote that indicates the depth of commitment to the human rights provision despite efforts from the White House and the World Bank to weaken it. Offered by a Republican (John Russelot, California), the amendment was rejected 161–200.

From the evidence of these votes and from other sources, we may observe that the House during the late 1970s voted conservatively on many foreign policy questions. In general it was more conservative than the Senate on the Panama Canal treaties, which were debated at this time. Thus it is not difficult to identify several conservative human rights proposals introduced in the House during this era (table 2.4).

The first of these conservative measures is an amendment offered by Congressman Clarence Miller (R., Ohio) to restrict international financial institution loans to Cambodia, Cuba, Laos, and Vietnam. It was rejected 165–190 in favor of more general language that did not name specific countries.

The next conservative measure pertains to the U.S. Export-Import

Table 2.4. Human rights roll call votes, 1977–84: House conservative proposals

Congress	CQ no.	Bill no.	Description	Type of pro– human rights vote
95th	115	HR5262	Prohibit international financial institutions from using U.S. funds for loans to Cambodia, Cuba, Laos, or Vietnam (*CQ*, April 9, 1977).	Yea
95th	344	HR12157	Delete Sullivan principles as condition for Export-Import Bank loans to South Africa (June 10, 1978).	Nay
95th	566	HR12931	Prohibit indirect U.S. aid to Uganda, Cambodia, Laos, and Vietnam (August 5, 1978).	Yea
96th	353	HR317	Disapprove president's exemption of Romania from human rights provisions in 1974 Trade Act (July 28, 1979).	Yea

Bank and indicates the complex choice offered in the House. Its supporters hoped to delete what was thought to be soft legislation on the subject of South Africa and the bank. Tough language forbidding bank activity with South Africa had been replaced with the Sullivan principles, which required the secretary of state to certify to Congress that loan recipients in South Africa followed policies of racial integration in their labor and management practices. This language greatly restricted the bank's activity in South Africa, since the secretary did not make the required certification for a number of years; yet it was still too much for some representatives. Congressman John Ashbrook (R., Ohio) pressed for elimination of the Sullivan principles but lost 116–219.

The third conservative proposal again attempted to restrict indirect U.S. economic assistance in the name of human rights, this time to Uganda, Cambodia, Laos, and Vietnam. Even the addition of noncommunist Uganda to the list of leftists did not save this measure from defeat (198–203), but it made the vote closer than the first, and related, conservative measure of a year earlier.

A final conservative proposal is complex. Under the Jackson-Vanik amendment to the 1974 Trade Act, a nonmarket society unreasonably restricting emigration is to be denied most-favored-nation status in its trade with the United States. But the president can waive this provision for twelve months if a particular country is loosening its restrictions. Even though emigration may not be free, the president can, in effect, declare that the country is moving in the right direction. Such a presidential waiver is subject to congressional review under the terms of the 1974 act. When President Carter issued such a waiver for Romania in 1979, several representatives moved to disapprove of the presidential action. This effort failed 126–271, with even southern Democrats voting against it 13–65.

Data and Methods

For analysis, voting on each of these measures was coded, with paired votes coded the same as actual votes. Two human rights scales were created for each house, one for what has been termed "liberal" human rights votes, the other for "conservative" ones.

The Variables.—Constructing the dependent variable human rights scales posed a problem because of the eight-year span of the study. Many members were not present over this period spanning three congressional elections. The scale score is therefore the number of pro–human rights votes divided by the total number of human rights votes cast, or paired for, by each member. Thus, the range extends from 0 to 100, with 100 representing a perfect pro–human rights voting pattern.

The advantage of this measurement is that it allows all members to be compared. The disadvantage is that the comparisons are rough, especially for members whose terms do not overlap. It is the only system, however, that allows a longitudinal perspective on these votes.

Independent variables include a measure of voting on national security issues compiled by the American Security Council. On this so-called National Security Index, a high score generally indicates voting for higher military spending and usually a conservative slant on foreign policy. Party affiliation and seniority are other salient political aspects of the member. Constituency characteristics used here include a fivefold regional categorization (South, East, Midwest, Far West, and border states). Four dummy variables are used, with the Far West omitted. The three constituency factors examined are the electoral margin in the member's most recent election, the amount of military spending in the district, and the district's mean level of education.

Methods.—To examine the characteristics that distinguish persons favoring human rights measures from those opposing them, I first constructed a simple causal model. I hypothesize direct relationships between the dependent variable and each of the independent constituency and political variables except for party identification. For methodological rather than theoretical reasons, this first model does not assume that party affiliation has a direct effect on human rights voting. A high multicollinearity between party and the National Security Index makes it impossible to obtain a reliable figure for the direct impact of party identification on voting.[4]

I posit an indirect effect of constituency, party affiliation, and seniority variables through NSI voting. Since the NSI measure is constructed from previous votes on national security issues, it is logical that the other political and constituency variables affected the NSI score and thus have an indirect effect on human rights voting.

Though it can be refined, this first model has advantages, one of which is replication of the earlier study. In a second model, I examined the direct effects of party affiliation on human rights voting by dropping the NSI as an independent or intervening variable. Doing so solves the problem of high multicollinearity between party and the NSI in a second way. It also allows us to test the extent to which party has an effect on national security voting. By dropping the NSI and interjecting party affiliation into a direct relationship with human rights votes, one can see the extent to which the findings from model two differ from those from model one.

Findings

The Senate.—Our first model explains voting on the Senate human rights issues fairly well, with total R^2 of 0.45 and 0.60 for conservative and liberal voting, respectively. As one might expect, votes on conservative and liberal human rights measures mirror one another. The factors that predict a pro–liberal human rights score also predict an anti–conservative human rights score and vice versa.

Attitudes toward national security, as indicated by the NSI, are the best indicators of who will vote for or against human rights measures (significant links are presented in figure 2.1). A high NSI score is strongly related to pro–conservative (beta = 0.56) and anti–liberal human rights voting (beta = −0.71). The magnitude of the effect is similar, the two unstandardized coefficients being 0.52 and −0.59, respectively. How one votes on a general series of foreign and military issues is thus an excellent predictor of how one will vote on more specific human rights issues.

Other direct effects on human rights voting are minimal. Seniority is related to a more conservative position on the liberal human rights scale, but the effect is modest. Those winning election by a substantial margin are less likely to support conservative human rights issues. Perhaps greater electoral security allows freedom from supporting bills aimed at leftist regimes. However, this effect is very small. No other direct effects are significant.

Despite these minimal direct effects from factors other than NSI voting, we can see from figure 2.1 that various factors indirectly affect our human rights scales, the strongest effect that of party affiliation. It is highly related to NSI voting, with a beta value of over 0.7. Its indirect effect on human rights voting, through NSI, is therefore substantial: 0.51 in the case of liberal human rights voting and −0.40 in the case of the conservative scale. Democrats are substantially more likely to support liberal human rights measures, Republicans conservative ones.

Other significant indirect paths through the NSI include those of region and amount of military spending in the district. Contrary to predictions, military spending is *negatively* related to NSI voting. Legislators with more military spending in their district are more likely to support *liberal* human rights measures (indirect effect = 0.14) and less likely to support conservative human rights measures (indirect

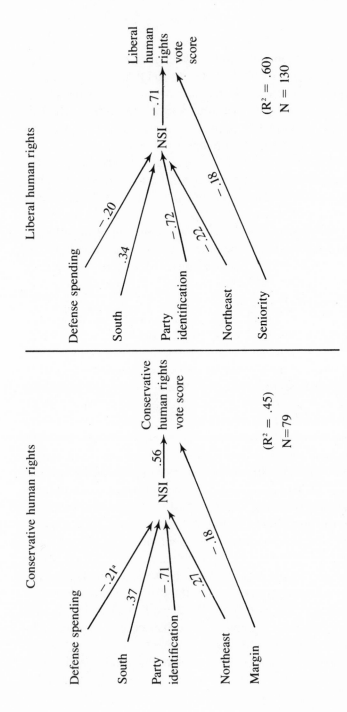

Fig. 2.1. Path model of human rights voting in the Senate (significant paths only)

a. Significant at .052. Others significant at ≤ .05. Coefficients are betas.

Note: R² with NSI the dependent variable, .64.

effect $= -0.11$). As predicted, southerners are more likely to support conservative measures, northeasterners liberal ones. This last finding comports well with regional differences in conservatism in Congress.

Thus, voting on human rights bills seems to be driven by ideological and partisan considerations: Democrats who vote "liberal" on national security issues also support liberal human rights measures and oppose conservative ones. Republicans who vote "conservative" on national security issues support conservative human rights measures and oppose liberal ones.

These results raise a question of whether human rights voting is *only* an extension of larger ideological contests. Are there no individuals supportive of human rights measures across the political spectrum, who want to punish or reform regimes violating human rights whatever their political orientation? To answer this question, I calculated a mean score for the two human rights scales to form a composite index of support for human rights. This measure gave equal weight to liberal and conservative scores no matter how many votes on each a member had participated in.

An analysis of this new scale shows that our model explains little of the variance, only 7 percent. No variable was significantly related to this overall measure. Thus, *overall* partisanship and national security factors do not predict support for human rights. This low R^2 indicates that it is necessary to look at different kinds of human rights voting to be able to predict and understand voting patterns on this issue.

Some members such as Dennis DeConcini, Gerald Ford, Richard Schweiker, and several others, strongly supported human rights across the board. At the other end of the scale were senators whose support for only one kind of human rights position netted them a low overall score. This mixed group included liberals such as Ted Kennedy and Charles Percy, who scored very low on the conservative human rights measures, and conservatives such as John Tower, Jake Garn, and John Stennis, who scored very low on the liberal measures. No members scored low on both liberal and conservative human rights scales, indicating again the basic ideological underpinnings of these votes for most members.

The House.—There are striking similarities between voting in the House and in the Senate. Overall the model predicts House votes nearly as well as Senate conservative human rights votes, but it serves less well in predicting liberal votes (fig. 2.2). As in the Senate, NSI

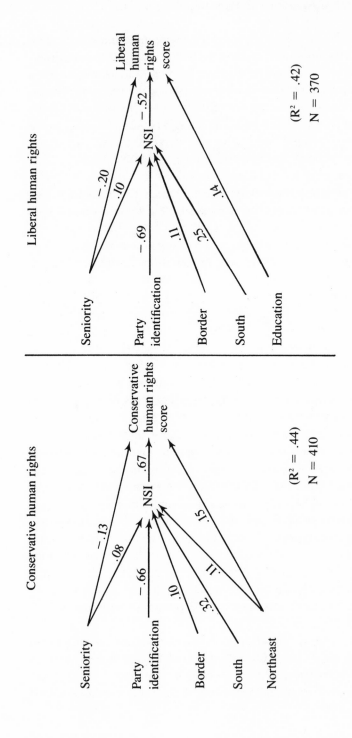

Conservative human rights

Liberal human rights

Fig. 2.2. Path model of human rights voting in the House (significant paths only)

Note: R² with NSI the dependent variable, .52 for conservative scale, .55 for liberal.

voting behavior was the best predictor of human rights voting, and in the same direction as in the Senate. Seniority had a stronger effect in the House; senior members were less predisposed to vote for either liberal or conservative measures. This is the one exception to our mirror-image generalization, where characteristics predicting a strong liberal human rights vote predicted a weak conservative one. Senior members of the House are less interested than others in protecting human rights at the possible expense of other foreign policy goals. Education was related weakly to a liberal pro–human rights voting pattern; and northeasterners in the House, unlike those in the Senate, had a higher conservative human rights voting record. This result was unexpected, since in both chambers northeasterners as a group are more liberal than legislators from other regions.

As in the Senate, party affiliation had a strong, indirect effect on human rights voting, while region and seniority had weaker ones. The generalizations made about the Senate hold true for the House: in the House, human rights voting is most strongly predicted by ideology and partisanship.

I also examined a mean scale score of conservative and liberal human rights votes similar to the Senate scale. Again, the model was poor in predicting human rights voting *overall*, with an R^2 of only 0.10. While three members had perfect human rights voting scores, patterns of ideology or partisanship were not apparent overall. As in the Senate, both liberals and conservatives scored low on human rights voting.

The findings from the second model are represented in tables 2.5 and 2.6. When I remove the National Security Index as an independent or intervening variable and examine the direct effect of several independent variables (including party affiliation) on human rights voting, I find that political party identification in the Senate is significantly related to each scale in the expected direction. If we take all human rights measures, we find that Democrats are more likely to vote to support human rights bills (beta $= 0.33, t = 2.76$). No other variable significantly influenced overall human rights voting. Hence the R^2 of all independent variables is a modest 0.16.

Looking next at liberal human rights measures, one can see that party affiliation more powerfully predicts voting (beta $= 0.54, t = 7.18$). Other variables, too, significantly predict voting. Living in the South is strongly and negatively related to a liberal pro–human rights

Table 2.5. Predictors of human rights voting

	All			Liberal on human rights			Conservative on human rights		
	b	beta	t	b	beta	t	b	beta	t
Senate (N = 79, 126)									
Party	10.3	.33	2.76*	30.57	.54	7.18*	−13.14	−.22	−1.92*
Seniority	−.17	−.09	−.73	−.52	−.15	−2.00*	.04	.01	.10
Education	−.40	−.18	−.91	−.41	−.09	−.74	−.52	−.12	−.65
Margin of last victory	−.25	−.18	−1.45	−.03	−.01	−.12	−.41	−.15	−1.29
Military spending/ district	−.00	−.14	−.90	.00	.16	1.84	−.00	−.25	−1.64
Region									
Northeast	−3.26	−.08	−.60	14.99	.19	2.36*	−19.96	−.24	−2.00*
Midwest	−3.62	−.10	−.73	7.56	.12	1.39	−11.87	−.16	−1.30
South	−11.57	−.32	−1.56	−28.02	−.41	−2.98*	9.68	.14	.71
Border	−2.80	−.06	−.30	−12.31	−.12	−1.15	−2.94	−.03	−.17
R^2		.16			.44			.24	

House (N = 321, 370)

Party	-1.77	-.05	-.99	17.31	.31	6.65*	-23.41	-.42	-8.98*
Seniority	-.44	-.22	-3.87*	-.89	-.26	-5.57*	-.27	-.08	-1.64*
Education	.22	.12	1.85*	.53	.17	3.12*	.03	.04	.92
Margin of last victory	.09	.06	1.11	.17	.08	1.54	-.04	-.02	-.34
Military spending/ district	-.00	-.03	-.43	-.00	-.02	-.43	.00	.06	1.16
Region									
Northeast	4.16	.12	1.58	5.57	.09	1.50	4.73	.07	1.19
Midwest	-.88	-.03	-.31	3.70	.06	.95	-1.84	-.03	-.44
South	-.84	-.02	-.27	-15.47	-.22	-3.53*	15.07	.23	3.70*
Border	-5.85	-.10	-1.64	-12.50	-.12	-2.40*	-.21	-.00	-.04
R^2	.11			.27			.21		

*Significant at .05.

Table 2.6. Changes in R^2 when NSI substituted for party affiliation in model

	Total human rights scale		Liberal human rights scale		Conservative human rights scale	
	House	Senate	House	Senate	House	Senate
Model 2 R^2, party has direct effect	.11	.16	.27	.44	.21	.24
Model 1 R^2, NSI has direct effect, party indirect	.10	.07	.42	.60	.44	.45
Effects of party in model 1[a]	−.05	.04	.36	.51	−.44	−.40

a. Indirect effect equals the effect of party on NSI times the effect of NSI on the voting scale. All other variables listed in table 2.5 have been controlled in calculating these effects. The R^2 listed are the totals for the entire equation.

position; living in the Northeast has the opposite effect. And, as expected, seniority has a significant negative relationship with liberal human rights.

Patterns are nearly the reverse on Senate conservative human rights measures. Republicans become the most pro–human rights members, while northeasterners are the least supportive. Southerners do not show a distinctive position on this scale, and military spending in the district continues, surprisingly, to have a negative effect——although the correlation remains insignificant.

As expected, this model more accurately predicts voting on liberal and conservative human rights measures than on overall human rights voting. Forty-four percent of the variance is explained in liberal human rights voting, 24 percent in conservative voting.

In the data on the House, we see similar but not identical patterns. The predictive power of the independent variables declines in each case, especially on the liberal human rights scale. There, our predictors explain only 27 percent of the variation compared to 44 percent in the Senate.

When considered wholly, party affiliation does not influence human rights measures in the House. An examination of the other two scales indicates why: party affiliation relates powerfully, in opposite directions, to each of the other two scales. Democrats are much more likely than Republicans to vote in favor of liberal human rights measures, while the reverse is true on conservative bills. In the Senate, party voting was much stronger on liberal measures, with the effect that Democrats voted in a more pro–human rights direction on the general scale.

Beyond the effect of party identification, the other independent variables show more or less the same significance and direction as found in the first model. Southern representatives, however, gave significantly more support to conservative human rights proposals than did southern senators.

If we compare the two models, it is clear that inclusion of the NSI (with party affiliation considered an indirect influence on human rights voting) allows us to explain more about human rights voting. The differences are presented in table 2.6. While party affiliation does directly affect voting, it explains between 42 percent and 60 percent of the variance in human rights voting on liberal and conservative proposals when combined with orientation toward security issues. The explanatory power of either model remains low for all human rights proposals considered.

Party, Ideology, and Human Rights

In this chapter I have analyzed congressional voting on human rights during the years 1973–84, drawing on an earlier study that compiled information from 1973 to 1976. My main finding is that, when taken as a whole, human rights votes are difficult to predict. As a group, they are not a function of obvious partisanship, ideology, or constituency factors.

Yet when these votes are divided into what I have termed liberal and conservative human rights proposals, voting patterns become quite distinct. Republicans and conservatives tend to vote in favor of human rights policies protecting rightist regimes and punishing leftist ones.

Democrats and liberals tend to vote the opposite way. Both party affiliation and voting record on national security issues are good predictors of these two forms of human rights voting.

As we expected, constituency factors are generally weak predictors of human rights voting. Even when indirect links through national security votes are examined, factors such as region and other constituency characteristics have little or no effect on voting. Rather, human rights voting stems clearly from party affiliation and ideology.

A few individuals vote for human rights across the spectrum, but they are isolated cases and are not easily predictable. Few members of Congress vote consistently against human rights; rather, many vote against human rights bills that seek to impose negative sanctions on a favored regime.

From one point of view, these conclusions are hardly surprising: human rights legislation offers an opportunity for liberals to vote with other liberals and for conservatives to vote with other conservatives. From another point of view, our findings show that few members of Congress manifest either a clearly strategic view in their voting on human rights or a clearly ethical one. Unlike Henry Kissinger, few members would always downgrade human rights in the belief that strategic considerations should predominate over the "domestic" matter of human rights. But few would elevate human rights to a consistently high position in U.S. relations with regimes of every stripe.

Human rights voting in Congress is largely but not completely a partisan and ideological matter, a prospect that cannot be viewed with optimism by the victims of politics in various foreign nations. While members of Congress will occasionally unite to approve human rights measures concerning South Africa, for example, on many human rights resolutions party and ideology prove to be divisive.

Chapter 3

The Fate of General Human Rights Legislation

It seems sort of foolish to have to say "and we meant it" with respect to various legislation. Even so, there may have to be legislation that says "and we meant it." That is, if the administration seems to flout guidelines in the law as to U.S. programs, then the Congress simply has to have outright prohibitions and not merely discretionary determinations by the administration.

—Aryeh Neier,
spokesman for Americas Watch,
in congressional testimony, October 1983

I will examine general human rights legislation by looking first at the "big three" subjects for human rights linkages: security assistance, economic assistance, and international financial institutions. Statutes in each of these areas supposedly denied U.S. foreign assistance when a "consistent pattern of gross violation of internationally recognized human rights" obtained. Then I will analyze the congressional effort to revise U.S. refugee law, to link communist trade privileges to emigration, and to use the U.S. Export-Import Bank as an instrument for human rights.

I will show that despite assertiveness in approving human rights legislation, Congress has great difficulty forcing the executive branch to comply with its requirements. The Reagan administration shows especially well how a determined executive branch can frustrate the apparent will of Congress. During the 1980s Congress has been neither attentive enough nor unified enough to see that general legislation on human rights was implemented. In the case of the big three mandates, the Reagan administration not only violated the law systematically but said openly it was doing so. On revision of the refugee law, Congress was badly splintered, and on the Export-Import Bank it showed little enthusiasm for restricting American exports because of human rights violations abroad (except in South Africa). Only on communist emigration did Congress persevere and effectively oversee what it had originally legislated. As usual, communist violations of human rights were a case apart.

While Congress may not be able to oversee its general legislation effectively, it can compel an administration to follow its will in particular cases. An administration may choose to ignore general legislation, but the intent of the legislation may be applied to particular countries by Congress. The Reagan administration refused to link U.S. foreign assistance to human rights considerations, said so openly on occasion, and got away with it in general; but it also found itself facing legislated bans on security assistance to Guatemala, on economic assistance to Chile, and so forth. This latter phenomenon is treated in subsequent chapters.

Security Assistance

Section 502B of the Foreign Assistance Act of 1961, as amended, reads in part that "no security assistance may be provided to any country the government of which engages in a consistent pattern of gross violations of internationally recognized human rights . . . unless the President certifies in writing to the [Congress] that extraordinary circumstances exist warranting provision of such assistance." This measure, offered in 1974 as a sense-of-the-Congress resolution, was made binding in 1978. The law further states that if the president certifies extraordinary circumstances, "The Congress may at any time thereafter adopt a joint resolution terminating, restricting, or continuing security assistance for such country." Among other provisions, Section 502B states that "licenses may not be issued under the Export Administration Act of 1979 for the export of crime control and detection instruments and equipment" to a gross violator of human rights unless the president certifies the need otherwise (see Appendix A).

The Carter administration was the first to have the responsibility for implementing Section 502B as law, and it is now clear that it paid some attention to this statute—much more so than the preceding Republican administration had done at a time when the section was not so clearly binding.[1] The Carter administration never formally named a gross violator nor formally certified extraordinary circumstances, and even within the Department of State it was not completely clear how Section 502B affected executive decisions. To some participants in the department, it seemed that the section was applied to twelve countries: Argentina, Bolivia, El Salvador, Guatemala, Haiti, Nicaragua, Paraguay, Uruguay, the Philippines, South Korea, Iran, and Zaire. The last four seemed to fit the category of extraordinary circumstances; security assistance was actually terminated to the first eight.

It also seemed clear that the State Department bureaucracy, especially in the geographical bureaus, did not want to implement this statute. It *is* clear that the higher officials, while they might pay some attention to the statute, would not execute the letter of the law by publicly naming consistent violators or by formally certifying exceptions.

There were also times when Section 502B was largely ignored. Indonesia's security assistance was never restricted, yet its government held thousands of political prisoners for long periods and engaged in protracted brutal actions in East Timor. The Carter administration recommended increased military assistance to El Salvador in 1980 and early 1981 though accounts of flagrant violations there were undenied. At approximately the same time, the administration sought increased military sales and the transfer of military equipment to Guatemala despite the continuation of massive violations of human rights.

These actions by the Carter administration went effectively unchallenged in Congress, except those concerning Guatemala. Congress held hearings on human rights violations, including those in Indonesia and East Timor, but only congressional denial of proposed military items to Guatemala in 1980 for 1981 delivery forced a change in executive policy.

Information on the transfer of crime control equipment, including items that might be used for torture, mistreatment, or general repression, is classified by the government. Interviews in Washington indicated that the Carter administration did seek to implement this provision. The Bureau of Human Rights maintained a list of nations seeking such equipment and pressed the Department of Commerce to restrict sales to certain countries. American companies and the Department of Commerce wanted the transfers, thinking human rights restrictions an idealistic interference in business practices that would give competitors a trade advantage. Yet officials in the Bureau of Human Rights and others in the Carter administration sometimes blocked such transfers on the basis of part of Section 502B. The confidential reports sent to Congress seemed to satisfy the few members of Congress and their staff members who monitored these events.

The Reagan administration changed overall policy drastically, wanting to increase security assistance to anticommunist countries. It refused to reduce security assistance or sales because of human rights considerations, thus ignoring the spirit and letter of Section 502B, and there were two reasons for its refusal. First, the United States faced a clear and present danger from the Soviet Union, its allies, and proxies, so it should respond with more, not less, security assistance. Second, repressive allies of the United States, by definition, were better than communists because they would eventually move toward democracy; therefore, by definition they did not engage in a consistent pattern of gross violations of human rights.

This view, called by some the Kirkpatrick thesis on dictatorships and double standards,[2] was in fact the first Reagan administration's policy on most of Section 502B. Elliott Abrams, the assistant secretary of state for human rights and humanitarian affairs, repeated it consistently during the period 1981–84: he said in 1983, "It sometimes seems to me that the essential difference between the Reagan administration and its critics comes down to the single fact that we believe the world to be an exceedingly dangerous place while our critics do not seem to."[3] His statement implied that there was no room to maneuver, that one simply did not have the luxury of manipulating security assistance for human rights reasons. In an interview in 1983, Abrams also said, "You could make the argument that there aren't many countries where there are gross and consistent human rights violations except the communist countries because they have the system itself. It is certainly a plausible way of reading the statute."[4] He added, "What portion of the population in Country X, a Third World country, a Latin American country, if you will, is killed or tortured? It will vary, of course, it is not 100 percent; whereas, in a communist country the portion of the population whose political and civil rights are destroyed of course is 100 percent because it is a dictatorship."[5]

This line of argumentation was followed sometimes in congressional hearings by Abrams and other administration spokesmen. In noncommunist regimes, which are the only ones to receive U.S. security assistance, any statistic or event would be cited to show that a pattern of human rights violations was not completely consistent. No matter how poor the human rights record, there was always the interpretation of improvement. It followed, for the administration, that if anything positive occurred in a right-wing country, Section 502B did not apply. This tactical and legalistic position supported a more fundamental view that, given the communist threat, security assistance and sales should go forward as existing or proposed.

From 1981 to 1984, the Reagan administration reduced or terminated no security assistance for human rights reasons. Indeed, security assistance rose 300 percent from 1980 to 1984.[6]

Congress approved this increase in security assistance and did not object to the Reagan administration's burial of the core provisions of Section 502B. Some persons criticized the administration's treatment of this and other human rights statutes involving the phrase "consistent pattern of gross violations of internationally recognized human rights." These critics were found mainly in a few private groups and House committees or subcommittees dealing with foreign affairs. But with the exception of certain Latin American countries, the administration generally got the security assistance it wanted. Congress did use country-specific legislation to limit, or to block for a time, military assistance or arms sales to Argentina, Chile, El Salvador, and Guatemala. Many members of Congress or their staff members indicated in interviews in 1984, however, that the core of 502B was moribund. The administration would not implement the law, and Congress would do nothing to force compliance. Hence, congressional action shifted to country-specific legislation primarily involving Latin America.

The Reagan administration did, by contrast, seek to implement that part of Section 502B dealing with crime control equipment. In this respect it resembled the Carter administration. In fact, Reagan's human rights team may have exceeded Carter's in vigor and effectiveness, although it is difficult to know since the overall picture remains classified. Interviews toward the end of the first Reagan administration revealed that, in one year, Reagan's people at the Department of State blocked the export of more crime control equipment in the name of human rights than had Carter's. In fiscal year 1983, the Department of Commerce sent 238 applications for export licenses worth $12.7 million to the Department of State for review. It denied licenses worth $1.2 million on human rights grounds. The list of denied countries was said to be reasonable, including such states as the Philippines, Paraguay, and Syria. By contrast, the Carter administration had denied, for fiscal year 1980, ten cases totaling $680,000, mostly affecting rightist governments in Latin America but also the Soviet Union and Iran.

Under the Reagan administration, however, several controversial transfers were approved only to be rescinded under negative publicity. Shock batons—said to be for cattle control but obviously used by police forces against persons—were approved for both South Africa and South Korea, and equipment that could be used for torture was approved for export to all NATO countries, including Turkey, where torture was a fact admitted even by the administration. These approvals were variously attributed to insensitivity by the Department of Commerce, laxness by the Department of State, or other causes. Congress played a role in pressuring the executive branch to change these specific approvals. Congressional interviewees from both parties seemed satisfied with the Reagan administration's overall record on this particular part of Section 502B, probably because there had been no major change from the Carter period, although some interviewees were incensed that shock batons and torture equipment could still be approved initially to South Africa, South Korea, and Turkey.

To summarize actions regarding Section 502B from 1978 to 1984, one can see similarities between the Carter and Reagan administrations. Both wanted to maintain executive flexibility in diplomacy and therefore did not want to name gross violators or formally certify exceptional situations. Both thought the strict requirements of this law pertaining to military assistance and sales were counterproductive to U.S. strategic needs. Neither wanted to offend client states or make relationships more difficult in the future by publicly applying the letter of law. Both administrations, however, blocked the transfer of crime control equipment to an apparently sizable number of countries. Such barriers could be erected in a classified process that normally avoided public embarrassment for both Washington and the client state. And such equipment could be seen sometimes as a genuine human rights issue, separate from the question of defense from external aggression or subversion. Even so, the Department of State under both presidents had to contend with strong support for unrestricted transfers by the Department of Commerce.

There was a real difference between the administrations as well. The Carter people were willing, on occasion, to reduce or terminate security assistance in part for human rights reasons. The record was neither clear nor consistent, but there was the possibility from 1977 to 1980 that Section 502B would be used within the executive branch to justify a reduction or termination. The situation changed under Reagan, and from 1981 to 1984 there was no such possibility.

Whereas Congress had changed Section 502B from 1974 to 1978 to make it more binding and more explicit, it was unable through the legislative process to compel the president to follow the letter (Carter) or even the spirit (Reagan) of this law. Some members were uninterested in the issue, some were sympathetic to the president's arguments, some did not want the responsibility of substituting congressional for executive judgment about the necessity of security assistance.[7] Congress was prepared to disallow what the executive branch wanted in the security field only with regard to a small number of Latin countries, and it did so not by passing a joint resolution under Section 502B but by passing country-specific legislation. Even though Section 502B had been amended and strengthened in 1978, by 1984 it seemed that its direct impact would be nil.

Economic Assistance

The Harkin amendment, or Section 116 of the Foreign Assistance Act of 1961, as amended, prohibited economic assistance to "the government of any country which engages in a consistent pattern of gross violations of internationally recognized human rights . . . unless such assistance will directly benefit the needy people in such country" (see Appendix B). This ban was extended to the Food for Peace Program and to U.S. insurance for American investors abroad. Congress gave itself the authority by joint resolution to override an executive decision on these matters.

Section 116, signed into law in 1974, was not given much attention during the Kissinger years. The Carter administration altered this state of affairs. The so-called Christopher Committee, named after Deputy Secretary of State Warren Christopher, moved actively to coordinate assistance policy. Human rights was one of the factors in the decision to provide economic aid. Section 116 was thus brought to bear on American foreign policy, and the Carter administration occasionally reduced some aid levels because of violations of internationally recognized human rights. The administration did not make these decisions public.[8] Moreover, the Agency for International Development, a supposedly independent organization tied closely to the Department of State, tried to honor the wording of Section 116 concerning "needy people." If it is correct that most AID programs are for "needy people" or meeting basic human needs (BHN), some AID activity is directed, nevertheless, to promoting national economic growth in a more general sense. During the Carter administration, AID, in consultation with the Department of State, altered some of this activity to conform with the intent of Section 116. That is, some AID programs were directed away from a handful of regimes because of their poor human rights records and because the assistance did not meet basic human needs or benefit the most needy in that country (Guinea, Haiti, Indonesia, Liberia, Somalia, and Zaire). Furthermore, AID required six countries to sign special agreements permitting extraordinary U.S. supervision of Public Law 480 food distribution because of human rights problems (Bangladesh, Indonesia, Liberia, Mozambique, Pakistan, and Somalia).

The Reagan administration altered State Department policy regarding Section 116 but not so much AID policy. It was clear from the public and private record that the administration was as reluctant to manipulate economic as security assistance in the name of human rights. Assistant Secretary Abrams said in 1983, "We are reluctant to use economic aid as a tool for our [human rights] policy."[9] The Christopher Committee was effectively disbanded despite a congressional resolution urging its continuance. A lower-ranking coordinating committee met periodically. Occasional memoranda circulated on the subject of human rights and economic aid, but the entire subject was downgraded. The Bureau of Human Rights, like the rest of Reagan's Department of State, did not want to restrict economic aid for human rights reasons.[10] The administration was prepared to restrict aid to some leftist regimes (Nicaragua, for example, which had its aid terminated the day after Reagan took office). Sometimes human rights were cited as the reason for such restrictions, sometimes strategic concerns.

The Agency for International Development, for its part, continued to alter some of its programs to deny general development aid to certain gross violators.[11] The short list in this regard varied, but during the Reagan administration a working group made up of AID, the Bureau of Human Rights, and the regional bureau involved restricted economic aid temporarily to Ethiopia, Uganda, Indonesia, and a few other nations.[12] Since most AID programs were seen as essentially basic human needs programs, the programs and countries so affected were few. AID continued to alter Public Law 480 programs to meet the requirements of Section 116. Halfway through the first Reagan administration, AID testified that Food for Peace programs had to meet special supervisory requirements in Guinea, Haiti, Liberia, Pakistan, Somalia, and Zaire.[13]

Some members of Congress focused, by holding hearings, on one Reagan action related to Section 116. In 1983, while civil unrest born of government repression raged in Chile, the administration signed an agreement with the Pinochet regime permitting future insurance for American investors under the Overseas Private Investment Corporation (OPIC). The administration did not at this time certify progress on human rights as required by other congressional legislation, but it moved ahead with the OPIC general agreement anyway. Several representatives challenged the propriety of this action. Administration spokespersons argued that the signed agreement did not violate Section 116 because no specific OPIC contracts had been signed. Concerned members argued that the general agreement was the wrong signal to send to Chile, given its continuing violations of human rights.[14] As of late 1987, no specific OPIC contracts had been concluded with Pinochet's Chile.

Another part of Section 116 was implemented by AID during the Reagan administration. Congress, not the president, initiated the idea of a positive use of economic aid linked to human rights. In 1981 Congress wrote into law Section 116(e), which provided $1.5 million for the promotion of civil and political rights in developing countries, provided that the money was not used to influence any election. In 1984 it increased that sum to just over $3 million. AID willingly implemented this small program, approving a variety of projects such as providing human rights materials to libraries, helping to train monitors for elections, and helping to pay the costs of human rights seminars for lawyers.[15] Some AID officials noted privately the difficulty of finding projects that could be executed safely in developing countries where working for civil and political rights could appear subversive to the ruling authorities.[16]

Despite the fact that the so-called Harkin amendment was passed in binding form as early as 1974 and was a symbol of congressional assertiveness vis-à-vis the executive branch concerning human rights and foreign policy, by 1984 Congress had expressed little interest in the subject. If a president refused to implement the law, Congress as a whole barely reacted. No attempt was made to pass a concurrent resolution overriding an executive decision under Section 116. The dollar amounts involved were small, and economic aid could be continued to a gross violator anyway provided it went for basic human needs. Some liberal members watched closely such aid programs to right-wing regimes in Latin America. Hearings might relate to Section 116, but any resulting action by Congress was usually country-specific.

A study in 1985 concluded that spending for both security and economic assistance during the Carter and Reagan years was largely maintained at consistent levels and not adjusted significantly for human rights or other reasons.[17]

Multilateral Banks

In the International Financial Institutions Act of 1977, Congress instructed the executive branch via Section 701 to use its "voice and vote" in international financial institutions (IFIs) "to channel assistance toward countries other than those whose governments engage in . . . a consistent pattern of gross violations of internationally recognized human rights . . . unless such assistance is directed specifically to programs which serve the basic human needs of the citizens of such country" (see Appendix C). This language was always controversial; proposed first in 1976 and again in 1977, it was opposed by the president as an unwise restriction on executive authority and a politicization of the multilateral banks. After 1980, the language became the focal point for a lengthy debate between the Reagan administration and its critics concerning human rights.

The forum for much of this debate was the Subcommittee on International Development Institutions and Finance of the House Committee on Banking, Finance and Urban Affairs. It became the place for general debate on the human rights policy of the Reagan administration for several reasons. The language of the International Financial Institutions Act was similar to other human rights legislation, containing the phrase "consistent pattern of gross violations of internationally recognized human rights." More important, there were personnel reasons fueling the debate. On the Subcommittee on International Development Institutions, both the chair and the ranking minority member were interested in human rights, possessed of formidable intellectual powers, and critical of Reagan policy: The chair was Jerry Patterson (D., California); the ranking Republican was Jim Leach (Iowa). They were more informed, active, and critical from 1981 to 1984 than others who might have used their positions to stimulate human rights debate or legislation.

The chairmanship of the Human Rights and International Organizations Subcommittee of the House Foreign Affairs Committee had been given to a moderate Democrat, Gus Yatron (Pennsylvania), when Don Bonker, the former activist chair, changed subcommittees. Representative Yatron, of Greek origin, could be counted upon to interest himself vigorously at least in human rights in Turkey.[18] Under his chairmanship, the Human Rights Subcommittee held hearings on a variety of subjects but did not oversee human rights legislation as actively as under his predecessors. But Patterson's subcommittee sometimes grew assertive, holding joint hearings with subcommittees of the Foreign Affairs Committee. On the Senate side there was no focal point for human rights debate. Republicans held the majority of seats in 1981–86 and were reluctant, with exceptions, to criticize the policies of a Republican president. There was no human rights subcommittee. Therefore, the House, especially the Subcommittee on International Development Institutions, sought to oversee much general human rights legislation.

The Carter administration, despite having opposed the 1977 International Financial Institutions Act, gave some attention to its provisions on human rights from 1978 to 1980 but certainly did not emphasize this kind of legislation.[19] It did abstain or vote against a number of loan proposals in international financial institutions for human rights reasons, and the list of targeted states included right-wing allies (see table 3.1)[20] All loans to the states listed in table 3.1 were eventually approved. It is evident that the United States did not pressure its voting partners to block these loans. Hence the Carter delegation could go on record as voting a concern for human rights without really interfering with international financial institutions' programs. Nevertheless it could at least be said that the Carter administration did not flaunt the International Financial Institutions Act.

The same could not be said for the Reagan administration. In 1981 it began to change U.S. policy in the multilateral banks by voting for loans to right-wing allies while voting against loans to certain left-wing developing countries. Moreover, it did so initially without what Congress thought was the adequate consultation required by law.[21] The two

Table 3.1. Number of loans per year opposed by United States (Carter administration) on human rights grounds

	1977	1978	1979	1980
Argentina	5	6	7	10
Benin	2	—	—	—
Central African Empire	1	—	1	—
Chile	1	3	—	4
El Salvador	—	1	1	—
Ethiopia	2	1	—	—
Guatemala	—	—	1	1
Guinea	1	—	—	—
Laos	1	2	3	3
Paraguay	—	3	4	1
Philippines	1	4	4	3
South Korea	1	—	—	6
South Yemen	—	4	1	2
Uruguay	—	1	1	6
Vietnam	—	6	—	—

actions together produced a vigorous response from Patterson's subcommittee and eventually some revision of the 1977 legislation. An extended analysis of these events illustrates the substance of the debate and some of the inherent weaknesses of Congress.

It is useful at the outset of this analysis to have a clear picture of the changes made by the Reagan administration in U.S. voting in the multilateral banks. The Carter record has been given. The record of the first Reagan administration is summarized in table 3.2.[22] It is clear that the Kirkpatrick thesis on dictatorships and double standards progressively became U.S. policy in international financial institutions. Violations of human rights by anticommunist authoritarian states were overlooked (Section 701 of the International Financial Institutions Act notwithstanding), and human rights violations by communist or Soviet-aligned countries were emphasized. The Department of the Treasury had never liked the intrusion of human rights into banking matters, and Reagan's Department of State was willing to use the leverage of human rights only against leftists.

Members of Congress who were concerned about this policy ex-

Table 3.2. Number of loans per year opposed by United States (first Reagan administration) on human rights grounds

	1981	1982	1983	1984
Angola			4	1
Benin		1		2
Bolivia	1			
Guatemala	1			
Laos	1		1	
Paraguay	1			
Philippines	1			
South Yemen	1	4	1	
Syria		1		1

pressed some reservation about having to change the policy by country-specific legislation. Despite being an activist member Chairman Patterson said, "I would not want to legislate country by country. I would prefer to leave that determination up to the President and to the administration." [23] But as the policy and hearings continued, it became clear that the Reagan administration was not going to implement Section 701. One spokesperson said candidly for that administration in 1981:

Mr. Bosworth: I would only add that I think that it would be unfortunate if there were a straight-line identification drawn between reports of torture and the U.S. votes and the MDBs [multilateral development banks] on loans, because in the human rights reports for 1980, if one reads those carefully, one will find that torture occurred in some 15 to 20 countries in Latin America, and in many more countries around the world. Now, this administration continues to oppose torture as a fundamental issue of human rights. But that does not mean that in each of those countries we consider that we should reflect that concern in our voting, in our pattern of voting on their loans in MDBs. [24]

Even though there was a consistent pattern of torture, the administration was thus not going to let that fact influence its vote in the multilateral development banks. As noted, the administration sometimes argued tactically that any alleged improvement in the human rights situation negated the existence of a consistent pattern of gross violations of human rights. Those arguments provoked Chairman Patterson to say in 1981:

> A key issue here is what constitutes a consistent pattern of gross violations. Another key issue is whether the administration can use apparent improvements as a justification for changing policy, even though admitted violations continue to occur. . . .
>
> Frankly, I have some difficulty with this argument. I doubt that it really meets the test of the law. I also have some problem with the view that one of these countries can hold 850 people in prolonged detention without trial, and the State Department can say there is no consistent pattern of violations because the number of such detainees has declined in recent years. I have some difficulty in addition, comprehending the legal basis of the argument that evidence of torture and other gross violations need not affect U.S. votes in the multilateral banks if somebody downtown decides this might not be the most effective procedure for handling the problem.[25]

As time passed, administration spokespersons repeated their arguments. In 1983 a representative from the Department of the Treasury, which actually instructs U.S. delegations to international financial institutions, said: "We are told [by the State Department] to use the vote to express certain human rights views. In general, however, we think that is a bad idea because if we do it, there is no reason to think that everybody else won't do it. Then these institutions will . . . fall apart."[26] Another said, "We have tried in this administration to delink, if you will, our vote in these institutions from the various sorts of political considerations [such as human rights] that we are talking about here today."[27] Of course, the administration was willing to "politicize" the banks by voting against loans to leftist regimes. One could assume from other statements that this was because a communist regime by definition constituted a consistent pattern of gross violation of internationally recognized human rights. But U.S. votes against loans to nations like Angola, Laos, and South Yemen could have been born of more general ideological opposition.

In 1983, a joint hearing was held before Patterson's subcommittee and the Subcommittee on Africa of the House Committee on Foreign Affairs. The chair of the latter subcommittee was Representative Howard Wolpe (D., Michigan). The following exchange occurred with Assistant Secretary Abrams:

> Chairman Wolpe: Let me ask you this. Do you believe that Angola is, in the language of the statute [Section 701] . . .a gross violator of human rights?
> Mr. Abrams: I have never formed an opinion about that.
> Chairman Wolpe: More importantly, nor has your own Human Rights Bureau.
> Mr. Abrams: We don't actually form opinions about that question because it is not a useful way to spend our time.[28]

In such unguarded moments, Reagan officials admitted that they ignored not only Section 701 but also other legislative acts requiring a judgment about a consistent pattern of gross violations of internationally recognized human rights. In more guarded moments, these officials argued that improvements interrupted a consistent pattern of violations. This argument prompted Congressman Leach on more than one occasion to remark that one could still have a consistent pattern of gross violations even if there were some improvements: "It is as if one were to argue in the days of Nazi Germany that the closing of Dachau and Auschwitz, while leaving Buchenwald open, would represent sufficient 'improvement' to warrant a legal determination that a 'consistent pattern' of gross violations no longer existed."[29]

Patterson, Wolpe, Leach, and other members stressed the logic and legislative history of the law; they were joined by various human rights groups that testified in opposition to administration policy. Section 701 (and other acts) required certain "determinations" based on certain facts. In 1983 they persuaded Congress to drop the word "consistent" from the International Financial Institutions Act. The intention was to signal the administration to stop using the "improvement doctrine" to justify continued assistance, especially in international financial institutions, to those right-wing governments with a pattern of gross violations of human rights. As Chairman Patterson said in testimony, "The deletion clarifies and strengthens, rather than drastically changes, congressional intents and helps clear up ambiguities which have dogged efforts to encourage even-handed enforcement of Section 701."[30] But the administration maintained its double standard of supporting loans to right-wing regimes while voting against loans to leftists. One might force an administration to change its tactical arguments, but one could not, by legislation, force an administration to alter a deeply held view of the world.

Toward the end of the first Reagan administration there appeared some confusion in U.S. policy in international financial institutions, at least with regard to Chile. In 1984 and 1985, in a context of considerable public debate, the administration first voted for a loan to Chile in the Inter-American Development Bank despite a clear pattern of violation of fundamental human rights by the Pinochet dictatorship. Later, the administration threatened to vote against a loan, with a spokesperson explaining that the denial would be based on human rights arguments. Shortly thereafter, the administration indicated further support for the Pinochet regime in several ways, thus calling into question the reason for the threatened vote. Policy seemed confused, although one could not discount an effort, which might have been reversed by others in Washington, by the Bureau of Human Rights to stress human rights violations.[31]

Critics of the administration were in a weak bargaining position regarding Section 701. They could try to shut off funding to international financial institutions, but this move would hurt the oppressed perhaps as much as their oppressors. Most of the critics were liberals who supported multilateral development banks as a good way to help developing countries. They did not want to cripple the banks or hurt the lesser developed countries by denying funds because of Reagan's human rights policies. Hence the critics could exercise only limited leverage, as they admitted publicly[32] and as Reagan officials perceived all along.[33]

The critics could also seek country-specific legislation. But some members thought that this kind of legislation usurped executive authority. And it was an awkward process: a legislative ban would have to be repealed if the situation changed, or renewed each year if it did not. Thus, the administration could stand firm in its fundamental policies.

The best that critics could do was delay what the administration wanted. At one point, Patterson's subcommittee mounted considerable criticism of a projected multilateral loan to Guatemala for the construction of a rural telephone system. The subcommittee challenged the notion that this was a basic human needs loan and thus permissible even though Guatemala's human rights record was atrocious. The loan was stalled for a time but eventually approved with an affirmative U.S. vote in the World Bank.[34]

To summarize the actions surrounding Section 701 of the International Financial Institutions Act, one can say that the Carter and Reagan administrations, especially their Departments of the Treasury, disliked the provisions on human rights. The Carter team did not interfere with loans, but it did not flagrantly violate the law; it used its vote in international financial institutions to signal concern about the human rights situation in a balanced list of countries. The Reagan team basically ignored the law except when it used human rights as a weapon against a leftist regime.

At times, high-ranking officials were candid about their violation of the law. Secretary Abrams said in 1983, "I think 701 does not call for a decision pattern. It calls for us to try to decide among the various means of influencing human rights conditions in a variety of countries. We have to choose when and where to use tools, including these votes."[35] While Section 701 called explicitly for the executive branch to channel multilateral assistance away from regimes with a consistent pattern of gross violations of internationally recognized human rights, Abrams was saying they would do so against leftists but not against rightists. Other tactical arguments were used in support of this fundamental view.

Congress, led by a House subcommittee on banking that vigorously challenged the president, tinkered with the wording of the law but was unwilling to shut off funds to international financial institutions because of Reagan's double standard regarding human rights.

Indeed, Section 701 met the same fate as that of 502B and 116. While all of this general legislation mildly influenced the Carter administration, which was predisposed anyway to do something about human rights, it failed to sway the Reagan administration. The main problem was that any general legislation could be avoided by the executive branch with specious arguments. This point was emphasized in testimony by Michael H. Posner of the Lawyers Committee for International Human Rights: "As a general rule I am concerned that the general human rights provisions, sections 502B and 116 of the Foreign Assistance Act and section 701 of the Banking Act, are couched in very general terms. These words lose meaning when the discussion is limited to broad concluding comments as to what constitutes a consistent pattern. One person's consistent pattern is, to another, an occasional violation." [36]

There being no precise method for making such determinations, the executive branch could stand firm in its policies. As one Carter official from the Bureau of Human Rights remarked in private, only half-jestingly, "We used the straight face test. If you could go up on the Hill and testify and keep a straight face while making your arguments, you could probably get away with it. If your argument was so silly you couldn't keep a straight face, your policy was in trouble." [37]

The situation regarding 502B, 116, and 701 was summed up by Aryeh Neier, Americas Watch, in testimony in 1983: "It seems sort of foolish to have to say 'and we meant it' with respect to various legislation. Even so, there may have to be legislation that says 'and we meant it.' That is, if the administration seems to flout guidelines in the law as to U.S. programs, then the Congress simply has to have outright prohibitions and not merely discretionary determinations by the administration." [38]

Refugee Policy

After World War II, the United States adopted a Cold War approach to refugee policy. Persons fleeing communist countries were viewed as refugees and welcomed to the United States. Those fleeing noncommunist repression met great difficulty in achieving legal admission. This distinction was codified in U.S. law. Growing congressional attention to this state of affairs pushed the Carter administration into an overhaul of refugee policy. [39] The result was the Refugee Act of 1980, a complicated statute that sought to bring balance and fairness to refugee policy but produced, instead, heightened controversy and a still unbalanced policy.

This act employed the United Nations' definition of a refugee, "one who is outside his native or habitual country and is unwilling or unable to return because of a well-founded fear of persecution." [40] This was a legally proper definition, faithfully reflecting the 1967 Protocol on Refugees to which the United States was a party. But it also meant that many persons would seek admission to the United States. The 1980 statute provided two general means of legal access for the growing number of world refugees.

If persons claiming to be refugees under the United Nations' definition were first relocated in a foreign country—say, Guatemalans in Mexico, Ethiopians in the Sudan, or Vietnamese in Malaysia—the United States accepted the label of legal refugee affixed by the host country or the Office of the United Nations High Commissioner for Refugees. Such a label did not obligate the United States to accept a refugee, since it still had discretionary authority to accept or reject such persons as it wished. The 1980 statute allocated a minimum of 50,000 entry permits for such persons, and it allowed the president, in consultation with Congress, to adjust the figure upward and to allocate entrants among various regions or countries. U.S. law also specified which of these refugees were to be given preferential entry into the United States.

If persons claiming to be refugees were found in the United States as the country of first recourse, the United States initially withheld the label of refugee. Such persons had to establish refugee status, then request political asylum. The resulting elaborate process, established by the 1980 legislation, set no numerical floors or ceilings, leaving the numbers and aspects of asylum policy to executive determination. But if the executive branch found the person to be unable or unwilling to return because of a well-founded fear of persecution, the United States was obligated under international law not to send the person back to the situation of persecution.

Shortly after the adoption of the 1980 Refugee Act, the Mariel boatlift from Cuba and rising numbers of Haitian migrants led Congress to be dissatisfied with what it had just legislated.[41] Some members worried about the increased numbers of Latins reaching the United States. Others, like those in the Black Caucus, protested that Haitians were discriminated against while Cubans received favorable treatment. The Carter administration defended itself with claims that resurfaced in the next administration: that Haitians were largely seeking economic improvement; that each had to demonstrate personal persecution by the Duvalier regime; that State Department studies showed no pattern of persecution of those who were returned to Haiti. Hence, in the Carter administration there was already a clear tendency to welcome Cubans fleeing communism but to exclude Haitians leaving a noncommunist country. Crosscutting pressures were already forming in Congress. Senator Strom Thurmond (R., South Carolina), despite being an anticommunist, wanted more restrictions on Cubans fleeing Castro. Others wanted fewer restrictions on Haitians. Still others wanted to know who was going to help the states pay the bills for potential refugee assistance and relocation.

The Reagan administration thus inherited a sizable problem concerning refugee policy. A difficult situation worsened with increasing applications for admission to the United States from persons fleeing martial law in Poland in 1982 and turmoil in the Horn of Africa during the early 1980s. For refugees identified in foreign host countries and "processed" by the Office of the United Nations High Commissioner for Refugees, the administration proposed progressively lower numbers for entry into the United States. Inheriting an entry figure of 217,000, the Reagan administration was proposing by 1985 that the United States accept 70,000—just 20,000 more than the minimum figure set by the 1980 act. Moreover, the administration modeled its policy firmly on Cold War tradition. For these foreign-based refugees, it allotted 50,000 spaces to Southeast Asia, where most refugees fled communist governments in Vietnam and Cambodia, and 9,000 spaces to Eastern Europe. By contrast, only 3,000 were set aside for all of Latin America, where emigrants left mostly right-wing regimes.[42] In fact, administration officials testified to Congress that despite the law requiring individual determination of persecution, groups fleeing places like Vietnam were presumed to be refugees while those fleeing Haiti were presumed not to be.[43]

As for persons claiming refugee status and then asylum in the United States, the Reagan administration denied as many claims as possible. In this regard it continued the policy of the Carter administration (notwithstanding Carter's rhetoric in favor of human rights). Also, the Congressional Select Commission on Immigration and Refugee Policy recommended a "cautious" approach to the number of refugees allowed into the United States.[44] There was concern that the number of persons asking for refugee status and asylum was simply too large. There were "political" complications as well. Since Haitians, Salvadorans, and Guatemalans fled governments supported—sometimes strongly—by the United States, it was obviously embarrassing to admit officially that such regimes persecuted their citizens. Some observers in the United States thought that granting political asylum to such emigrants would alter U.S. domestic politics, perhaps leading to large numbers of future votes supporting "leftist" politicians or "generous" welfare policies.

Therefore, the Reagan administration—through the Immigration and Naturalization Service, as advised by the Department of State—denied almost all claims to political asylum by persons from Central America and the Caribbean. Spokespersons said that such claimants were mostly "economic migrants" seeking better jobs. In effect, the policy demanded that claimants not only show a general denial of human rights in places like Haiti but prove that they had been personally targeted by the regime for persecution.

The administration took two more steps to deter immigrants from south of the border. First, it sought to make life in the United States pending a determination of their status as unpleasant as possible. Immigrants were no longer paroled into society but were detained, sometimes in unpleasant conditions. New detention facilities were constructed, and the one in Louisiana was located far from urban centers—and from legal counsel, who might assist the immigrants in defending their rights.

Second, the Reagan administration instituted the policy of interdicting Haitians in particular before they could reach U.S. jurisdiction. The U.S. Coast Guard, with the permission of the Haitian government and with an official of that government on board, turned back Haitians before they could reach U.S. waters, thus preventing them from making effective claims to refugee status in U.S. courts. The administration argued that an official from the Immigration and Naturalization Service on board was capable of making a sound determination at the time of interdiction. These and other policies were obviously intended to keep the number of successful claimants to an absolute minimum.

In moving to reduce the number of refugees and asylum seekers entering the United States, the Reagan administration acted in conformity with the views of important members of Congress. In July 1981, Senator Alan K. Simpson (R., Wyoming), chair of the Senate Subcommittee on Immigration and Refugees and one who emerged as a key figure in debates on immigration and refugee policy, showed Congress's inclination for greater restrictions when he told Reagan officials:

> Let me say very clearly that I have a strong belief that the primary obligation of government . . . is to promote the national interest; that being the long-term well-being of the majority of its people and their descendants. . . . [T]he interest of the American people . . . is not merely economic. . . . [T]here are other . . .

interests, including the maintenance of freedom, the protection of our citizens from violence and fear, and a responsive and stable political system. And even more basically, I think the national interest includes the preservation of the public cultural qualities and national institutions that make these specific benefits possible.

If legal immigration is continued at a high level and if we do not stop illegal immigration, we'll find that a substantial portion of the influx of new human beings into our land are not able to assimilate into our society and accept our public culture. . . .

For today, the vast and growing world population means that we live in a world of limits, and tragically that may come to mean limits to compassion. . . .

I have referred to that potential unwillingness to respond to others as "compassion fatigue," and the signs I think are all around us that this is already happening.[45]

Nevertheless, persistent criticisms arose that Haitians and others fleeing noncommunist situations were not being treated according to the intent of Congress when it passed the Refugee Act of 1980. Rep. Ramano Mazzoli (D., Kentucky), chair of the House Subcommittee on Immigration and another key player in refugee debates, complained to Reagan officials: "Sometimes it is the governments we are for versus the governments that we are against which seems to determine the [refugee] policy. If we are against a kind of government, then their people, their rejectees, are refugees. Those governments that we are supporting or are for, their rejectees, their flotsam and jetsam, become just another one of the problems of society."[46]

Members of Congress attributed this double standard in U.S. refugee policy to the Department of State, which was accused of playing "political games" with refugee determination. In speaking to a representative of the Department of Justice, Congressman Mazzoli urged greater effort in bureaucratic battles: "Let me encourage you to remember that the Department of Justice is, I believe, a co-equal department of Government, along with the State Department. I do not think they acted in a co-equal way in the spring [of 1981]. I think they got overwhelmed, run over, and stomped on by the State Department. I do not think they should have. I think that ought to be part of your feeling."[47] State Department officials had provoked this criticism in several ways. Some had testified honestly about the administration's policy,

James N. Purcell of the Department's Bureau of Refugee Programs, for example: "If by unequal distribution [of refugees from second countries] that means we have fewer Africans or ones from the Western Hemisphere or the Near East than Indochinese, I think that is a matter of national interest. . . . While I think we have a uniform system, the application of that system has to vary by region depending on the politics and the requirements."[48] He also testified candidly that even when those fleeing Indochinese countries cited economic motivations, the Department of State still treated them as victims of political persecution. He argued that their economic deprivation was a matter of class and, hence, political and that they would be persecuted if sent back.[49]

Even after a U.S. court had found systematic persecution by Haitian officials against those returned by the United States, State Department officials—presumably with straight faces—testified to Congress that Haitians were economic emigrants who faced no problems upon return.[50]

Thus, while the dominant mood favored lower numbers of entrants of all categories, there was unease over State Department policies reflecting Cold War biases in U.S. refugee policy that obviously continued beyond the 1980 Refugee Act. But other concerns cut across this unease. Members of Congress from Florida and sometimes those from elsewhere wanted to maintain restrictions on Haitians even if it reflected a bias, and many members were concerned about the costs of incarceration and assimilation. These ideas undercut concerns about balance and fairness because implementation of a really balanced policy would lead to *more* Haitian and Salvadoran immigration. The only way out of this dilemma—to deny entry to greater numbers of persons fleeing communism in Europe, Asia, and Africa (Ethiopia)—seemed equally unappealing.

Given congressional moods and divisions, several private groups turned to the courts rather than to Congress for alterations in the executive branch's interpretation of the 1980 Refugee Act. Especially on the subject of refugee status for those from Latin America and the Caribbean, the private groups could intervene at several points in the long process of determination. Decisions by the Immigration and Naturalization Service could be reviewed by an immigration judge, then by a Board of Immigration Appeals, then by U.S. District Courts and Courts of Appeals. Several rulings went against the administration, encouraging the private groups who had taken up the cause of the

Haitians or Salvadorans to concentrate their efforts further on the judicial process.[51]

In sum, Congress was aware of the need for revisions in immigration and refugee policy, but it could not agree on precisely what should be done. Election year politics exacerbated the difficulties. The Simpson-Mazzoli bill, which simplified the handling of asylum claims by, among other things, reducing the State Department's role, failed to pass in the election year of 1984.[52] But court cases and continued activity by private groups plus the level of awareness of the general problem ensured that further efforts would be made to refine U.S. refugee policy. In the meantime, the Reagan administration continued its policies of lowering the number of immigrants and giving preference to refugees from communism. A new immigration bill finally passed both houses in 1986 and took legal effect in 1987, but refugee law remained unchanged.

Communist Emigration

The Jackson-Vanik amendment, named after Senators Henry Jackson (D., Washington) and Charles Vanik (D., Ohio), or Section 402(a)(b) of the 1974 Trade Act, prohibits the granting of most-favored-nation status in trade, as well as U.S. credits, to countries with nonmarket economies that restrict unreasonably the right of emigration for their citizens. The president has the authority to waive these restrictions for twelve months if such a waiver would promote the objectives of the act. Congress can disapprove of such a waiver by a simple resolution in either chamber. Neither the 1974 act nor its legislative history clearly defines unreasonable restriction, and the letter of the statute only pertains to emigration. This is the so-called human right of last resort—the right to leave a situation of abuse or persecution.

Congress, mostly with the Soviet Union in mind, approved linking human rights questions to trade with communist countries. Since 1974, however, the Jackson-Vanik amendment apparently has exerted little impact on Soviet emigration policies. In 1973 emigration from the USSR was about 34,000 persons. Immediately after passage of the 1974 Trade Act, the Soviet Union repudiated the Jackson-Vanik amendment; it withdrew its request for most-favored-nation status and reduced emigration. By 1978 Soviet emigration had fallen to about 20,000. But in 1979, without any legislative change in the amendment's status, Soviet emigration rose to about 50,000.[53] Despite a temporarily negative effect on emigration from the USSR, the Jackson-Vanik provision did not impede levels of emigration over time. Whether the Soviets allowed emigration to increase because of hopes of influencing American opinion on other issues, such as the ratification of the SALT II treaty, is a matter of conjecture. During the Reagan administrations, Soviet emigration declined slightly, and there was constant harassment of persons applying to emigrate.[54] The USSR did not renew its request for most-favored-nation status.

Three communist countries achieved most-favored-nation status by the mid-1980s. Romania was so named by the Ford administration, and the Carter administration issued subsequent waivers. The Carter administration added Hungary and the People's Republic of China to the list of nonmarket economies with reasonable emigration procedures. Waivers for all three countries were renewed initially by the Reagan administration. Congress, which reviewed the status of the Jackson-Vanik amendment annually, concurred in all these actions.[55]

After considerable debate over the wisdom of the Jackson-Vanik amendment in 1973–74, there arose a consensus in support of the amendment both in principle and in applying it to particular countries. Certain countries such as the USSR, East Germany, Czechoslovakia, and Bulgaria clearly restricted the right of emigration in a fundamental way, and there was no question but that they fell under the restrictions of Section 402. Other countries, such as Hungary and China (after U.S. normalization of relations in 1979), clearly permitted emigration as a general rule and were thus clearly entitled to most-favored-nation status.

During the Reagan administrations, however, controversy over Romania resurfaced. Emigration policies in that country had never been so clear-cut as in Hungary. Yet as of mid-1982, three administrations of two political parties had judged that Romania had made enough progress in allowing reasonable emigration so that a waiver was in order. Congress had agreed.[56] In the summer of 1982, two conservative senators, Jesse Helms (R., North Carolina) and Steven Symms (R., Idaho), introduced a resolution that would have blocked most-favored-nation status for Romania. A variety of people testified against the resolution, including Senator Jackson himself, spokesmen for Jewish and Christian organizations, businessmen, and representatives from the Departments of State and Commerce. It was historically clear that Romanian emigration had jumped significantly after Jackson-Vanik: from 4,469 in 1973, to 12,633 in 1978, to 16,893 in 1980, and to 19,000 in 1984. Many problems remained, but because such a clear pattern permitting more emigration had emerged, because Romania had maintained a foreign policy independent of the Soviet Union on a number of issues, and because trade with Romania had increased, giving a number of American businesses a stake in a renewed waiver, the Helms-Symms proposal at first got nowhere.

Shortly after the Reagan waiver of 1982 took effect, the Romanian government imposed, along with other financial obligations, a so-called education tax on those wishing to emigrate. This action led to considerable concern at both ends of Pennsylvania Avenue, especially since executive and congressional officials had been in touch with Bucharest and had been led to believe that remaining problems concerning emigration would be attended to. In March 1983 the president, in the context of congressional criticism of Romania's action, indicated that most-favored-nation status would be denied when the current waiver expired in June of that year.[57] The Romanian government then revised its emigration policies, including the elimination of the education tax, which was to have been paid in hard currency—an extra difficulty for Romanians for whom the possession of foreign currency is illegal. Congressional officials traveled to Romania and informed authorities that the president's denial of the waiver would be sustained by Congress.[58] The Romanian government then again revised its emigration policies.

While the Jackson-Vanik amendment had thus done little for emigration from some communist countries, it had been important in dealing with Romania. There was general agreement in Washington on its use. Congress played an active role both in monitoring executive interpretations and in discussing matters with foreign governments. A few members of Congress and some ethnic groups had especially wanted to punish Romania for its communist policies apart from emigration. Some felt that there remained too many unreasonable restrictions on emigration procedures. But these views failed to command much support through 1986. (In mid-1987, however, both houses voted to suspend Romania's most-favored-nation status, despite generally unchanged emigration policies. Members of Congress were seeking to punish Romania for religious persecution.)

Jackson-Vanik became, by the mid-1980s, that rare item in Washington: human rights legislation supported by both parties and both branches that at least on some occasions could be seen as helpful in promoting certain human rights. But when applied to Romania, Jackson-Vanik had become controversial by 1987. Congress finally accepted the view that most-favored-nation status should be governed by more than the right to emigration.

Export-Import Financing

Brief mention can be made of the rapid rise, limited use, and rapid decline of the idea that the U.S. Export-Import Bank should be a weapon in the fight to promote human rights in U.S. foreign policy. It has been noted that Congress authorized the president to deny Export-Import Bank credits to human rights violators where the U.S. national interest would be so advanced. In such cases, foreign parties could not obtain an Export-Import Bank loan to purchase goods or services from American companies.

The early form of this authorization was supported in principle by the Carter administration, but that administration never viewed economic sanctions as a major weapon in the struggle to protect human rights abroad,[59] with the major exception of its support for U.N. economic sanctions on Rhodesia. It had to be forced by Congress into a coffee embargo on Uganda.[60] The Carter administration denied or delayed Export-Import Bank credits to only four countries: Argentina, Chile, South Africa, and Uruguay.[61] Even this limited use of the bank for human rights purposes proved highly unpopular with the American business community and its champions in Congress. Some also saw an unacceptable double standard used by the Carter administration when Argentina and Uruguay were denied Export-Import Bank credits at the same time that most-favored-nation status in trade relations was given to Hungary and the People's Republic of China despite their obvious violations of civil and political rights.[62]

Given this reluctance in both branches to use the Export-Import Bank extensively in the human rights cause, it is not surprising that, during the Reagan administration, the bank ceased to be even a limited instrument for protecting human rights. In an era of U.S. trade imbalances and growing concern about the American ability to compete successfully in world markets, Washington cared little about curtailing American exports in the name of human rights. Indeed, in congressional hearings on the Export-Import Bank during the first Reagan administration, the subject of human rights had no consequence whatsoever.[63] Needless to say, the administration did not act under the authorization granted to it to link the bank with human rights.

Only on the subject of South Africa was there a continuing desire in the Congress to prevent Export-Import Bank credits in the name of human rights. In 1978, at perhaps the apogee of congressional activism on human rights, Congress adopted the Evans amendment, named after Thomas Evans (R., Delaware), binding the Sullivan principles to Export-Import Bank loans in South Africa.[64] In general, the principles constituted a voluntary code for U.S. firms doing business in South Africa, and over 175 firms signed on. Their performance was then monitored by the Arthur D. Little Company of Cambridge, Massachusetts, which made an annual report to Reverend Sullivan. Congress made the principles mandatory for any South African agency and any American firm in that country that sought credits from the Export-Import Bank. No bank loan could go forward until the executive branch certified that progress was being made in the implementation of the principles.

The Carter administration implemented this law, a posture consistent with not only its verbal attacks on South African apartheid but also its 1977 vote in the U.N. Security Council in favor of a mandatory arms embargo on the Republic of South Africa. That administration, however, did not favor a general economic embargo on the Republic—or economic sanctions on Uganda in response to human rights violations there.

The Reagan administration also followed the Evans amendment, despite its shift to the policy toward South Africa of "constructive engagement," which emphasized positive rather than negative approaches to ending apartheid. No certification was made that would have allowed Export-Import Bank loans to governmental agencies or American firms, although the Reagan administration did change executive export regulations to allow more sales to the South African government, including its military and police. Because such executive actions called into question the administration's commitment to ending apartheid (Ambassador Kirkpatrick met with high-ranking South African military officials in a departure from U.S. practice), parts of Congress kept close watch over South African policy in general, including the fate of the Evans amendment.[65] There was some discussion of making the Sullivan principles legally binding for all American firms in South Africa, not just any who might seek Export-Import Bank credits.

It is not known exactly why the Reagan administration did not certify progress on human rights or try to repeal the Evans amendment. That administration "massaged" the facts to certify progress on human rights in El Salvador and Haiti (as will be seen), and it sought the repeal of the ban on U.S. aid for foreign policy training (a partially successful effort, covered in chapter 5). Perhaps the issue was too minor. Members of Congress, while refusing to extend the mandatory nature of the Sullivan principles, did progressively move toward support for general economic sanctions against South Africa. Quite possibly, therefore, the Reagan administration decided to implement the Evans amendment in order not to antagonize Congress, even though the amendment was inconsistent with its stated "constructive" approach to South Africa. In 1987, Reverend Sullivan called for abandoning his principles; in his view they had not had the desired effect so he came to favor general economic sanctions, including a withdrawal of foreign investment.[66]

Chapter 4

Country-Specific Legislation: Central America

[I]n your [State Department's] human rights report you document some progress on human rights in El Salvador. In 1981, although not clearly pointed out in your report, there were something like 10,000 to 12,000 noncombatant deaths; in 1982, maybe 6,000 to 8,000 noncombatant deaths. That is good progress, but it is like closing Buchenwald and keeping Auschwitz open. . . .

My question to you is, under section 502B do you feel the U.S. Government . . . can continue military assistance to the Government of El Salvador?

—Representative Jim Leach (R., Iowa)
Human Rights in El Salvador, House Committee on Foreign Affairs,
1983, 5

Congress enacted not only general but also specific legislation on human rights. After the Chilean coup of 1973, for example, it passed a number of measures on Chile, some of them specifically predating much of the general legislation. Country-specific legislation on human rights came to prominence in congressional deliberations relating to Central America during the period of this study.

When it wished, Congress could influence foreign policy through specific legislation, as events pertaining to El Salvador, Guatemala, and Nicaragua bear out. At the same time, Congress could ignore some specific legislation once it was passed. One act might require a presidential certification of progress on human rights matters in El Salvador and another in Haiti, but there was a world of difference in how Congress treated those two requirements.

El Salvador

During the period under study, El Salvador presented one of the most salient foreign policy problems before Congress. Indeed, Lebanon and Poland, Nicaragua and South Africa, arms control and immigration all claimed substantial attention. But El Salvador consumed much congressional time especially during the first Reagan administration, and the human rights question was the center of the debate.

In El Salvador, the Carter administration inherited a situation common to much of Central and South America. For years, a small aristocracy had allied with senior military officials to rule the country for their benefit, in the process denying basic human rights to the overwhelming majority of the population. In 1979 junior army officers, perhaps trying to avoid the fate of their brother officers in neighboring Nicaragua, deposed the Romero government, established a civilian junta, and tried to reform the country. But a rebellion already under way (which included Marxists) merged with a rightist backlash against the attempted reforms. The rebels committed mayhem in the name of the left; the ultrarightists—undeniably including the important political figure Roberto d'Aubuisson—threatened coups against the civilian junta, attacked the U.S. embassy, and killed supporters and beneficiaries of the reforms.[1]

The Carter administration supported the 1979 coup and tried to build up the political center while opposing the extremes on both sides. For most of its tenure the administration opposed military aid to the Salvadoran military, believing the rebels relatively weak and the military a distinct threat to the political and economic reforms presumably needed to undercut the rebels' appeal. Uncertain of the military's commitment to reform, the administration withheld military assistance to gain leverage for Salvadoran human rights and other reforms.[2]

Toward the end of the Carter administration, however, several events altered U.S. policy and increased congressional concern. On December 4, 1980, four American churchwomen were raped and murdered in El Salvador. Since they had been helping the poor, they were viewed as "political activists" by a number of people, including the future U.S. representative to the United Nations Jeane Kirkpatrick and Secretary of State Alexander Haig. It is highly probable they were ordered killed by ultraconservatives.[3] In response to the murders, the

Carter administration suspended economic assistance to El Salvador. The following January, two American labor advisers assisting in the land reform policies of the junta were also killed, again presumably by rightists. For many Americans, including many members of Congress, these murders spotlighted human rights abuses in El Salvador.

In that same winter of 1980–81, two other events pushed the Carter administration in new directions and attracted the attention of Congress. First the rebels proclaimed their "final offensive." It fizzled, but it raised the question of whether the rebels could win militarily. When their international supporters, including Communist Vietnam and Ethiopia, sent them more aid, using Cuba and Nicaragua for transshipment,[4] the Carter administration resumed economic aid shortly after suspending it and, for the first time, sent small amounts of military aid—$10 million, half of it in lethal equipment. The lethal aid was provided one day after the U.S. ambassador in San Salvador, Robert E. White, said that no progress was being made by Salvadoran authorities in the investigation of the murder of the American churchwomen.

At this point the Reagan administration entered office, and some of its early actions caused both houses of Congress to take a greater interest in El Salvador, joining a debate that was to last, off and on, for at least four years. If events during the winter of 1980–81 had not stimulated Congress to monitor U.S. policies in El Salvador, the new Reagan administration took several steps that guaranteed congressional activism. First, the administration abruptly removed Ambassador White from San Salvador and effectively forced him into retirement. This action assured him a hearing in Congress, an opportunity that he used fully to express his views. Second, the administration broke with Carter policies and lobbied for a $20-million military assistance program accompanied by more American advisors on the ground. This step was pursued even though some evidence showed that Napoleon Duarte and other civilian members of the junta really were opposed to it, notwithstanding their formal request for military aid.[5]

Both the House and Senate held extensive hearings on El Salvador as early as March 1981. Democrats in the House were especially well positioned to raise questions about Salvadoran policy. The House Inter-American Subcommittee of the Foreign Affairs Committee was chaired by Michael Barnes (D., Maryland), a critic of emerging Republican policy. The larger Foreign Affairs Committee, while initially more cautious under Clement Zablocki (D., Wisconsin) and, later,

Dante Fascell (D., Florida), turned out to be overwhelmingly critical. When the 1981 foreign aid bill and subsequent continuing resolutions on funding went to the House Appropriations Committee, they had to pass through the Subcommittee on Foreign Operations, chaired until 1985 by Clarence Long (D., Maryland), a crusty critic of Reagan's policies on El Salvador.

Each of these bodies had conservative members who welcomed the administration's attacks on communism and its support for military assistance in El Salvador. Charles Wilson (D., Texas), Henry Hyde (R., Illinois), Jack Kemp (R., New York), and others contested the majority Democratic view, but it became clear that many in the House had reservations about the course of U.S. policy.

That these same reservations should be voiced with some effectiveness in the Senate as well indicates that they were not generated solely by Democratic party loyalty. After the Republicans took control of the Senate in January 1981, Charles Percy (R., Illinois), new chair of the Foreign Relations Committee, professed support for the administration's foreign policy, but he broke with the administration on the nomination of Ernest Lefever to be assistant secretary of state for human rights. Percy was at the center of those opposing Lefever's view that U.S. human rights policy should be consolidated into an anticommunist policy.[6] The Republican majority in committee did not save Lefever from a 13–4 negative vote, and the administration withdrew his nomination.

The Foreign Relations Committee's Subcommittee on Western Hemisphere Affairs was chaired by Jesse Helms (R., North Carolina), one of the most conservative senators and one who had supportive ties to d'Aubuisson. Helms, like d'Aubuisson, opposed the junta's nationalizations and land reform, and he regarded Christian Democrat Duarte as too far to the left. Yet Helms was far to the right of his own subcommittee, which was made up of critics Ed Zorinski (D., Nebraska), Paul Tsongas (D., Massachusetts), and Christopher Dodd (D., Connecticut) as well as moderates Richard Lugar (R., Indiana) and Nancy Kassebaum (R., Kansas) and conservative S. I. Hayakawa (R., California). On the larger Foreign Relations Committee there were many liberals or moderates, including Democrats Claiborne Pell (Rhode Island), Joseph Biden (Delaware), John Glenn (Ohio), Paul Sarbanes (Maryland), and Alan Cranston (California). On the Republican side, Charles Mathias (Maryland) was liberal while Rudy Boschwitz (Minnesota) and Larry Pressler (South Dakota) were independent moderates. Given this committee makeup and lingering fears of another Vietnam, it was not surprising that the administration's policy on El Salvador encountered greater scrutiny in the Senate as well as in the House. Senate Republicans voted repeatedly against the administration on El Salvador.

In the debate between the Reagan administration and its congressional critics, the lessons of Munich and of Vietnam were argued. The main point, in Secretary of State Alexander Haig's words, was that El Salvador represented a "textbook case" of communist aggression.[7] State Department spokesmen followed this line, alluding to appeasement at Munich in 1938 and subsequent totalitarian aggression:

> If there was some reason to think that, if they [the Communists] succeeded with this in El Salvador, their appetite would be satisfied, would be sated, and they would never do it again, perhaps that would be one situation. But we know they don't see things that way. They concentrate their efforts where there is an area of weakness and they will, at least on all precedents, continue to do that. We have to keep this perspective of El Salvador as part of a much bigger issue, an issue which goes to the basis of what we stand for in this country, and we cannot lose sight of the fact that it was the Communists who first engaged in a massive military intervention in El Salvador by supplying weapons.[8]

Secretary Haig wanted to go to "the source" and use military force against Cuba, advice rejected by President Reagan.[9] While the administration refused to go to the source, it nevertheless continued to see the primary issue in El Salvador as a communist threat to U.S. security. It professed interest in curtailing human rights violations by ultraconservatives, but it stated publicly that it would do whatever was necessary to defeat the communist insurgency.[10] Logically, this position could encourage ultraconservatives to continue their violence, since they knew that the Reagan administration would make specific human rights secondary to anticommunist action. The Department of State spoke out against a rightist coup and distanced itself from d'Aubuisson, and the administration argued that movement toward democratic elections and better training for the security forces would correct human rights problems on the anticommunist side.[11] It argued that specific human rights legislation restricting foreign aid would have a "stop-and-go" effect on U.S. efforts, leading to rebel successes.[12] The administration wanted more foreign assistance from Congress, but it also wanted a free hand to deal with human rights problems through executive diplomacy.

Administration critics drew frequently on the supposed lesson of Vietnam, namely that the United States should not get deeply involved in the name of anticommunism on the side of brutal shaky governments in developing countries. Such governments made weak allies by alienating the people they were supposed to be saving from the communists. This view was well represented by a series of questions directed at an administration spokesman in 1981 by Senator Joseph R. Biden, Jr.: "Have we picked a winner this time? Can we win? Is our side going to prevail, or are we going to mount another horse and ride it gallantly into a swamp and sink with it as we seem to have done so many times in the past in Democratic and Republican administrations?"[13]

Critics of the administration's policies were sensitive to the problems of how to curtail reactionary violence by the extreme right without contributing to the political success of the extreme left.[14] Yet these critical members of Congress were unwilling to leave specific human rights problems to administration diplomacy. They were unwilling to provide U.S. foreign assistance without any human rights conditions, especially since right-wing atrocities had continued during the Reagan administration. (In 1981 and 1982 there was little response to the murder of Americans, and reactionary violence against Salvadorans was uncurtailed.)[15] In general, congressional critics feared that the administration would wind up with Americans engaged in combat on behalf of a brutal and corrupt regime, as they had been in Vietnam.

Throughout 1981, right-wing violence in El Salvador continued (as did left-wing violence, but with fewer civilian deaths attributed to the rebels). There was ample reason to suspect that U.S. military assistance was strengthening reactionary elements. As early as April, the House Foreign Affairs Committee voted 26–7 to ban further military assistance until the junta was able to suppress the killing of civilians by forces associated with the government. This stand was too restrictive for most members of Congress, and at the end of 1981 a different approach received majority support.

In the 1981 foreign aid bill (covering fiscal year 1982–83), Congress voted to require the president either to certify progress on human rights matters in El Salvador or to terminate economic and military assistance. The president was required specifically to certify each 180 days starting in January 1982 that the government of El Salvador was (1) making a "concerted and significant" effort to protect "internationally recognized human rights," (2) achieving "substantial control" over its security forces so as to end human rights abuses, (3) making "continued progress" in land reform and other socioeconomic reforms, and (4) moving toward supervised elections and negotiations with all political factions that renounced violence.[16]

With these strings attached, Congress finally voted more economic and military assistance to El Salvador for fiscal year 1982–83, much less than the administration wanted but more than some thought it could get. The administration had resisted the certification requirement but accepted it after the Republican Senate voted for it 54–42. (The Foreign Relations Committee had voted 11–1 in favor of it.) Congress did not put much faith in its general legislation on human rights (such as Sections 502B or 116E) to restrict the executive branch; nor did it turn to the War Powers Act to keep the executive from further involvement in El Salvador. While some members mentioned these general acts, most debate concentrated on what kind of country-specific legislation to adopt.

On four occasions the Reagan administration submitted certification statements to Congress under the 1981 legislation. Each time it tried to put the best possible face on a poor situation in El Salvador. And each time congressional critics of U.S. Salvadoran policy held hearings and heaped scorn on the administration's statements.[17]

In 1983 Congress elaborated the certification requirement. Henceforth the president had to certify also that the Salvadoran government was making a "good faith" effort to investigate the deaths of the four American churchwomen and "to bring to justice" the perpetrators of the deed and that it was taking "all reasonable steps" to investigate the killing of another American, Robert Kline, shot in the fall of 1982.

Some members of Congress and private human rights groups pressed for suspension of U.S. military aid to El Salvador, using the argument that the presidential certifications were bogus and that only a termination of aid would bring the repressive security forces to heel. Most members preferred to maintain the certification process. By passing the certification requirements, Congress reminded the president of its commitment to human rights but did not interfere with the executive branch's struggle against Marxist rebels. The certification mechanism allowed Congress to take its stand for human rights without the risk of being held responsible for the rebels' successes. It seemed a convenient halfway measure; it periodically burdened the executive branch but left it with the responsibility for a possible failure of policy.

By the summer of 1983, a stalemate had developed over U.S. policy. The administration would get some aid to El Salvador, more economic than military, though more of both each year than the year before. But Congress would turn down about 50 percent of the administration's requests and attach conditions to those it approved. Thus the executive branch could pursue the outlines of its desired policy, but Congress made it difficult to achieve policy goals. Since some members of Congress favored greater restrictions, its future actions could not be taken for granted.

Doubtless weary of this deadlock and of making dubious certifications, President Reagan tried to use a pocket veto on the certification requirement in the fall of 1983 (that is, he did not sign the 1983 foreign aid bill before Congress went into recess). At this time, Congress had backed off somewhat in overseeing the presidential certifications; questioning of the fourth certification had not been notably tough.[18]

Challenged by the president's veto, Congress altered its approach to Salvadoran policy but not as the executive branch wanted. In 1984 it withheld 30 percent of the funds authorized for El Salvador until specific human rights concerns were addressed. Chief among its requirements was bringing to trial those accused of murdering the American churchwomen. In addition, it voted a new certification requirement and continued to reduce the administration's aid requests by about half. The attempted use of the pocket veto thus left the president with a more assertive Congress, and he still had to go through a certification process.

Some members of Congress had become unhappy with the certification process, and the president's open challenge to congressional prerogatives produced a new majority favoring assertiveness. Typical was the frustration expressed by Congressman Ted Weiss (D., New York) to a group of critical witnesses during 1983 hearings:

All of you have expressed your sense of frustration at this process that we have engaged in over the course of the years. I think we all share that frustration with you. . . .

[A] certification process [should not] legitimize what, in fact, has been transpiring. . . .

[I]t is very difficult for the Congress to limit the way in which the President makes foreign policy. Most of the initiative rests with the executive branch.

The only real weapon that the Congress has in shaping foreign policy is control over the purse. I would simply urge that the Congress, or that members of Congress, express their disapproval of what is going on in El Salvador and of the administration's backing for the forces that are committing all these murders simply by using every possible occasion to try to block funds for the Government of El Salvador.[19]

During 1984 the Department of State labored to arrange the trial of five lower-ranking military people in El Salvador, and as a result the authorized military and economic assistance was released. To be sure, higher officials were never charged; indeed, a U.S. report suggesting a cover-up in the case by higher Salvadoran officials was suppressed by the Department of State.[20] Nevertheless, by withholding aid, Congress had forced a trial when no trial had been forthcoming. The Reagan administration also complied with the general certification requirement in 1984.

Other events in 1984 caused the problem of El Salvador to recede a little from American politics, mainly the presidential election in May in which the Christian Democrats under Napoleon Duarte won a plurality and, hence, the presidency. The U.S. government, through both the CIA and the Department of State, supported opponents of d'Aubuisson and his ARENA party. After the 1982 elections, the United States had worked to set up a constituent assembly and to prevent d'Aubuisson from assuming its presidency. Despite well-publicized U.S. financial and diplomatic interventions,[21] Congress took the view—over Senator Helms's strong objections—that the Salvadoran elections had been fair and free. The 1984 elections, combined with a subsequent visit to Congress by Duarte, satisfied a number of members that overall progress was being made in El Salvador. Congress began to relax its vigorous monitoring of executive policy in El Salvador, yet it did not give the president a free hand. It continued to reduce the administration's aid requests, and for fiscal year 1985–86 it withheld $5 million of authorized funds until concrete steps were taken by Salvadoran authorities toward a trial of those responsible for the deaths of the two American labor advisers.

In sum, Congress kept some pressure on the administration from 1981 to 1984 to do something about human rights violations by Salvadoran security forces and their political associates. At first the administration downgraded such concern in the name of U.S. security interests relative to international communism. But then congressional demand for certification and the accompanying debates, followed by the withholding of a percentage of authorized aid, probably pushed the administration to do more about rightist human rights violations than it otherwise would have done. Testimony made clear that the administration would always argue that progress was being made even when it was not, that the government in San Salvador was cooperating even when it was not, and that, in general, improvement lay on the horizon. A skeptical Congress was wary of these presentations, and, goaded by the president's pocket veto, began to withhold money; this action produced some change in El Salvador, incomplete though it was. By moving from general certification requirements to withholding specific funds, which the executive branch could not evade, Congress forced changes in American policy. The president could not be sure that it would not move to a complete ban, at least on military assistance, as it did for a limited time in the early 1980s on funds for the anticommunist rebels in Nicaragua.

By 1985, however, the administration had achieved much of what it set out to do in Salvadoran policy. It had broken with the Carter policy by greatly increasing assistance to El Salvador: in 1981, U.S. economic aid was $106.6 million, in 1984, $329.3 million. Military aid had grown from $35.5 million to $196.5 million. The Marxist rebels seemed no stronger in the mid-1980s than in the winter of 1980–81, although this could have been attributed to continued land reform as much as to increased military assistance and training. The administration's emphasis on elections as a solution to human rights abuses had been vindicated politically if not factually. There was more congressional satisfaction with U.S. policy after Duarte's election in 1984, even if it could not be proved that those elections were fair and free or that the new civilian government was clearly in control of "its" security forces. Indeed, many observers saw Duarte's power as much circumscribed by security forces after the election as before.[22]

By the end of the first Reagan administration, both Congress and the president had achieved much of what they wanted. U.S. policy seemed more sensitive to human rights abuses by rightists than it had been in early 1981, socioeconomic reforms continued, and American combat forces had not been introduced. U.S. military assistance and training had increased; the Marxist rebels, while not defeated, seemed less threatening; and a centrist government had been elected. The dialectic of the congressional–executive branch struggle had produced a synthetic policy that was not unreasonable from the point of view of reformists in El Salvador like Duarte. Congress still did not trust completely the Reagan administration's policy; in the mid-1980s it passed legislation so that a right-wing coup would produce automatically a total ban on U.S. assistance to El Salvador.

Nicaragua

The Somoza dynasty in Nicaragua, created and supported for half a century by the United States, finally provoked its long-suffering citizens to revolt in the 1970s. The Somoza family had so suppressed, repressed, and oppressed the Nicaraguans that, after a bloody civil war, a broad-based opposition installed itself as a new government in mid-1979.

The Carter administration played an important role in the final phase of this process. True to its image, the administration vacillated in its approach to Anastasio Somoza Debayle during 1977 and 1978, sometimes criticizing the dictator, sometimes providing him foreign assistance as a "reward" for his "progressive reforms." As the Sandinista revolution came to its denouement in 1979, however, the Carter administration worked diplomatically to end the Somoza regime, finally offering the head of state political asylum if he would relinquish power. In its own ambiguous style, the Carter administration thus sought to end a long era of U.S. support for gross violations of human rights in Nicaragua.[23]

Moreover, the Carter administration recognized and tried to normalize relations with the new government in Managua despite the presence of Marxists in the broad Sandinista National Liberation Front. The administration, hoping to co-opt the Sandinista government, granted it discretionary economic assistance of some $60 million to aid the country's economic development after the civil war and to keep Managua out of the political orbit of Havana and Moscow. In the 1980 appropriation, the Carter administration sought an additional $75 million from Congress for foreign aid to Nicaragua.

Congress, however, was deeply divided about the wisdom of the co-optation strategy. In the House of Representatives, some conservatives were suspicious of the left wing of the Sandinista National Liberation Front and feared the creation of a Cuban-model state. Some conservative members like Charles Wilson (D., Texas), Robert E. Bauman (R., Maryland), and John Murphy (D., New York) had long supported the Somoza regime in the name of anticommunism and had been close socially to the last dictator. After the revolution of 1979, they sought to block foreign aid to Managua by proposing that none could be provided without prior congressional approval. This measure lost in the House by a narrow margin, signaling rough times for co-optation.[24]

When Carter proposed the $75 million aid package for 1980, the Senate went along, only Senator Helms strongly opposing it. In the House, on the other hand, a bipartisan conservative coalition fought hard to derail aid for Nicaragua. One tactic used was delay, another loading up the bill with crippling amendments. As a result Carter got his aid bill of $75 million some seven months after he sought it, with a dozen stipulations attached. Indeed, the Nicaraguan aid bill of 1980 may be a classic example of Congress attaching strings to an aid program.[25] The aid was to be terminated if the president found that Nicaragua supported terrorism or that Soviet or Cuban combat troops in Nicaragua constituted a security threat to the United States. No aid was to be used for any project related to Cuban personnel; 60 percent of it was to go to the private sector and 1 percent to publicize in Nicaragua that the aid came from the United States.

There were also human rights provisions among the restrictions on Nicaraguan aid. The executive branch was to report to Congress every six months on human rights conditions, and it was to evaluate the human rights situation when administering aid. It was to urge support for free and fair elections, and aid was to be terminated if the president found a consistent pattern of gross violations of human rights in Nicaragua.

The Carter administration and its supporters in Congress accepted these conditions as the only way to get the aid. The administration then implemented the aid program and fulfilled the technical reporting requirements. But the provisions had been motivated not so much by genuine concern for the rights of Nicaraguans as by a desire to use human rights matters and other restrictions for strategic ends. In the House, according to the *Congressional Quarterly,* "the spectre of communist subversion from Cuba was the overriding concern." [26]

Within days of assuming office, the Reagan administration suspended virtually all U.S. foreign assistance to Nicaragua, thus killing the co-optation approach. It moved toward a strategy of confrontation in which human rights criticisms eventually played a prominent role. It can be argued persuasively that the administration saw the human rights issue in the same way conservatives in the House did: a tactical means to a strategic end. If one is genuinely interested in the well-being of Nicaraguans, one does not support rebel attacks resulting in the murder and rape of noncombatants, and one does not veto multilateral bank loans intended for the construction of rural roads. [27] It might be argued, on the other hand, that such military and economic coercion is intended to block communist denials of civil and political rights.

In its early rhetoric about Nicaragua, the Reagan administration stressed security interests. It charged the Sandinista government (increasingly dominated by Marxists after the defection of the non-Marxists who had helped make the revolution) with subverting neighboring states, especially El Salvador. Some facts bolstered this allegation. As the Reagan administration moved to support and partially direct the armed attacks on Nicaragua, it insisted that attacks by the contras were for the purpose only of changing Sandinista policy. They were supposedly a countervailing pressure to force Managua to stop its interventions in El Salvador.

In late 1983 President Reagan began to speak of human rights violations in Nicaragua. [28] Other persons in his administration had spoken of human rights violations under the Sandinistas, but in late 1983 high-ranking officials began to mention Nicaraguan human rights matters more frequently. It became increasingly difficult to say with assurance what bothered the United States more—the Sandinistas' revolutionary foreign policy or their imposition at home of a Marxist party-state that violated human rights.

Insofar as one saw U.S. Nicaraguan policy as responsive to both of these issues, one did not have to choose. [29] But the distinction remained important. If the major concern was the Sandinistas' revolutionary foreign policy, then one could have normal relations with a Marxist Nicaragua that moderated its foreign policy objectives. If the major concern was the nature of the regime itself, then there could be no accommodation until the government in Managua was purged of Marxists.

This latter concern appeared to dominate Reagan's policy from 1983 onward. The president himself declared that the Sandinistas would have to "cry uncle" before the United States would ease the pressure—that is, they would have to surrender power.[30] And the administration in general dropped its arguments that the contra (or rebel) attacks were not designed to overthrow the Sandinistas but rather to pressure them to behave in foreign affairs. Moreover, the administration refused to accept the legitimacy of the 1985 presidential elections in Nicaragua and continued to stress human rights violations, especially those pertaining to the Miskito Indians in northwestern Nicaragua. Yet the administration maintained diplomatic relations with Managua, and Secretary Shultz said on television in 1985 that the issue was not the Marxist nature of the regime at home but rather its revolutionary goals abroad.[31]

The administration's public vagueness and shifting criticisms may have derived in part from congressional opinion. Given the earlier House sentiment on this question, it is surprising that many representatives were highly critical of Reagan's policy toward Nicaragua. The issue was not the termination of economic aid. Indeed, Congress had passed another country-specific measure in 1981 that again tied foreign assistance in Nicaragua to human rights (and U.S. security) concerns. A long and explicit provision in this bill reminded its readers that the Sandinistas had promised attention to elections and other human rights and stipulated that the government in Managua was "to establish full respect for human rights in Nicaragua in accordance with the United Nations Universal Declaration of the Rights and Duties of Man [sic] and the Charter on Human Rights of the Organization of American States."[32] As if this provision were insufficient, despite the fact that no Latin American state had ever fully implemented both standards, Congress further required the free movement of the Inter-American Commission on Human Rights in Nicaragua and fair and free elections for offices from the highest to the lowest rank. It appended restrictions regarding U.S. security and other matters. Given this congressional sentiment on foreign aid in late 1981, it was not surprising that Congress had deferred quietly to the suspension of most economic aid by the Reagan administration earlier that year. During 1982, only $6.3 million reached Managua from Washington.[33]

The main controversy in Congress stemmed from CIA involvement in military attacks against Nicaraguan territory. A near majority in the House had feared Carter's co-optation strategy; from 1981, a clear majority there opposed covert involvement against Nicaragua. Beginning in 1981, the Democrat-dominated House was willing to halt CIA "dirty tricks" in Nicaragua, and it had voted to do so four times by 1985. Whereas the previous Senate deferred to Carter's co-optation, from 1981 the Republican-controlled Senate would not go along with a cut-off of CIA activity. A compromise was struck in which Congress agreed to authorize funds for CIA activity linked to the contras but not for the purpose of overthrowing the Sandinistas. This was the surface meaning of the so-called Boland amendment of 1982, named after Richard Boland (D., Massachusetts), the Democratic chair of the House Select Committee on Intelligence. The measure supposedly restricted the executive branch and was supported by critical Democrats in the House; but to comply with its language, all the president had to do was say that his intention was to influence, not overthrow. Congressional conservatives realized it was not a major problem. The amendment passed in the House 411–0, indicating that it was not viewed as a serious restriction on the president's decisions pertaining to Nicaragua.

During Reagan's two terms, congressional debate on Nicaragua concentrated more on certain actions of the CIA than on general questions about initiating covert activities. Congress debated human rights in Nicaragua and the nature of Sandinista foreign policy as well. But it did not address consistently the question of whether either of these subjects merited military attacks on Nicaragua involving the U.S. government. Rather, Congress debated whether U.S. dirty tricks should be allowed to violate international law, as did the mining of Nicaraguan harbors. It debated whether the CIA was keeping it informed of covert actions in a full and timely way and whether U.S. support should be limited to "humanitarian" assistance to the contras—that is, funds for nonlethal purchases. But Congress did not consistently focus on whether Sandinista intervention and subversion justified contra attacks or whether the violation of human rights in Nicaragua somehow justified those attacks.[34]

The Reagan administration itself treated the first of these points in a way that suggested that Sandinista foreign policy was not terribly revolutionary. Reagan officials admitted publicly at one point that Sandinista arms shipments to rebels in El Salvador had been sporadic, not massive and consistent.[35] Furthermore, the administration refused to participate in the World Court case brought by Nicaragua charging the United States with illegal intervention and aggression. This refusal suggested strongly that the administration did not have the evidence to support its allegation that the military attacks on Nicaragua constituted collective self-defense of El Salvador in response to illegal Nicaraguan intervention there.[36]

On the extent of human rights violations, the Reagan administration maintained a harsh line. Observers generally agreed that serious human rights violations had occurred.[37] Managua had suppressed the Miskito Indians with a heavy hand (and a Sandinista spokesman had admitted as much while averring a commitment to change). People's courts that denied recognized procedures for due process had been instituted. Reports of torture and mistreatment during interrogation were made credible by the fact that the International Committee of the Red Cross was not allowed access to places of interrogation.[38]

But the administration's treatment of the human rights issue lacked a sense of balance, proportion, and contextual analysis. Some members of Congress tried to get at these points.[39] Senators Dodd and Zorinsky both indirectly raised the issue of whether the Miskitos were being organized and armed by the CIA or Honduras and whether Managua might therefore have some legitimate security interest in displacing those Indians from their traditional villages. This line of questioning was weak, leading nowhere in Senate proceedings.

Some members of the House, like Representative Peter Kostmayer (D., Pennsylvania), made some legitimate points about the Sandinistas: they had a better record on protecting the right to life than many of their Central American neighbors whom the United States was supporting; they had detained members of Somoza's national guard humanely; they did not commit political murder or engage in forced disappearances as general policy; and they had provided social and economic services far beyond what had been provided under

Somoza.[40] Likewise Congressman Leach challenged the administration's versions of human rights violations and in so doing gave an interpretation of human rights matters in Nicaragua that offered a sharp contrast to Ambassador Kirkpatrick's treatment.[41]

The exchanges about human rights under the Sandinistas that occurred in both Senate and House hearings remained largely disconnected from the fundamental questions about U.S. policy toward Nicaragua. The debates concentrated on the micromanagement of the CIA rather than on why the CIA should be joining in attacks on Nicaragua at all. To be sure, good reasoning urged an examination of the CIA role. Why should anyone expect the Nicaraguans to rally to a force made up to a significant degree of former members of Somoza's detested National Guard and directed to a large extent by the same Yankee colossus that had supported the repressive Somoza dynasty?[42] But such tactical questions tended to displace the more important questions of whether human rights violations could justify military attacks and whether Sandinista subversion in Central American was serious enough to justify those attacks. Congress, of course, did limit and restrict funding to the CIA, and by so doing it raised questions about the direction of U.S. policy.[43] But the administration continued to misreport the human rights situation in Nicaragua, to make unsubstantiated statements about Sandinista subversion, and to violate international law as determined by the World Court. The two pieces of country-specific legislation on human rights, from 1980 and 1981, died soon after becoming law, bypassed by events and executive decisions.

Guatemala

In Central American terms, Guatemala is an important nation because of its location, size, population, and professional army. It is far more important in geostrategic terms than either El Salvador or Nicaragua, yet it usually received far less attention in Washington than either of these other two Central American nations. As Lars Schoultz has noted, Washington is more sensitive to human rights affecting what it perceives as U.S. security than to human rights per se.[44] Guatemala had not drawn much attention because it has been ruled since 1954 by a noncommunist military elite, which alleviated Washington's security worries. Extensive political murder and other repression by the government went almost unnoticed, despite the fact that the regimes stemming from the CIA-installed 1954 government were as brutal as those in Nicaragua under the Somoza dynasty. Over the years, opponents and critics of the regimes were eliminated, and the large Indian population remained nonpolitical.

U.S. relations with Guatemala changed in 1977 when the Carter administration announced that Guatemala had one of the worst human rights records in Latin America and targeted it for a reduction in military assistance. This step was part of the emerging Carter policy of taking concrete action on human rights in countries where lack of major U.S. economic interests and lack of communist threat made such steps attractive. But before Washington could implement this policy, Guatemala itself broke off the military assistance program, charging interference in its domestic affairs. From this beginning, an embargo on formal military assistance grew to transcend the changing of power in the White House. The embargo on military goods was not complete, however, and during the Carter administration some $8.5 million worth of military assistance reached Guatemala by way of U.S.-approved export licenses to private companies.[45] Also during that administration, U.S. bilateral economic aid slowed to a trickle, as table 4.1 shows.[46]

Thus the Carter administration implemented, with the help of Guatemala itself, a policy of disassociation because of violations of human rights. The major overt exception constituted a small amount of economic aid intended to benefit the neediest civilians. This exception was consistent with the letter and spirit of general congressional legislation on bilateral economic aid, as well as legislation on indirect aid through multilateral banks like the World Bank and the Inter-American Development Bank. Congress supported this policy direction, especially after the 1978 coup, which brought General Lucas Garcia to power. Under his four-year rule, human rights violations remained not only major but obvious. He seemed oblivious to any need to conceal his repression, apparently indifferent to whether relations with Washington improved or not.[47]

The Reagan administration, despite a consistent pattern of gross violations of human rights in Garcia's Guatemala, tried to do there what it had tried in other countries—namely, to end the policy of disassociation and support the anticommunist regime. The basic arguments were familiar to persons who had observed the administration's views toward general human rights legislation as well as toward other countries like El Salvador: the major issue was communist insurrec-

Table 4.1. U.S. loans and grants to Guatemala, 1976–80 (in $ millions)

Year	Develop- ment aid	Economic Support Fund	Food for Peace	Misc.	Total eco- nomic aid
1976	29.0	0	12.5	2.0	43.5
1977	14.3	0	4.5	2.0	20.8
1978	4.5	0	4.6	1.5	10.6
1979	17.4	0	5.3	2.0	24.7
1980	7.8	0	3.3	1.9	13.0

tion, the policy of disassociation was counterproductive, and general human rights legislation would not be implemented because it was not effective.[48]

State Department spokespersons had to devise some new arguments for Guatemala. There they could not plausibly pretend that there was sufficient progress in protecting human rights to justify full U.S. support. Indeed, in 1981 a department spokesperson observed that the human rights situation was deteriorating,[49] refusing to answer when asked about governmental violations of fundamental human rights.[50] Hence the Reagan administration, through the Department of State, began to argue that the Guatemalan government had developed a siege mentality because of its negative approach to human rights issues and that more U.S. aid, not less, was needed to gain positive leverage with it. This was the doctrine of constructive engagement applied to friendly Central American regimes.[51]

But Congress rejected this argument. When the Reagan administration permitted an export license to be issued for some military trucks and jeeps in 1981, House Democrats in particular and others like Congressman Jim Leach criticized the move.[52] Congress maintained the export licenses, but each subsequent year it turned down the administration's request for military assistance. Even in 1982 following a coup in Guatemala, after a United Nations rapporteur submitted a somewhat favorable report about Guatemala, and after the Reagan administration seized upon that report to argue that "substantial improvement" was occurring in the human rights situation,[53] Congress still turned down an administration request for $25,000 in military assistance. Key members of Congress found the U.N. report out of line with testimony from Amnesty International, Americas Watch, and other private human rights groups.[54] They simply did not believe the assertions of overall improvements, and they did not believe that renewing military assistance would better protect human rights. The Reagan administration did what it could on its own, issuing export licenses for $6.3 million worth of private military sales.

A coup in March 1982 brought General Rios Montt to power, and the Reagan administration tried to claim that the Montt regime was making substantial improvements. The president himself proclaimed that Montt had been given a "bum rap" by his critics.[55] Those with more knowledge and objectivity, however, had noted in the rural areas a conscious policy of atrocities designed to intimidate the Indians, who were beginning to be more active politically.[56] Montt quickly lost favor with his military colleagues, partly because of his evangelical Protestantism in a strongly Catholic nation, and he was overthrown in August 1983 by General Mejia Victores. These events seemed to thwart temporarily the administration's attempts to pry formal military assistance out of the Congress. Having presented Montt so strongly as the savior of the Guatemalan situation, it was difficult if not impossible to present Mejia Victores in the same light. By 1983, Congress was so skeptical of the Guatemalan government that it required U.S. development aid to be administered by private organizations.[57]

The administration persisted, however, in trying to implement the theory of dictatorships and double standards that Jeane Kirkpatrick had articulated so well. Each year it would request for Guatemala higher levels of economic assistance and some type of military assistance, thus nibbling around the edge of the problem and hoping to reduce the resistance of Congress. In 1984, for example, the administration requested $35 million in economic support funds, which are used in relation to military expenditures. It requested $300,000 in military training, and it tried to get $10 million in concessionary military loans to underwrite sales of military equipment.[58] But Congress would not budge. For fiscal year 1985, it approved no formal or direct military assistance and no economic support funds, no military training funds (IMET), and no concessionary loans (foreign military sales).[59] It insisted on disassociation as pressure for Guatemalan human rights improvements. Its main tool was the budget bill, but it did attach the 1983 country-specific requirement pertaining to administration of economic aid through private organizations.

Since the rebellion in Guatemala was so weak, Congress could stick to its policy of disassociation without much fear of being tagged by the Reagan administration with causing the loss of Guatemala to the communists. Moreover, through 1984 few clear signs of overall progress in human rights appeared. These factors made the situation in Guatemala different from that in places like El Salvador. In the second Reagan administration, Mejia Victores and other key military officials in Guatemala seemed to be at least improving their image and perhaps even making real improvements in the human rights situation. A civilian president was finally elected in reasonably fair and free elections. To the extent that this was due to congressional pressure, it showed that a policy of disassociation might produce progressive changes in an isolated regime. If true, it would disprove the Kirkpatrick thesis, since change would have been brought about by U.S. pressure combined with international pressure,[60] not by a U.S. embrace.

Guatemala in the late 1980s thus presented a situation similar to that in Honduras, Paraguay, and certain other Latin American states. It possessed at least a facade of democracy, with elections, some freedom of association, and a legally unrestricted press. But the military was still an independent force not fully controlled by laws or civilian officials, and numerous violations of personal integrity occurred. In this situation, the Reagan administration advocated a full embrace, while members of Congress like Senator Mark Hatfield advocated continuing U.S. scrutiny and pressure to solidify the fragile democracy. Senator Hatfield wrote, "To do otherwise is to succumb to the unforgivable naiveté that the military network that perpetuated a systematic torture of suspected adversaries has somehow magically 'disappeared'—like so many thousands of Guatemalan citizens."[61]

Chapter 5

Other Country-Specific Legislation

Well, I think it is terribly important that our government . . . makes
clear that we stand for democracy, and that we are not supporting the kind
of repression that the people of Chile have been subjected to. If there is a
lesson that we can learn from other comparable situations, it is that when
it is over . . . we don't want it to be perceived that we were part of the
problem.

—Michael D. Barnes (D., Md.),
Human Rights in Argentina, House Committee on
International Relations, 1976, 182

Western Hemisphere Countries

We have previously seen that specific legislation can affect the executive branch's conduct of foreign policy in places like El Salvador, Nicaragua, and Guatemala. In this chapter I will show that outside of
Central America this may or may not be true. A great deal depends on
congressional politics and the seriousness of congressional oversight.

Chile.—Congressional interest in human rights in Chile dates from
the mid-1970s, the time of the first wave of congressional activism on
human rights in general. The Marxist Allende government was overthrown in 1973. If Congress had deferred to moves by the executive
branch in Chile before and during the Allende period and had looked
the other way when President Nixon and National Security Advisor
Kissinger acted to destabilize Allende,[1] it was not inclined to ignore the
abuses of human rights that accompanied the subsequent Pinochet dictatorship. It was characteristic of the imperial presidency that Nixon
and Kissinger were able to disrupt the Chilean economy covertly and
to urge Chilean military officials to move against Allende—and get
away with it. Executive testimony in Congress about the nature of U.S.
foreign policy toward that nation constituted a buffer against reality.[2]
But it was a sign of the new Congress that President Ford and Secre-

tary of State Kissinger were not to have their way so easily from 1974 onward.

The Pinochet regime sought to eliminate its opposition through murder, detention and torture, forced exile, martial law, and other means of extreme repression during the period from 1973 to 1976. These actions went unopposed by the United States; indeed, when the U.S. ambassador in Santiago brought up the subject of human rights, Kissinger reprimanded him.[3]

Congress, stirred not only by events in Chile but also by a growing wariness of Kissinger, moved gingerly at first, requesting in late 1973 that the executive branch pursue the subject of human rights with the Pinochet government. This typically cautious first move had a predictable, which is to say imperceptible, effect on Kissinger. In 1974 Congress took more decisive action, placing a ceiling of $25 million on economic aid to Chile and banning new military assistance. When the violations of human rights in Chile continued, it banned the remaining military relationships in 1976. While not terminating all economic assistance, it moved very far in trying to disassociate the United States from the severe repression in Chile.

The basic problem for Congress was that Kissinger would not implement the law; meanwhile Pinochet liquidated his opposition. For each limit or restriction that Congress placed on aid (especially economic aid), Kissinger would produce a State Department lawyer with legalese exempting the programs he wished to continue. As a close observer of these events has concluded, "The case of economic aid to Chile demonstrates that an administration with a will can find a way to circumvent congressional limitations in foreign assistance legislation. By the time Congress became aware of and closed the loopholes, the Pinochet regime had exterminated its opposition and no longer required the support of the United States economic aid program."[4] Furthermore, Congress was unable to prevent Kissinger and Ford from close diplomatic relations with, and probably covert support for, Pinochet.

But events in 1976 changed U.S. relations with Chile. In September, Chilean secret agents murdered Orlando Letelier, who had been Allende's foreign minister, and his assistant in Washington, D.C. In November, Jimmy Carter won the presidential election.

Unlike his predecessors, Carter implemented congressional restrictions against Chile. His administration moved to reduce further what economic assistance was still permitted. It used quiet diplomacy to try to protect particular persons in Chile, and one can assume that Carter reduced covert support for the junta. The administration voted against multilateral loans to Chile even if the loans in institutions like the World Bank were approved. Major violations of human rights continued in Chile, however, for the duration of the Carter presidency. If the worst human rights abuses had ended by then, it was only because Pinochet had brutally crushed his opposition.

From 1977 to 1980 the impact of U.S. policy on Pinochet was slight despite congressional and presidential agreement on the goals and tactics of policy. Both branches sought disassociation through manipulation of bilateral assistance. But bilateral aid was not a powerful enough weapon against Pinochet. By 1980 U.S. economic aid was only $10.2 million (mainly for the Peace Corps and Food for Peace programs).[5] While direct aid declined, indirect aid through the international banks continued,[6] and private lending to Chile increased during the Carter period.[7] In both 1978 and 1980 Pinochet held and won plebiscites on his rule. Foreign criticism had generated support for the junta, as had the desire of the important Chilean middle class for order and economic growth.

Upon taking office in 1981, the Reagan administration clearly sought to end the policy of disassociation. In February and March of that year, the new administration signaled its intentions in three concrete ways. By executive order it decreed that Chile could resume joint military exercises and that the Export-Import Bank would conclude a technical agreement with Chile opening the way for a possible resumption of loans. In Geneva the U.S. delegation in the United Nations Human Rights Commission voted against a French resolution calling for continuation of the UN special rapporteur investigating violations of human rights in Chile. (The resolution passed, with only three Latin American states joining the United States in opposing it.) U.S. Ambassador to the United Nations Jeane Kirkpatrick clarified the meaning of these steps when she called for normalization of relations with Chile.[8]

Liberal Democrats in the House were not ignoring the emerging policy toward Pinochet and, as early as March 1981, held hearings to raise criticisms of Reagan's policy.[9] Since Secretary of State Haig was emphasizing U.S. opposition to terrorism around the world, congressional critics focused on the Letelier murder and tried to paint the Pinochet government as supporting terrorism. That government had refused to extradite the suspected murderers, who had been indicted by a U.S. grand jury, and it refused to prosecute them within Chile. In 1981, when the Reagan administration asked Congress to repeal the 1976 ban on military assistance to Chile, critics of the policy were able to give the president what he wanted while, at the same time, taking it back.

After repealing the ban on military assistance, Congress legislated that

(1) no assistance may be furnished under [specified sections of] the Foreign Assistance Act of 1961 to Chile;

(2) no sale of defense articles or services may be made under the Arms Export Control Act to Chile;

(3) no credits (including participation in credits) may be extended and no loan may be guaranteed under the Arms Export Control Act with respect to Chile; and

(4) no export licenses may be issued under section 38 of the Arms Export Control Act to or for the Government of Chile;

unless and until the President submits to the . . . House . . . and . . . the Senate a detailed report certifying—

(A) that the Government of Chile has made significant progress in complying with internationally recognized principles of human rights;

(B) that the provision of such assistance, articles or services is in the national interest of the United States; and

(C) that the Government of Chile is not aiding or abetting international terrorism and has taken appropriate steps to cooperate to bring to justice by all legal means available in the United States or Chile those indicted by a United States grand jury in connection with the murders of Orlando Letelier and Ronni Moffitt.[10]

Congress thus forced the executive branch to continue disassociation from the Pinochet government as far as overt economic and military assistance was concerned, with some minor exceptions. The executive branch was left with the normal conduct of diplomacy, as well as with whatever covert relations existed, to signal its support for an anticommunist government. It also voted for multilateral loans to Chile. In the Inter-American Development Bank, Chilean loans jumped from zero in 1980 to almost $181 million in 1981 and $182 million in 1982.[11]

Toward the end of its first term, the Reagan administration showed some public confusion over its human rights policy toward Chile, and this confusion perhaps confirmed reports that Elliott Abrams and the Bureau of Human Rights and Humanitarian Affairs were in favor of a tougher policy toward Pinochet.[12] In the context of State Department public statements endorsing movement toward democracy, the administration voted for a loan to Chile in the Inter-American Development Bank but then said further affirmative votes would depend on Chile's progress in human rights. Had this been the real policy, it would have reflected a change in the administration's position, for it had never opposed or blocked a loan to Chile previously. In the end, it voted for all loans to Chile despite the lack of overall progress there on human rights matters.[13] This voting record, to many observers, violated the 1977 law linking U.S. action in the multilateral banks to promotion of human rights. But there was no specific law banning such loans to Chile. The executive branch thus continued to associate the United States with Pinochet erratically when not prevented by the Congress from doing so.

The second Reagan administration toughened U.S. policy toward Chile. Internationally, the fall of Marcos in the Philippines and Duvalier in Haiti increased the prominence of dictatorial Chile, where the extreme left renewed its violent attacks against a Pinochet regime that refused to move significantly toward restoration of civil and political rights. The Reagan administration tried to advertise itself as an opponent of tyranny whether of the left or right, but this image making— designed partly to generate congressional support for the contras in Central America—made its connection with Pinochet embarrassing. For these reasons and perhaps others, the second Reagan administration shifted its position and publicly criticized Pinochet's Chile.

The Reagan administration grew active at the United Nations Human Rights Commission not in defense of Pinochet, as it had at the start of Reagan's first term, but in criticizing him, and the United States voted for a condemnatory resolution. In Washington a number of critical public statements were made, and one can safely assume that the decibel level of quiet diplomacy rose as well. In all of this, the Reagan administration probably saw the denial of civil and political rights as injurious to its efforts to undermine the extreme left. This had been the case in the Philippines as well, where the administration belatedly rallied to the side of the human rights movement after it noticed the growth in power of the Marxist New Peoples Army. In Chile also, the Reagan administration finally recognized that the Kirkpatrick doctrine was incompatible with the steps needed to undercut the radical left's resurgence. Probably this reason more than any other caused U.S. policy to shift in the direction that congressional voting had been taking since 1973. While the Reagan administration did not formally endorse disassociation from Pinochet, it took minor steps toward that end in the mid-1980s.

Congress did not force a change in U.S. policy toward Chile; rather, executive perceptions of Chilean politics confirmed the wisdom of what Congress had endorsed. (It is possible that Congress had interrupted normal relations with Chile because of moral fervor and that this action only chanced to coincide with more careful calculations of U.S. national interest. This possibility cannot be proved or disproved, since the legislative history of congressional Chilean measures does not reveal the dominant reason for congressional votes.) It is also probable that the decisions of high-ranking Reagan officials finally reflected what Elliott Abrams had been recommending for some time as assistant secretary for human rights or for inter-American affairs—namely, that support for civil and political rights in Chile was in the U.S. national interest.

Argentina.—In 1976 the Argentine military overthrew an inept civilian government amid much chaos and confusion in the public life of that country. The resulting junta proceeded to institute a "dirty war" against an exceedingly broadly defined left. Among the major problems was the institutionalization of the practice of forced disappearances: governmental forces did not acknowledge responsibility for the detention of innumerable persons, which left the captors free to engage in torture, murder, and other gross violations of human rights. Many parts of Argentine society looked the other way rather than confront these abuses, as did the U.S. government during 1976.[14]

This situation drew the attention of the Carter administration in 1977, and the Congress supported a tougher policy. The administration reduced military assistance because of human rights violations; Argentina itself then broke off the military assistance program, whereupon Congress legislated a total ban on such assistance and on military sales. The administration and Congress also terminated direct economic aid. Moreover, the Carter administration voted in the multilateral banks against Argentine loan applications, and in a more erratic way interjected its human rights concerns into the operations of the U.S. Export-Import Bank.[15]

By 1978 the Carter administration and Congress were thus united in a policy of disassociation from the Argentine junta because of gross violations of human rights. It was also hoped that the denial of assistance would pressure the junta into reforms, but that did not occur. If political murders declined after the first couple of years of military rule, it was largely because the opposition—or perhaps more accurately those targeted in the dirty war—had been controlled or eliminated. During the late 1970s, many Argentinians supported the junta in the hope of improved order and economic growth. Private investments and bank loans continued to flow into Argentina despite the cutoff of official U.S. aid, and the junta developed military and economic ties with European states. When the Carter administration applied a grain embargo on the Soviet Union after its invasion of Afghanistan, Argentina increased grain sales to the USSR.

U.S. foreign policy toward Argentina under military rule was thus largely consistent but also largely ineffective during the Carter administration. The combined effects of negative pressure plus disassociation did not bring about structural change. Against this background, the administration's quiet diplomacy did save some lives, including that of the journalist Jacobo Timerman.[16] The policy of disassociation, at least, made clear that the United States did not have the responsibility for Argentine events, a point of some importance in the aftermath of brutally harsh regimes.

The Reagan administration tried to alter U.S. policy toward Argentina in 1981. Its efforts to improve relations were consistent with its other steps in Latin America to emphasize anticommunism and deemphasize human rights violations by anticommunist regimes. The administration sent troubleshooter General Vernon Walters to Buenos Aires for private discussions, and Secretary of State Haig received high-ranking Argentinian officials in Washington. In Geneva the U.S. delegation to the U.N. Human Rights Commission voted to defend the junta against international pressure. The administration tried to shift more military and economic assistance toward Argentina and also asked Congress to repeal its ban on economic assistance.[17]

Congress appeared to give the Reagan administration what it wished when, in 1981, it repealed Section 620B of the Foreign Assistance Act of 1961. But then it attached a certification requirement that effectively negated the repeal. In late 1981 Congress passed a country-specific measure including the following provisions:

(b) Notwithstanding any other provision of law, assistance may be provided to Argentina under chapter 2, 4, 5, or 6 or part II of the Foreign Assistance Act of 1961, credits . . . may be extended and loans may be guaranteed with respect to Argentina under the Arms Export Control Act, defense articles and defense services may be sold to Argentina under the Arms Export Control Act, only if the President has submitted to the Speaker of the House of Representatives and the chairman of the Committee on Foreign Relations of the Senate a detailed report certifying that—

(1) the Government of Argentina made significant progress in complying with internationally recognized principles of human rights; and

(2) the provision of such assistance, credits, loan guarantees, defense articles, defense services, or export licenses is in the national interest of the United States.

(c) The Congress welcomes the actions of the Government of Argentina to adjudicate numerous cases of those detained under the national executive power of the Argentine Government, and the Congress hopes that progress will continue, especially with regard to providing information on citizens listed as "disappeared" and prisoners remaining at the disposition of the national executive power. In the process of making the determination required in paragraph (1) of subsection (b), among other things, the President shall consider

(1) efforts by the Government of Argentina to provide information on citizens identified as "disappeared"; and

(2) efforts by the Government of Argentina to release or bring to justice those prisoners held at the disposition of the national executive power (PEN).[18]

Congress thereby replaced a total ban on economic and military assistance with legislation leaving foreign policy determinations squarely to the executive branch, though with guidelines as to congressional interests. Congress wanted both economic and military assistance to be contingent on progress in human rights matters, and it specified its primary human rights concerns.

Given the strong support for this legislation in both houses, the Reagan administration did not try to certify progress on human rights in Argentina for the remainder of 1981 and into 1982. But it does appear that the administration manipulated matters so that it might eventually move to certification and, hence, a resumption of foreign aid. In its 1982 Country Report on Argentina dealing with human rights, the administration reported that the junta had begun to inform relatives about the fate of many detainees.[19] When this report was published in early 1983, a number of watchful members of Congress disputed the State Department's version of events, as did several private human rights groups. Hearings were held in the House, and the department could not substantiate the contents of its report.[20] The hearings also served notice that subcommittees with responsibility for human rights in Argentina were watching carefully what the administration did in that regard. The issue of Argentine certification also drew attention in the elite press. When, for example, in late 1982 rumors had circulated that the administration was about to certify progress on human rights and hence to resume military aid, the *New York Times* carried an op-ed piece critically reviewing the state of human rights under the junta.[21]

The Reagan administration wanted to normalize relations with the Argentine junta and to handle human rights matters through quiet diplomacy, but Congress frustrated this desire initially, and the use of force by the junta in the Falklands/Malvinas war completed the process. The country-specific legislation therefore had an impact on U.S. foreign policy until the junta fell through its own failures at home and abroad. Growing unrest at home over the human rights issue, where several Argentine private groups had bravely taken up the cause, a deteriorating economy, and finally the British victory in the war removed the junta and made the certification legislation a moot point.

Upon Argentina's free and fair election of a civilian government in 1983, the Reagan administration certified progress in human rights. There was no opposition in Congress. The administration offered military assistance to the new Alfonsin government, which rejected it. Moreover, Alfonsin withdrew Argentine military personnel from Central America, where they had been operating in close conjunction with U.S. policy. The Reagan administration thus encountered considerable coolness from Buenos Aires after the fall of the junta. Some congressmen like Rep. Michael Barnes (D., Maryland) had anticipated this problem and had tried to warn the administration of the dangers of becoming too cozy with repressive regimes,[22] one of the reasons that many in Congress had resisted Reagan's policies in Latin America. Congressional resistance over policy toward Argentina not only greatly affected the policy but proved correct in the long run. It was especially clear that a double standard favoring anticommunist dictators and ignoring their gross violations of human rights did not endear the United States to the democratic forces in Argentina that succeeded the military regime.

Haiti.—In the words of one observer, Haiti was "the human rights basket case of the Western Hemisphere."[23] Other contenders for this dubious distinction were El Salvador, Guatemala, Argentina under military rule, Chile under Pinochet, Paraguay under Stroessner, and Bolivia in anarchy. There is no denying, however, that the human rights situation in Haiti was very bad in the period under study—and before, for that matter.

Haiti has never known an extended period of respect for civil and political rights. Especially under the rule of "Papa Doc" Duvalier, forced disappearances, torture, and mistreatment were added to the customary denials of political participation and due process of law. With the passing of rule from father to son in the early 1970s, the more egregious violations of personal integrity were reduced but the structure of repressive rule did not change. As for economic and social rights, Haiti was clearly the most deprived nation in the Western hemisphere. In the 1980s illiteracy was still around 80 percent, unemployment near 50 percent. Annual per capita income was about $270, with manual workers receiving approximately $2.65 a day. Life expectancy was forty-five years on the average.

Congress deferred to the executive branch on Haiti for a number of years. Predictably, the Nixon-Ford-Kissinger era produced no new initiative pertaining to human rights there, as it posed no geostrategic threat to the United States. The Carter administration, with relatively greater interest in human rights, took some new steps. It proscribed foreign military sales although military training (IMET) continued on a small scale. It maintained a moderate level of economic aid, but the aid was directed away from general economic development toward meeting basic human needs. Haiti, in short, was on the Carter hit list. As a result, impoverished Haiti hired a Washington lobbyist at a fee of $2,000 per month to try to clean up its image.[24]

The election of Reagan produced a nominally more assertive Congress on the question of human rights in Haiti. By the fall of 1981, it seemed clear that the administration was going to ignore the general legislation on human rights that might be applied to Haiti. Therefore, Congress, led by House Democrats but followed by Senate Republicans, legislated the following:

It is the sense of the Congress that up to $15,000,000 of the funds available for the fiscal year 1982 . . . should be made available for development assistance for Haiti, subject to the limitations of subsection (b) of this section.

(2) To the maximum extent practicable, assistance for Haiti . . . should be provided through private and voluntary organizations.

(b) Funds available . . . may be expended for Haiti, and credits and guarantees extended . . . only if the president determines that the Government of Haiti

(1) is cooperating with the United States in halting illegal emigration from Haiti:

(2) is not aiding, abetting, or otherwise supporting illegal emigration from Haiti;

(3) has provided assurances that it will cooperate fully in implementing United States development assistance programs in Haiti . . ., and

(4) is not engaged in a consistent pattern of gross violations of internationally recognized human rights.

(c) Six months after the date of enactment of this act, the president shall prepare and transmit to the Congress a report on the extent to which the actions of the Government of Haiti are consistent with . . . subsection (b) of this section.

(d) Notwithstanding the limitations of this section, funds made available under such act . . . may be used for programs with Haiti to assist in halting significant illegal emigration from Haiti to the United States.[25]

A plausible understanding of this statute is that if Haiti cooperated with the United States by controlling illegal emigration, aid could be continued for that purpose; but if a consistent pattern of gross violation of internationally recognized human rights remained, aid would no longer be forthcoming for any purpose. A presidential report was to be the triggering event.

The administration chose to read the statute differently. Given the strong emphasis on illegal emigration evident in the statute, the Reagan team decided it could continue other forms of aid as well so long as progress was made on the emigration issue. As it had done in other cases, it avoided making a judgment about a consistent pattern of gross violation of internationally recognized human rights. Instead, administration spokesmen argued in effect that there was some progress on human rights in Haiti that broke any possible pattern of gross violation.

This was the meaning of the presidential certification presented by the administration in 1982 as it administered $112 million worth of economic and military assistance to Haiti. Of this, $80.7 million was economic aid. The remaining $31.3 million worth of military aid was a large increase from the 1981 figure of $8.9 million allocated by Carter. The reason for this increase was unclear, Haiti being under no external or internal threat. The administration in effect said that the human rights situation was better in some respects than before even though human rights violations continued. More clearly, the administration was able to claim that Haiti cooperated in emigration control, for it was true that Haitian and U.S. officials were turning back Haitian nationals before they could reach U.S. jurisdiction and claim refugee status.

No part of Congress reacted vigorously or effectively to the Reagan administration's interpretation of the 1981 statute regarding Haiti. Some of the private human rights groups followed events closely. But Congress seemed preoccupied with El Salvador and Nicaragua as far as human rights matters were concerned, where they were combined with an alleged threat to U.S. security.

In 1983, however, Congress again turned to issues of human rights in Haiti. In an attempt to force the administration to deal with such issues more specifically, the part of the statute on human rights was revised. The executive branch had to certify that

The government of Haiti . . .
(3) is making a concerted and significant effort to improve the human rights situation in Haiti by implementing the political

reforms which are essential to the development of democracy in Haiti, including the establishment of political parties, free elections, and freedom of the press.[26]

Congress thus reintroduced the idea of presidential certification on human rights, among other things, and moved away from language about "consistent pattern of gross violation of internationally recognized human rights" to language about requisites for democracy. The new language was both more specific and more in keeping with the administration's own rhetoric about a general push for democracy.

The 1983 country-specific legislation, however, did not cause a change in administration policy. Two certification statements, one in January 1984 and one in May, continued the pattern of the past. While those statements noted human rights abuses, no aid was held up, much less cut off, notwithstanding that events in Haiti did not allow a reasonable argument that significant steps had been taken by the government toward genuine democracy. Private human rights groups and parts of the American press made clear that the Haitian government of Jean-Claude Duvalier was highly authoritarian and was tightly controlling its opponents and dissidents.[27] While the political climate was more tolerant than in the brutally harsh days of "Papa Doc," no private party maintained that significant steps had been taken toward democracy.

In 1984 some congressmen criticized the administration's stand on certification of progress on human rights in Haiti. Clarence Long (D., Maryland), chair of the Subcommittee on Foreign Operations of the House Appropriations Committee, and Michael Posner of the private Lawyers' Committee for International Human Rights opposed the certification. They charged the administration with violating the law.[28] But in the end the administration had its way.

A number of members of Congress worried more about controlling the entry of Haitians into the United States than about the human rights sitation in Haiti, apparently not seeing or not wanting to see the relationship between the two. No doubt others thought human rights in Haiti unimportant as long as Haiti presented no security threat to the United States. Perhaps some liberal members thought that because Haiti was so desperately poor, U.S. aid should be continued as long as economic aid reached its poor citizens. But there was no broad sentiment to cut or delay military aid either, which Congress approved in slightly larger amounts each year.

By the middle of the 1980s the Reagan administration had significantly increased military assistance to Baby Doc's Haiti and had administered economic aid without interruption. AID had redirected some economic assistance from general economic development toward basic human needs because of human rights violations. Apart from that, it was business as usual between the United States and Haiti. Officials in the U.S. embassy in Port-au-Prince did stay in touch with opposition figures, inviting some of them to embassy functions to show displeasure with the Duvalier regime. But this quiet diplomacy paled against the background of business as usual. Its effectiveness was highly questionable.

The country-specific legislation had made no visible impact on American foreign policy. Congress could get legislation on the books, but it could not effectively oversee enforcement to achieve its original intent. There was simply no consensus or will in Congress to "get tough" with Haiti either over gross violations of human rights or for lack of significant steps to implement genuine democracy, especially in light of Haitian cooperation in reducing illegal emigration to the United States. It made no difference that the measures used in emigration control probably violated the human rights of some Haitians, as established by the 1967 International Protocol on Refugees and the U.S. Refugee Act of 1980.[29]

As is well known, the regime of Baby Doc Duvalier fell in the spring of 1986 in the face of mounting domestic upheaval. Events proceeded beyond the control of the United States, as they had in the Philippines at approximately the same time. The role of the U.S. executive branch seemed limited to providing a military plane on which Duvalier fled to France and to helping install a caretaker government partially made up of military men from the ancien régime.

In Haiti, as in other countries, U.S. policy was basically wedded to the status quo in the name of anticommunism. Congress made noises about pushing for change on human rights, the Carter administration took some minor but ineffectual steps toward that change, and the Reagan administration (with congressional approval) pumped military assistance into Duvalier's regime even as it collapsed. Once again, U.S. policy had clung to a geostrategic fixation until it was swept away by reality. People in other countries take their own human rights seriously—at least sometimes or eventually. When U.S. policy ignores that political reality, policy yields to the force of change. Congress recognized this in the abstract and fashioned legislation on that principle, but it failed to oversee the policy in a timely way. The record of the Reagan administration was even worse.

Other Developing Countries

Countries in the Western hemisphere generally drew more attention from Congress than those in other regions. (In 1985 Congress added more human rights legislation for two Latin American countries: it blocked military assistance to Paraguay unless the president certified that torture and abuse of detainees had ceased and that procedures had been established to prevent these violations from recurring, and it decreed that in Peru, instruction in international human rights would be an important part of military training provided by the United States.) This hemispheric focus may have stemmed from geostrategy, economics, or tradition. Country-specific legislation was on the books in the early 1980s regarding Pakistan, Mexico, Korea, and Uganda, but none of it had much impact on American foreign policy.

About Pakistan, Congress stated in law that "in authorizing assistance to Pakistan, it is the intent of Congress to promote the expeditious restoration of full civil liberties and representative government in Pakistan." [30] But in the same statute, Congress expressed concern about a response to the Soviet invasion of neighboring Afghanistan, mentioned other U.S. interests such as controlling the proliferation of nuclear weapons, and reiterated the importance of security assistance. The law may have reflected well the myriad interests of the United States with regard to Pakistan, but it did not really emphasize human rights and it provided no guideline as to how human rights were to be integrated with other interests. Some congressional interest in human rights in Pakistan stirred, [31] but the country-specific legislation was useless. It was law, it was country-specific, and it proved irrelevant to the conduct of American diplomacy.

As for Mexico, Congress at one point showed concern for U.S. nationals detained there but couched its interest in more general language. Ostensibly, it wished to signal the U.S. president that he should integrate concern for detained Americans into our other interests with Mexico, such as controlling the traffic in illegal drugs. It legislated that U.S. policy on international trafficking in drugs "must be consistent with respect for fundamental human rights. The Congress therefore calls upon the President to take steps to insure that United States efforts to secure stringent international law enforcement measures are combined with efforts to secure fair and humane treatment for citizens of all countries." Congress then "requested" that the president express "the concern of the United States over treatment of United States citizens arrested in Mexico." [32] There is no evidence that this legislation affected U.S.–Mexican relations pertaining to either drugs or the rights of detained Americans.

Congress took the same sort of action regarding South Korea, approving the following language: "The Congress views with distress the erosion of important civil liberties in the Republic of Korea and requests that the President communicate this concern in forceful terms to the Government of the Republic of Korea within sixty days after enactment." [33] In this case, the country-specific legislation may have had some slight political importance. Private human rights groups and particular circles in Congress had long pointed out the denial of certain civil and political rights in South Korea. [34] That both houses passed this legislation verified congressional interest in human rights in South Korea even if the measure was brief and its language general. Given the history of other congressional action, the executive branch could not be sure that more specific or demanding legislation might not be forthcoming.

Some evidence suggests that the Reagan administration, like Carter's, had already quietly addressed South Korean leaders on some human rights matters. [35] The country-specific legislation pertaining to Korea signaled the administration to continue its efforts and the Korean government to ease its repression. The situation in Korea differed from that in Mexico in that Congress had shown, over a longer period, greater interest in human rights in South Korea, hence the possibility that something more concrete might follow the general language if no progress could be shown. Still, given Washington's desire to contain communism through defense of South Korea, this legislation could not have had more than slight impact on the administration's actions. It was only later, in 1987, that the second Reagan administration pushed hard for human rights in South Korea, in the context of major unrest in that country.

Uganda presented yet another situation to Congress, whose action was weak and, ultimately, useless. Because the United States lacked direct influence in that unhappy country, events bypassed all U.S.

efforts there. In Cambodia in the late 1970s, there was mass political murder verging on genocide and something only slightly less appalling in Uganda under the brutal rule of Idi Amin. Congress lumped the two countries together in a statute deploring those atrocities and urging the president to take the subject up with international organizations and foreign governments. The Congress then directed some language specifically at Uganda.[36]

But this language constituted only a congressional opinion, not law. Congress then suggested tying a U.S. visa for any Ugandan official to the judgment "that the Government of Uganda has demonstrated a proper respect for the rule of law and for internationally recognized human rights"—an interesting but not very powerful sanction. Finally, Congress suggested that the U.S. delegation to the United Nations take up a mandatory arms embargo in the Security Council. Congress had urged an economic embargo on Uganda during the Carter administration, supported that sanction when Carter finally took the step, and then watched from the sidelines as Milton Obote and the Tanzanian army overthrew Amin. There was little more that Congress could do, given the chaos in Uganda and the lack of compelling pressure points available to Washington. The Department of State was monitoring events there, but it was equally at a loss as to how to affect the course of events.

Communist Countries

The question of human rights in communist countries has long been perplexing to many in Congress because of the lack of effective leverage. Generally the United States has more security assistance, economic aid, and trade with noncommunist nations. Hence, aside from hortatory statements, it is seldom clear how congressional action can affect the human rights situation in communist countries. The Jackson-Vanik amendment concerning trade and human rights in command economies and the Helsinki agreement on human rights and other matters in Europe are taken up elsewhere. Two types of country-specific legislation will be noted here.

Congress has banned direct or indirect U.S. assistance to Cuba, Vietnam, and Cambodia, but there was no strictly human rights legislation.[37] Many motives supported this ban, but human rights considerations played some role. American MIAs in Vietnam, mass killing and failure to allow unrestricted humanitarian relief in Cambodia, and denial of civil and political rights in Cuba are issues that have been raised in congressional hearings on human rights matters pertaining to these countries.[38] Should any administration move to provide assistance to Vietnam as part of some negotiated agreement, there is no doubt that Congress would debate extensively the wisdom of that policy. Should any administration move to normalize relations with Castro's Cuba, the same would be true. Human rights in various forms would be part of that debate. In the period under study there was only a slight probability that the Carter administration, and even less probability that the Reagan administration, would move toward assistance to, or normalization with, the listed communist regimes. The country-specific legislation in question thus confirmed the obvious.

Congress has also put language on the books pertaining to human rights in the Soviet Union. It has used law to publicize the case of Raoul Wallenberg, a Swedish diplomat who allegedly died in the Soviet Union in the 1940s,[39] and it has commended Radio Free Europe, Radio Liberty, and the Voice of America for giving attention to religious freedom in the Soviet Union.[40] Hearings have been held on various human rights matters in the Soviet Union and Eastern Europe, most of which have not led to new legislation. The laws that have been passed have not had a demonstrable effect on Soviet-American relations.

Chapter 6

Function-Specific Legislation

> The Reagan Administration continued to take advantage of Congress'
> chronic inability to handle its foreign policy oversight chores through es-
> tablished procedures. The administration got much of the foreign aid it
> wanted, and headed off several moves to torpedo key policies, because
> Congress could not resolve its internal squabbles.
> —*Congressional Quarterly Almanac*, 1984, 71

Congress, in addition to other measures on human rights, has adopted
specific language instructing the executive branch to act. Some function-specific legislation has pertained to the president's administration
of human rights policy. Congress created a Human Rights Bureau, required country reports on human rights situations, created the Helsinki
Commission, and endorsed State Department interagency coordination
on human rights matters. These congressional actions tried to get at
the substance of the matter through procedure. Other function-specific
legislation has attacked this "substance" directly by prohibiting funds
for the training of foreign police, providing funds for specific human
rights activities such as Red Cross work with political prisoners, and
making human rights grants in South Africa.

Administrative Rules

One important congressional act on human rights created the Bureau
of Human Rights and Humanitarian Affairs in the Department of
State.[1] It was designed to give human rights a bureaucratic advocate in
the Washington turf wars. In its short history the bureau has had some
opposition, and it has had two distinct orientations. It seems to have
become fixed in the structure of the Department of State.

The bureau was created originally as part of the backlash against
Republican foreign policy in the 1970s. The move had been long dis-

119

cussed in foreign policy circles, with its opponents arguing two main points. One was that human rights and, more generally, morality in foreign affairs should not be separated from other foreign policy factors. Proponents of this view contend that an institutional home for human rights and humanitarian affairs would make policy coordination more difficult, that it would be best to integrate rights and morality with expediential interests like security and profit. The other point of opposition was that creation of the bureau would introduce too much consideration of morality into U.S. foreign policy; world politics differs from domestic politics because no authoritative central institutions oversee the nation-state system, so one must emphasize power rather than human rights. Others who disliked change opposed the creation of the bureau for less rational reasons. Like all large bureaucracies, the Department of State has often greeted change as if it were the plague.

Obviously Congress overrode opposition when it created the Bureau of Human Rights and Humanitarian Affairs. While not all dissent has disappeared, administrations of both parties have now accepted its presence; opponents are thus disadvantaged, and the bureau is likely to remain. In Congress there was certainly no move to reconsider the bureau. To understand why it has gained acceptance as a part of the Department of State, one must recall its different postures under the Carter and Reagan administrations.

Jimmy Carter was the first president to have the opportunity to name an assistant secretary of state for human rights and humanitarian affairs. He chose Patricia Derian, a white, female, southern activist on civil rights matters with little or no experience in foreign affairs. Under her leadership, the bureau became an independent monitor of human rights within the Department of State. Derian and the bureau saw it as their proper function to challenge other bureaus as well as other departments (like Defense, Commerce, and the Treasury) to give more attention to human rights. Moreover, while some traditional Foreign Service and Civil Service personnel were chosen for the Human Rights Bureau initially, the Carter administration also staffed it with persons who had been active in human rights as members of private groups and congressional staffs. The operating style of this first bureau team has been variously described in interviews as independent, assertive, brusque, and moralistic.[2]

During the Carter administration, coordination of human rights policy with other policies, especially economic, was in the hands of the Christopher Committee, an interdepartmental committee chaired by Deputy Secretary of State Warren Christopher. Derian was only one voice on this committee. How often human rights or the bureau or Derian carried the day when in conflict with other agencies and interests is not a matter of public record. The conventional view is that insofar as human rights could be separated from other U.S. interests, it lost more than it won at the hands of the committee.

There was a separate coordinating committee on arms transfers and human rights, a separate process on exporting crime control equipment and human rights, and no distinct and institutionalized process on general diplomacy and human rights. From the beginning, Derian's Bureau of Human Rights and Humanitarian Affairs and the Carter administration as a whole never found a way to interject human rights systematically into American foreign policy. That administration never resolved, for example, the general question about whether to work for particular or structural change on the issue. Should one concentrate on correcting violations of personal integrity (stopping torture, for example), or should one push for a change in the political system (to democracy)? This situation allowed the Latin American and East Asian bureaus in the Department of State, and other departments like Treasury and Defense, to oppose the bureau successfully.[3]

When the Reagan administration took office in 1981, rumors circulated that it intended to roll back most human rights legislation, including the statute that had established the Bureau of Human Rights and Humanitarian Affairs.[4] These reports generated considerable congressional concern, leading to close questioning of Reagan's first nominee to be head of the bureau. (Nominating someone to head it did not guarantee the bureau's future; at about this same time, Reagan nominated a secretary of education but indicated the possibility of dissolving that department.) The tardiness of the nomination as well as the person of Ernest Lefever, the nominee, were not reassuring to those concerned about the direction of human rights policy under Reagan. Lefever had publicly advocated erasing human rights legislation from the books and was seen by many as wanting to make human rights policy into simply an anticommunist policy. He had written that to do otherwise was to "trivialize" human rights.[5] These concerns were not alleviated by evidence that Lefever had accepted money from the Republic of South Africa to publish and circulate views favorable to that government. Nor did Lefever's conduct during his confirmation hearings erase suspicions. His nomination was withdrawn after the Senate Foreign Relations Committee, despite its Republican majority, voted 13–4 against consent.[6]

Because Reagan left the post of assistant secretary for human rights vacant for a time after the Lefever debacle, Congress still wondered about how Reagan saw human rights in foreign policy. It was in this context that Elliott Abrams was finally nominated and easily confirmed to head the bureau in the autumn of 1981. Abrams sailed through his confirmation hearings without a problem, possibly because he was more diplomatic or possibly because the Senate did not want to fight the president a second time on the position (and Abrams had previously been confirmed as assistant secretary of state for international organization affairs). Yet some members of Congress watched developments closely. After all, Reagan *had* nominated Lefever, and Abrams was the son-in-law of Norman Podhoretz, the hawkish editor of *Commentary* magazine. Apparently traumatized by violent protesters as a student at Harvard, Abrams shifted from the Americans for Democratic Action to the far right and remained thereafter active in right-wing causes. Like Derian, he had no direct experience in foreign affairs.[7]

The Bureau of Human Rights and Humanitarian Affairs under Abrams grew less independent, becoming more integrated into Reagan's and the State Department's emphasis on competing with communism, partially in the name of human rights. The administration's compliance—or lack of compliance—with the legislation analyzed in chapters 3–5 substantiates this generalization, as does a memorandum written by Charles W. Fairbanks and intentionally leaked to the press in the fall of 1981 at about the time of Abrams's nomination. In the memo it was argued that the Reagan administration should have a vigorous human rights policy for two primary reasons: it would emphasize the crucial difference between democratic capitalism and communism, and it would keep Congress from taking over that aspect of foreign policy.[8]

In pursuit of these objectives, Abrams's bureau approached most policy issues as did the other bureaus and political appointees in the Department of State. The Kirkpatrick doctrine of double standards favoring noncommunist dictators and tolerance for *their* violations of human rights did guide much policy. In this regard, available evidence suggests that the Bureau of Human Rights frequently resembled other executive actors in the foreign policy process. There is no bulk of evidence otherwise, and Abrams himself testified, for example, that the bureau favored the president's certification of progress on human rights in El Salvador as a condition for continued U.S. foreign assistance, just as did the other decision makers at the Department of State.[9] When most human rights organizations were criticizing South Africa's new three-tiered parliament for denying real political rights to the black majority, Abrams endorsed the move, as did other Reagan officials. Congressman Bonker complained that Abrams was less a spokesman for human rights and more a spokesman for Reagan's foreign policy in general.[10]

Some evidence seems to indicate that behind the scenes Abrams occasionally challenged policy in the name of human rights. Some reported that Abrams sought a tougher policy against the Pinochet regime in Chile.[11] For whatever reason, U.S. policy did shift after Abrams became assistant secretary of state for inter-American affairs. Some observers assert, however, that the push for public pressure on Pinochet came from elsewhere.[12] More clearly, the Bureau of Human Rights did resist Department of Commerce efforts to permit transfers of crime control equipment despite human rights violations by the designated recipient. Some persons interviewed, both career Foreign Service officers and congressional staff members for Democrats, indicated that Abrams worked behind the scenes in favor of democratic politicians in Latin America who were challenging dictators friendly to the United States. Various reports also claimed that Abrams had fought for a different policy toward Argentina and Guatemala.[13]

The fact that the second Reagan administration found Abrams acceptable as assistant secretary for inter-American affairs indicates that the Bureau of Human Rights had been fully integrated into U.S. foreign policy. It would have been unthinkable for Derian to have made that transformation, such was the vigor—some would say abrasiveness—with which she fought for human rights issues. Only partially in jest did one Foreign Service officer observe that Derian and her bureau personnel were the type of people you didn't like to see coming down the hall toward your office. Abrams certainly did not have such a reputation—or, as one of his critics remarked, at least not for the same reasons. One columnist noted that Abrams certainly did not have the reputation for being a zealot in behalf of human rights.[14] One of his most public critics, columnist Anthony Lewis of the *New York Times,* regarded him as little more than an intelligent and polished Lefever.[15]

Generally, Abrams's Bureau of Human Rights differed with the thrust of Reagan's public policy on few issues, and it was less an independent watchdog than part of a sled team. In this role it achieved more policy integration at the bureau level than when Derian had headed the bureau. Indeed, the higher interagency coordinating group (which had been the Christopher Committee) withered away during the Reagan administration. There was little need for it since Abrams's bureau rarely challenged other agencies and departments. But this policy integration at the bureau level sacrificed real concern for specific human rights in many foreign countries,[16] even if some quiet diplomacy and behind-the-scenes infighting of a more balanced nature did occur.

In sum, Congress created the Bureau of Human Rights and Humanitarian Affairs. The Senate was prepared in 1981 to challenge President Reagan and his nominee to head that bureau if it doubted that the bureau would actively oversee the law. The Senate generally does not like to deny confirmation to a presidential appointee; the president, having won an election, is thought to be entitled to his team no matter how unqualified. A case in point was the confirmation of Judge William Clark to high position at the Department of State even though he obviously knew very little about foreign affairs. Yet Lefever's nomination was overwhelmingly opposed in committee. Beyond that point, however, Congress had little influence over how the bureau was managed.

Congress may pass a sense-of-the-Congress resolution suggesting some administrative step. It did so in 1981 in endorsing the interagency coordinating group on human rights, a small step designed to support human rights in Reagan's foreign policy. The resolution was both nonbinding and ineffectual in keeping alive the coordinating committee.

Derian saw her role as that of an independent watchdog; Abrams saw his as that of an integrated team player. Congress almost certainly had Derian's model in mind when it created the Bureau of Human Rights, but it was powerless to prevent the Abrams model from emerging. Indeed, it was indifferent to how Abrams saw the bureau's role, though much interested in the resulting policy. As of late 1987, it is not clear which model the third head of the bureau, Richard Schifter, will follow or if he will create another one. It is not a matter Congress will determine.

Public Reporting.—Under different pieces of legislation, Congress required the Department of State to report to it on aspects of human rights policy. The Bureau of Human Rights consolidated much of this public reporting with its annual country reports on human rights situations. The first such statute requiring country reports in relation to U.S. security assistance was a congressional effort to get Kissinger's Department of State to pay attention to specific human rights. A master of bureaucratic maneuvering, Kissinger dragged his feet on this legal requirement. Just before leaving office in early 1977, he allowed short and superficial reports to be submitted to Congress. The Carter administration then began to publish more serious reports.[17] In 1977 the first major effort was made to collect pertinent information from American embassies around the world and compare it with data from private human rights groups and other nongovernmental sources.[18]

Congress then broadened the requirement, calling for human rights reports on all members of the United Nations. This move was led by conservative members of Congress whose motives are still debated. One is obvious: Since U.S. security assistance goes only to friends, the human rights policies of adversaries were not reviewed in the early reports. Congressional conservatives and others found this insufficient. A second motive may have been to make the reporting so voluminous as to be unmanageable, a possibility that, of course, is not recorded in public documents. But some observers thought some members of Congress might be interested in sinking the whole project in order to get back to such basics as power and profit.

The second intention, if it existed, has been frustrated—as much by Abrams's Bureau of Human Rights as by Derian's. The country reports, ever larger and more complex, continue to be published. The annual volume, regularly noticed by the national press when it appears, now runs some fifteen hundred pages. It is one of the major global reference sources on human rights.[19]

Congress has played an important role in these developments beyond commissioning the reports. Regularly, and with increased vigor in the early Reagan years, some part of Congress would hold hearings on the reports. In the early 1980s, the House Foreign Affairs Subcommittee on Human Rights and International Organizations scrutinized the reports, obviously harboring suspicions about Reagan policy in this regard.[20] At other times, a review of the reports would make up part of a more general hearing on human rights.[21] A congressional committee or subcommittee would work with various private human rights groups such as Amnesty International, Americas Watch, the Lawyers' Committee for International Human Rights, and Helsinki Watch to scrutinize State Department findings. Executive officials would be called on to explain how the reports were compiled and to justify particular wordings or conclusions.

During the Reagan administration, the Bureau of Human Rights grew more distant from many established human rights groups. These private agencies had contended with the bureau during the Carter administration, but in general there was a grudging respect and a modus vivendi from 1977 to 1980. One high-ranking Carter official remarked that while Amnesty International had been a "pain in the neck" on the subject of political prisoners in Indonesia, one had to admit that its information was largely accurate even if inconvenient for the U.S.- Indonesian alignment. From 1981, however, there was public friction between Abrams's bureau and such groups.[22] One can assume that Abrams's bureau tended, at least initially, to make less use of information from private groups when compiling the country reports than had been the case during the Carter administration. This assumption was reinforced when it became known that the Reagan administration at times attempted to discredit private human rights reports about such places as Central America.[23] It was especially important, therefore, from 1981 onward, that Congress made use of information and testimony from private groups when evaluating the administration's country reports.

Over time Congress became satisfied with the overall veracity of State Department reporting in the annual country reports. By 1984 Abrams and the Bureau of Human Rights had received praise from Democrats in Congress as well as from private human rights groups for the overall publication, although questions did arise over particular countries where some political bias or inaccuracy was alleged.[24] Vigorous congressional review of the reports seems to have induced accuracy, especially when human rights agencies with their own sources of information participated in the review process. What eventually became the main issue was not the accuracy of the reports but the relation between the facts presented in the reports and U.S. foreign policy toward a particular country. A number of country reports indicated a consistent pattern of gross violations of internationally recognized human rights, yet U.S. policy supported the government in question and economic and security assistance continued. In one study it was concluded that little correlation existed over time between reports of human rights violations and decreases in U.S. economic and military assistance. Once established, levels of assistance seemed instead to remain more or less fixed.[25]

The annual country reports were notable in several other ways. Abrams used the introduction to the reports from 1982 to 1985 to publicize a philosophy of rights.[26] During the Reagan administration, the reports urged that economic, social, and cultural rights should not be recognized, although they were internationally acknowledged in various treaties and declarations. Consequently, these reports contained information only on civil and political rights, though information on some economic and social conditions in various countries was presented. This method was not very different from the final reports from the Carter administration, which, while endorsing socioeconomic rights, also presented more economic data than information on economic rights. Since Congress did not appear terribly interested in socioeconomic rights either, this aspect of the reports did not lead to great debate.[27]

In sum, public reporting began as a congressional step to pressure Kissinger but within a decade became an institutionalized process of some importance. Every U.S. embassy is required to collect information on human rights in its area of jurisdiction. The Bureau of Human Rights then compares this information with that from other sources. Both Congress and news media like the *New York Times* watch the resulting synthesis, relying largely on information from private human rights groups to validate the reports' conclusions. Since the key step in linking the facts to substantive policy decisions goes beyond reporting, the country reports merely set the stage for further policy debates. Yet it is clear that, to a point, Congress has helped increase sensitivity to human rights in American foreign policy.[28]

Both country-specific and general legislation requires the Department of State to submit to Congress various reports and certification statements on a variety of subjects, sometimes as often as semiannually, usually once a year. Such reporting requirements burden the Department of State, but they seem to have overwhelmed Congress. It has been unable to keep track of its own legislated requirements in this regard and finally has had to ask the Congressional Research Service for a systematic overview of executive reporting requirements on human rights. Congressional staff responsible for human rights matters, when interviewed in 1986 about public and confidential reporting, could only reply that they were awaiting the Congressional Research Service study. Compounding the difficulty for Congress was the fact that the same staff members, not to mention their principals, were also supposed to be overseeing other executive branch reports on such subjects as voting in the United Nations, international drug enforcement, and nuclear nonproliferation standards.

The Helsinki Accord.—After the 1975 Helsinki Accord was signed by thirty-five states to promote security and cooperation in Europe, Congress created a unique body called the United States Commission on Security and Cooperation in Europe (CSCE).[29] It was to monitor developments under that diplomatic accord and to make suggestions for the future. It also came to deal with the particulars of implementing the provisions of the accord. The commission was unique in three ways: no other signatory created a similar agency, other states leaving matters to their foreign ministries or other governmental units; comprised of twelve members of Congress and three from the executive branch, it broke down the separation of institutions theoretically established in the U.S. Constitution; and it involved itself in casework such as handling the details of family reunification across East-West barriers in Europe. The commission, while theoretically responsible for security, economic, and human rights subjects, focused almost entirely on human rights.

Though the Department of State initially resisted the CSCE as an unnecessary (and one could add unconstitutional) infringement on its conduct of foreign policy, both branches have accepted it and it has been active. Many reports have been published about specific nations' compliance with the Helsinki Accord. There is thus a bipartisan and "bi-branch" governmental view of the accord, in addition to the private reports published by groups such as Helsinki Watch.

The CSCE has made many suggestions to the House Foreign Affairs Committee, which in turn offered most of them as simple or concurrent resolutions. (The first chair of the commission was Dante Fascell, an active member of the House Foreign Affairs Committee and its chair from 1984.) The House or Congress has adopted most of these resolutions. Though without direct legislative authority, the commission thus enlarged legislative activity and its own reports gave public attention to the Helsinki Accord. The impact of this legislative activity is difficult to gauge; much of it seems to fall into the category of "motherhood resolutions," mentioned in chapter 2. Few of the ideas originating with the commission have been made binding, and the executive branch— certainly under Reagan—was already prepared to criticize the Soviet Union and its allies publicly for violating provisions of the accord.

The staff work of the commission may reflect an institutionalization of what many members of Congress do individually; that is, many senators and representatives help American citizens who have a family or humanitarian problem that cuts across the Iron Curtain. They write letters to authorities in Eastern Europe, or they take up issues with the Department of State on behalf of a constituent. The CSCE has done some of this work, provided it falls under the section of the Helsinki Accord on specified human rights. Some persons in the Department of State welcome these developments; those in the geographical bureaus prefer dealing with the high politics of geostrategic issues, and those in the Bureau of Human Rights welcome the added help on particular problems.

It is usually difficult to establish precisely the extent of an agency's influence, and this is true concerning the CSCE. Letters of thanks or affirmative statements in hearings may be pro forma.[30] Yet the CSCE has had an impact on the executive branch and probably on Western European allies. At one point during the Carter administration it intervened to get a rewriting of the instructions to the U.S. delegation to a Helsinki follow-up meeting; human rights had been downplayed in the first version but were subsequently emphasized in the final version and at the meeting itself. At another point, personnel from the CSCE became the staff for Max Kampelman, U.S. representative to a Helsinki meeting; they pushed the subject of human rights in discussions with allies, and the General Accounting Office found influence for the CSCE in keeping with its mandate.[31] Whether any of this activity had an impact on East European states is impossible to tell.

Therefore, although some actions pushed by the CSCE would have probably occurred anyway, since criticizing human rights violations in Eastern Europe has long been a popular pastime in Washington, the CSCE seems to have affected U.S. foreign policy under the Helsinki Accord in small but important ways. By the mid-1980s, however, the commission seemed somewhat less important. Its chair, Dante Fascell (D., Florida), was a prominent force because he also chaired the House

Foreign Affairs Committee for part of that time and was a major figure associated with the State Department appropriations bill—so his views carried some weight in the Department of State. When other members of Congress assumed the chair, the CSCE seemed less active and influential.

Substantive Rules

Some function-specific legislation by Congress has dealt not with administration of the human rights policy but with substantive programs. A couple of these regulations on matters of substance were negative; most were positive.

One negative rule was the prohibition on the use of U.S. funds for the training of foreign police, prison personnel, and intelligence or surveillance agencies. This ban grew out of concern that U.S. officials were contributing to torture and other gross violations of human rights, especially in Latin America. The U.S. Office of Public Safety had been much criticized for its alleged role in training torturers for right-wing governments around the world. The same coalition of human rights activists that had opposed brutality toward political prisoners and other detainees under the control of the government of the Republic of Vietnam (South Vietnam) lobbied Congress vigorously in the 1970s on such training. They frequently cited close U.S. relations with security forces in places like Brazil and Uruguay, where gross human rights abuses were known to occur.[32]

Definitive proof was never marshaled in support of the allegations. Congress, nevertheless, in 1975 terminated U.S. training for foreign police and other internal agencies. Some saw this move as congressional hysteria directed against the imperial presidency or perhaps morality run rampant in U.S. foreign policy. Others saw it as responsible action, reflecting awareness of how some foreign policy is conducted. After all, if U.S. agencies were providing instruction in interrogation under coercion, that policy was unlikely to be found in any document or testimony by administration officials. If this latter view was true, one should not wait for definitive proof before acting.

The Carter administration deferred to congressional sentiment on this issue. The Reagan administration sought to rescind the legislation and succeeded, partially, in 1985. Reagan officials argued that if foreign agencies were guilty of gross violations of human rights, as were the Treasury Police in El Salvador, for example, an effective way to attack the problem was to provide better training. A majority in Congress was long reluctant to yield to this rationale, doubting the humanitarian impact of U.S. police training. This reluctance was fortified by reports, for example, that Salvadoran military units trained in the United States had repeatedly committed atrocities in the civil war in El Salvador.[33] Nevertheless, in 1985 Congress exempted El Salvador and Honduras from the ban on U.S. aid for foreign police. This ban occurred shortly after a fatal attack on off-duty marines in San Salvador by unidentified assailants. Then the Reagan administration sought to exempt both Panama and Guatemala. But Congress held firm into mid-1986. At the time of this writing, the general ban is still in place, with only two countries exempted.

A second negative rule that was quite specific pertained to UNESCO. The rule combined a nonbinding sense-of-the-Congress resolution with a binding threat. This congressional action arose in reaction to debates in UNESCO about a possible New World Information Order entailing, among other things, the licensing of journalists.[34] The UNESCO debate in the 1970s worried a number of people in Washington, since it was led by authoritarian governments of the Second and Third Worlds that had not hesitated to muzzle the press in their own countries. It was associated with the New International Economic Order, which had never been popular in Washington because of its association with the obligatory transfer of wealth from developed to less-developed countries. Also, the debate occurred in a UN agency increasingly accused of being unsympathetic to Western states and wasteful as well. Moreover, Western journalists publicized the debates widely, most of all the aspects that might curtail their freedoms.

Given these factors, it was not difficult for Congress to take a stand against UNESCO and the New World Information Order. It did so in 1976 by first endorsing Article 19 of the Universal Declaration of Human Rights, which affirms the right to a free flow of information across international borders, then by stating in a binding way that U.S. funds to UNESCO would be blocked if journalists were required to be licensed or otherwise unreasonably restricted. At the time of adoption of these two legislative statements, the push for international regulation of the private press had already peaked. Objectionable UNESCO resolutions had already been beaten back by the Western countries. The congressional action was thus mostly symbolic, at best demonstrating to outside parties that U.S. foreign policy was supported by consensus at home.

Congress's threat to withhold funds violated the constituent document of UNESCO, which requires states to meet the budget of the organization as apportioned by the organization. Contributions may not be withheld to exert political pressure. This congressional action was part of a broader trend in both Congress and the executive branch to ignore legal obligations contained in the constituent treaties of international organizations. The executive branch had done so in the past by withholding funds from the International Labor Organization in a dispute over policy. Congress would do so in the future by legislating a unilateral reduction in U.S. contributions to the regular budget of the United Nations if the General Assembly did not accept some version of weighted voting. It did not seem to matter that all of these actions violated clear international law. (There was also the Byrd amendment, which from 1971 permitted trade with Rhodesia and thus violated legally binding economic sanctions imposed by the UN Security Council on that white minority government.)

In the case of UNESCO, the congressional threat to withhold money became moot. The Reagan administration withdrew the United States from membership in 1984, citing a variety of reasons. Some members of Congress opposed this move (and the U.S. Advisory Committee on UNESCO, a group of private citizens supposedly advising the Department of State on UNESCO affairs, had voted overwhelmingly to stay in). But there was little organized congressional opposition.[35] The American withdrawal was a popular move, supported editorially even by the *New York Times*. Thus the United States withdrew its contribution of 25 percent of UNESCO's budget along with its membership, and the congressional endorsement of Article 19 of the Universal Declaration was bypassed by more drastic action by the executive branch. Indeed, the 1976 congressional action could have been taken as a green light, indicating to the Reagan administration that subsequent congressional opposition to withdrawal from UNESCO would be slight.

A third negative rule pertained to internationally recognized workers' rights; it had two essential dimensions. First, in 1984 Congress adopted human rights language pertaining to international trade under the General System of Preferences. According to these amendments to the 1974 Trade Act, no country could be designated to receive U.S. preferential treatment in trade unless it had implemented, or was moving toward implementation of, the rights of freedom of association, collective bargaining, freedom from forced labor, minimum wage, and safe and healthful working conditions. The president could, however, certify to Congress exceptional countries based on U.S. economic interests. By 1987 the executive branch had removed three countries from the GSP list of preferential trading partners—Nicaragua, Paraguay, and Romania—and had invented the category of probation for Chile. There was considerable debate about other trading partners such as Taiwan and South Korea, but at the time of writing the executive branch had neither removed them from the GSP list nor certified exceptional status.Second, in 1985 Congress amended the law governing the Overseas Private Investment Corporation (OPIC) so as to introduce the consideration of workers' rights into the functioning of that agency. Using the same rights enumerated in the Trade Act, Congress forbade the granting of governmental insurance to American companies operating in countries denying internationally recognized workers' rights. This law has been in effect only since 1986 and it was not clear by late 1987 how this amendment had affected OPIC, except that Nicaragua, Paraguay, and Romania were clearly barred.[36]

Several function-specific rules have been positive and relatively noncontroversial. One allocated special funding to the Inter-American Commission on Human Rights as a gesture of support for human rights within the Organization of American States. The commission, unlike certain other OAS institutions, has enjoyed a good reputation in Washington. Most persons who follow such subjects see it as actively and impartially implementing the rights guaranteed in the American Declaration of the Rights and Duties of Man and later in the American Convention on Human Rights. Its work in places like the Dominican Republic (1965–66) and Nicaragua (1977–78) has been acclaimed.[37]

Another such congressional act provided special funding for the International Committee of the Red Cross and its work with so-called political prisoners. The ICRC, little known but associated generally with the Geneva Conventions, had expanded its humanitarian work beyond war situations to include political prisoners. In fact, in a given year its work with those detained for political activity or belief could dwarf the work for persons protected by the Geneva Conventions of August 12, 1949, applicable to situations of armed conflict. The persistently high number of political detainees around the world severely strained the ICRC's budget. As a consequence, and in the light of its reputation for diligence and impartiality, the all-Swiss ICRC became the beneficiary of congressional largess.[38]

Congress created special funds for persons in South Africa whose rights were violated by apartheid. The oldest of these was the fund for educational assistance in South Africa, dating from 1980 when Congressman Stephen Solarz (D., New York) was the chair of the Foreign Affairs Subcommittee on Africa. It was a two-pronged program providing grants for education in South Africa at integrated facilities and for education in the United States. This South African educational fund was renewed subsequently, although a House staff study found some confusion and administrative tangles in the program.[39]

In 1984, Congress also created the South African human rights program. This initiative hoped to foster "a just society" in South Africa and to compensate victims of apartheid. Grants were made to nongovernmental organizations in South Africa to increase their capabilities so that they could influence the government in behalf of civil rights and "general tolerance of diversity." The long-term goal was to achieve full civil and political rights for all.[40] In addition, Congress began a program to assist the integration of the private sector and another to improve schools, hospitals, and other institutions for the general welfare at the local level.

These programs invested a combined total of $20 million in fiscal year 1986 in a positive approach to human rights in South Africa.[41] Congress formulated most of this composite initiative, though the Carter and Reagan administrations did not oppose it, and the Agency for International Development or the U.S. Information Agency implemented it through the U.S. embassy in South Africa. In addition, AID and the Bureau of Human Rights could funnel monies to groups in South Africa under section 116(e) of the Foreign Assistance Act, the Harkin amendment, for the promotion of civil and political rights.

One positive approach to human rights proved more troublesome. It involved what came to be called the National Endowment for Democracy, representing an attempt to promote at least some internationally recognized human rights structurally.

As indicated in chapter 1, many of President Reagan's supporters had criticized the Carter administration's approach to human rights. They believed it unsystematic, overly negative, and without sufficient attention to communist violations of rights. From late 1981 Reagan's policy, as fashioned by persons like Charles Fairbanks and Elliott Abrams, sought to act on the basis of this criticism. But in its own way Reagan's policy was itself uncoordinated on several points. There was, for example, little in Reagan's early policy that could be called positive or structural besides the recurrent attacks on Soviet-led communism.

In June 1982 Reagan gave a speech to the British Parliament in which he stressed the need to promote democracy in the world. Attacking the Soviet Union, referring to the Universal Declaration of Human Rights, resisting charges of cultural imperialism, Reagan called for a "crusade for freedom" in the tradition of Woodrow Wilson.[42] Great inactivity followed this rousing speech. Eventually Reagan officials resurrected an idea that had been discussed earlier by congressional Democrats, especially Dante Fascell and Donald Fraser. They had wanted to start a Program Democracy to encourage the evolution of democratic institutions, particularly in countries of the Third World. The Reagan administration proposed to Congress a Project Democracy for the same purpose.[43]

After much debate, in 1983 Congress authorized such a positive approach to political rights. Opposition came from fiscal conservatives who did not believe funds should go for such a purpose, from social liberals who did not trust the Reagan administration with management of such a program, and from a variety of members who opposed public funding for U.S. and foreign political parties (in early proposals the two major American parties were part of the administration of the program). But finally a National Endowment for Democracy was authorized with funding of just over $31 million to make grants to the U.S. Chamber of Commerce (one-third) and AFL–CIO (two-thirds), whose subsidiary institutes would then make grants to foreign private parties. Officially the intent was to promote democratic institutions, processes, and values, not to align the United States with particular candidates in elections—and the process was to be open.

The weakness in congressional support for the National Endowment for Democracy, despite its bipartisan origins, could be seen in the fact that appropriations for it were slashed to about $18 million in 1984, the start-up year. The continuing skepticism was bipartisan as well. Opposition was to remain bipartisan because the Reagan appointees to the National Endowment for Democracy acted in 1984 and 1985 in ways feared by social liberals but also by some conservatives. Acting through the AFL–CIO, the endowment made secret grants in at least two dubious situations. In democratic France, grants went to two right-of-center entities, one of which may have had undemocratic values. In Panama, a secret grant went to a political candidate backed by the military.[44] It appeared that the AFL–CIO Free Trade Union Institute had violated the authorizing guidelines of the endowment with the knowledge of endowment officials.

The resulting storm in Congress almost scuttled the endowment. The House voted to terminate all funding, though previously the Democratic House had been more favorable than the Republican Senate to funding the endowment. In a reversal, however, the Senate managed to save the endowment through a compromise in conference committee, and as of the mid-1980s the endowment still functioned to encourage democratic institutions and promote exchanges among democratic personnel. Congress increased its scrutiny of endowment operations, and one could assume that secret grants, especially in democratic Europe, no longer occurred.

In 1977, Congress passed one of those "soft" laws instructing the administration to seek an accounting for Americans listed as missing in action in Southeast Asia. All administrations had been active on this issue, though various beliefs persisted that the U.S. government had not done enough. As of the late 1970s, no firm information existed indicating that any of the MIAs were alive or being held prisoner as a result of the long U.S. military involvement in Southeast Asia. During the Reagan administration, improved cooperation by the Vietnamese authorities made possible the identification of the remains of some MIAs, which were returned to the United States. At best, Congress had communicated some popular sentiment to the executive branch by passing this bill. No member of Congress could oppose such a measure, and no president needed such a measure to produce action.

Chapter 7

Congressional Process and Impact

This flexibility . . . is the bright side of the invitation to struggle. . . .
This does not make for neat categories in practice, nor for predict-
ability.

Thomas M. Franck,
"Constitutional Practice until Vietnam," 18–19

The interrelationships among human rights matters, congressional actions, and U.S. foreign policy from 1973 to 1984 are not easy to summarize with confidence. If the Constitution invites a struggle between
the two political branches for the control of foreign policy, then it can
be said that Congress attempted much.[1] Different components of Congress did different things with different results. Four administrations
(counting Nixon's and Ford's as two) have dealt with Congress in different
ways because they confronted different human rights problems, interlaced with different security issues, in different cultures and economic
situations.

By the late 1980s, Congress played a larger role in making foreign
policy than at any time since the interwar years (1919–39). Its concern
for human rights matters has been unusually high also during the period under study. One could see both the general and the particular human rights trends played out daily. Foreign governments had to deal
with Congress almost as much as with the executive branch. Even the
other superpower evidently felt the need to have its officials testify in
Congress on such matters as the nuclear accident in the Soviet Union in
1986; the striking point was not what the Soviet official said but rather
his presence before a congressional body in the first place. As for human rights, foreign governments as well as nonstate parties (such as
armed rebels) tried to influence Congress directly through lobbying or

indirectly through timing their actions in accordance with the congressional schedule, particularly the budgeting process.

Despite this, Congress did not equal the executive branch in making human rights policy. It may have wanted to codetermine foreign policy and human rights, but it fell short of that goal. Generally it continued to be subordinate to the executive branch, but it became more assertive than it had been. The situation was well summarized by Congressman Stephen Solarz (D., New York):

> To say that the congressional role in foreign affairs has greatly increased over the past decade or two is not to say that the Congress has assumed co-equal status with the president in this area. Clearly, the primary responsibility for foreign policy still lies with the president, and is going to remain there. I think it is important to recognize that there are still significant constraints on the Congress' ability to formulate or implement foreign policy decisions that prevent it from assuming a primary role.[2]

Solarz went on to list three major constraints: the executive branch could get around general congressional directives; Congress was internally divided; and many members of Congress believed in the idea of bipartisanship, which caused them to support the president in foreign policy.

The Tools

There was nothing especially new in the tools used by Congress to make an impact on human rights policy. Congress could legislate general policy statements, but these were of dubious importance since the executive branch could circumvent them, as Solarz noted, if it wished not to implement them. The Senate could withhold its advice and consent on treaties and presidential appointments, and this it did with renewed assertiveness. Congress could legislate reporting requirements, legally compelling the executive branch publicly to justify and rationalize an action after the fact or to consult with Congress before a decision was taken.[3] Finally, the ultimate congressional weapon was, as always, the power of the purse; and in the era under review Congress did not hesitate to use foreign aid bills, continuing funding resolutions, and supplementary money bills to affect human rights in foreign policy. The use of these tools can be demonstrated by recalling some examples from the preceding chapters. They will be drawn from the first Reagan administration, one of the times of greatest conflict between Congress and the executive branch over human rights.

The Senate Foreign Relations Committee used the nomination of Ernest W. Lefever to make clear to President Reagan, through the advise and consent process, that it disagreed with turning the human rights policy into one simply of anticommunism. Of course Lefever's personality, or personality conflicts with certain senators such as Charles Percy, contributed to the withdrawal of his nomination. But it was also important that many senators on that committee disagreed with the administration's early statements downplaying human rights and human rights legislation while emphasizing, exclusively, the international communist movement. It appears that the executive branch did receive the message that the Senate, and Congress generally, would insist on trying to achieve at least a more even-handed human rights policy. In the fall of 1981 the executive branch acknowledged in a memorandum that the administration would have to formulate a separate human rights policy or lose control of that foreign policy issue to Congress. If the Reagan administration initially intended to scrap a human rights policy separate from anticommunism (as endorsed in print by Lefever, Jeane Kirkpatrick, Alexander Haig, and others), the Senate prevented this; and the Reagan administration changed directions at least somewhat by the autumn of 1981.

(It is difficult in late 1987 to say just how much the Reagan administration shifted in its general orientation to human rights issues because of congressional opposition to Lefever and all that he symbolized. A case can be made that, in its essentials, the first Reagan administration followed the policy that Lefever represented but did it in a more acceptable way under Elliott Abrams. As suggested in chapter 6, however, it seems more persuasive to see the Reagan administration moving incrementally toward a more balanced position on human rights. This shift became more pronounced in the second Reagan administration, to the point that it resembled the Carter administration in a number of ways. Congress played a major role in that shift, as did events beyond the control of either branch, for example, the revolution in Haiti.[4]

Reporting requirements took on added appeal in Congress, which imposed on the executive branch all types of certification requirements. This can be seen in action pertaining to Chile. These requirements, when exceedingly specific in nature, definitely affected U.S. foreign policy. The president could not "fudge" a certification that Chile had extradited two officials indicted for murder in the United States, which was made a condition for renewed economic and security assistance to Chile. Though the first Reagan administration wanted to normalize relations with Chile despite continuing gross violations of internationally recognized human rights, the certification requirement clearly prevented full normalization. The executive branch remained free to take certain diplomatic steps aligning the United States with Chile, and the Reagan administration did so. Constitutionally, the administration controlled the U.S. vote in international organizations; it was also entitled to make public statements of friendship and support and to control decisions on joint military maneuvers and whatever the Central Intelligence Agency was doing. But the certification requirement blocked most economic and security assistance and kept a certain amount of political pressure on the Pinochet regime, as much through symbolism as through denial of concrete goods.

Many examples of Congress using the power of the purse in behalf of human rights have been discussed here. One of the more striking pertained to El Salvador: Congress withheld 30 percent of U.S. economic assistance until a trial was held in the case of the four abused and murdered American churchwomen. Within months, such a trial took place. One could question the quality of justice in the case, since higher officials were not prosecuted and lower officials were convicted rapidly. But where no concrete progress had previously been made in the investigation of the murders, the U.S. embassy in San Salvador was able to prod the Salvadoran government into action once the power of the purse was brought into play. Congress also used the purse to affect U.S. policy toward Guatemala, refusing to authorize or appropriate most funds for security assistance as long as the various military governments engaged in gross violations of human rights. The Reagan administration wanted to normalize relations in the name of anticommunism, and Congress prevented it.

The process in which these tools are used is commonly broken down into legislation and oversight of administrative compliance with legislation.[5] No doubt that bifurcation has its utility, but I will not use it here in any rigorous sense. Legislation and oversight frequently become one process of trying to get the executive branch to do what Congress wants done. The ultimate stage in oversight is to write new legislation that either makes the law more specific, giving the executive branch less room for interpretation, or affects the funding available to the executive branch. At that point, yesterday's oversight becomes today's legislation. Although certain committees have oversight but not legislative authority, most committees active on human rights were both legislative and oversight committees, and the congressional process involved both activities in a more or less continual sequence (an exception is the Commission on Security and Cooperation in Europe, which lacked direct legislative authority).

The focus here is on legislation, oversight, and legislation in a usually seamless web, showing those elements as a continuum of stages of congressional activity. The first stage includes subcommittee and committee action, the second, congressional action after that (floor action in each house and conference committee deliberations). Both stages can and usually do entail both legislative and oversight activity. (Occasionally legislation can bypass the first stage entirely, as when the Harkin amendment, or Section 116(a) of the Foreign Assistance Act, was introduced on the floor of the House.)[6]

The First Stage.—The first stage of congressional action on human rights, whether pertaining to legislation or oversight, is unpredictable, especially for the Senate. Whether a human rights matter gets taken up in Congress de novo or under existing legislation is largely a matter of personalities.

In the Senate, no focal point exists for human rights activity. There is no subcommittee on human rights. For most of the period under review, one staff person dealt with human rights on the Foreign Affairs Committee. Under the chairmanship of Senator Richard Lugar, for example, this staff person had other duties as well, and interviews suggest that human rights came below subjects like terrorism on the list of important considerations. This situation meant a weak institutionalization of human rights as a distinct policy issue. The process depended largely on whether an individual senator, or a staff person somewhere, became interested in a particular human rights problem.[7] When Charles Percy, who was interested in human rights, yielded to Richard Lugar, who initially was not, Senate first-stage action on human rights declined. (By late 1987 it seemed that Lugar had become more interested in human rights after having been a member of the U.S. election supervision team in the Philippines in 1986 and after having played an important role in disassociating the United States from the Marcos regime.) Of course, certain senators did show a concern over time for human rights—Christopher Dodd, Dennis DeConcini, Richard Schweiker, for example. But the general point remains that Senate first-stage action on human rights was highly personalized.

Sometimes personality intertwined with party label, especially with reference to committee chairs. When the Republicans won control of the Senate in 1981, not only did Percy become chair of Foreign Relations but Jesse Helms became chair of the subcommittee on the Western hemisphere and Strom Thurmond became chair of the Judiciary Subcommittee on Refugees. These changes had profound implications for human rights action in the Senate. But, fundamentally, the matter still came down to personalities. Republicans like Percy, Larry Pressler, and James Abourezk were interested in internationally recognized human rights (as opposed to, say, Jesse Helms's personalized conception of human rights). Whether a senator became a chair was a party matter, but whether human rights interested that senator and what version of human rights he advocated was essentially a matter of personality and personal ideology. The Senate process was not highly institutionalized.

There was a move in the Senate in the 1980s to reduce the number of committees and subcommittees still further, in the belief that senators were overextended and were improperly trying to micromanage the executive branch. According to Senator Dan Quayle (R., Indiana), "Senators generally serve on three committees, for an average of 12 committees and subcommittees. Now, you tell me how you can accommodate 12 committees and subcommittees in a 24-hour day and have any time left over to sleep."[8] According to Senator John Tower (R., Texas), by 1984 "over 150 legislative prohibitions had been enacted, the impetus of which was either to restrict the president's ability to dispatch troops abroad in times of crisis or to proscribe his authority in arms sales, trade, human rights, foreign assistance, and intelligence operations."[9] In his view this led to micromanagement and taking up the president's time with negotiations with disparate power centers in Congress. Thus, it was unlikely that the Senate would move to create a human rights subcommittee.

On the House side, there was more institutionalization, but there was no escaping the personality factor; hence, one could not make firm predictions about this side of Congress either. The Foreign Affairs Subcommittee on Human Rights and International Organizations had, as usual, both majority and minority staff, in addition to the personal staff of its chair. Moreover, the parent Foreign Affairs Committee had staff persons greatly interested in human rights during the era under study. Several chairs of the Human Rights Subcommittee were highly active—in particular, Donald Fraser of Minnesota. He represented a classic case of how an unknown congressman acting from the base of a little known subcommittee can have a great impact on public policy. With his systematic hearings on human rights, Fraser put that subject back on the foreign policy agenda. During his time in Congress (he resigned to run for the Senate, lost, and became mayor of Minneapolis), he remained highly active on human rights issues. The same pattern of assertiveness characterized his successor, Don Bonker of Washington. But matters changed somewhat in 1983 when that chairmanship went to Gus Yatron of Pennsylvania. He was less assertive and brought less intellectual acuteness to the position than his two immediate predecessors. (Staff members loyal to Yatron argued that he was highly active behind the scenes.) Hence, the personality factor again came into play, although in the House human rights concern and momentum were more institutionalized than in the Senate.

Also on the House side, there was a diffusion of interest in human rights from the Human Rights Subcommittee to the geographical subcommittees of the Foreign Affairs Committee. Thus a "socializing effect" radiated from one subcommittee to the others involved in foreign affairs and, indeed, to other subcommittees like the International Financial Institutions Subcommittee of the Banking and Urban Affairs Committee. Here again one must note the personality factor. In the 1980s it made a difference that first the African, then the Asian Subcommittee under Foreign Affairs was chaired by Stephen Solarz of New York—a bright, capable, and highly assertive congressman much interested in human rights in places like South Africa and the Philippines. When Solarz changed subcommittees, Howard Wolpe of Michigan took over the African subcommittee and continued in the direction that Solarz had charted. Michael Barnes of Maryland became chair of the Western Hemisphere Subcommittee and displayed great interest in human rights in places like El Salvador. The combination of a human rights subcommittee and individuals much interested in internationally recognized human rights meant that the Democratically controlled House Foreign Affairs Committee gave much systematic attention to human rights issues from 1973.

Yet personality probably mattered more than institution; when Fraser began his push in 1973, his subcommittee was technically concerned with international organizations and movements. It was only later renamed to focus on human rights and international organizations, largely to reflect his personal interests. Moreover, other parts of the House that apparently had little to do with the Human Rights Subcommittee became active on the subject. Jerry Patterson (D., California) kept close watch on human rights issues related to the international banks, and Clarence Long (D., Maryland) became interested in human rights in El Salvador from his position as chair of the Foreign Operations Subcommittee of the Appropriations Committee.

Third, there was the Commission on Security and Cooperation in Europe. While officially a bipartisan and "bi-branch" agency, it may be treated here as if it were a House commission because its first chair, Dante Fascell, served for nearly a decade. Since he also chaired the House Foreign Affairs Committee from 1984 and, before that time, served as one of its ranking and active Democratic members, the commission frequently appeared to function as an appendage of the House Foreign Affairs Committee. The CSCE systematically oversaw human rights issues arising under the 1975 Helsinki Accord, and it was able to produce legislation indirectly through the Foreign Affairs Committee. But personality factors had to be taken into account here as well. Under Fascell the commission was not the same as under, say, Senator Alfonse D'Amato (R., New York), who assumed the CSCE chair in 1985. D'Amato was neither as interested nor as assertive as Fascell, although one must acknowledge a declining interest in Helsinki issues in general after ten years of debate on the subject.

On balance during the period 1973–84, the Democrat-controlled House gave much first-stage attention to human rights issues, whether for reasons of personality or of structure. The introduction and monitoring of new legislation and the seeking of follow-up legislation were not entirely partisan matters, although much voting was (as demonstrated in chapter 2). The Democrats were certainly not reluctant to challenge the Nixon, Ford, and Reagan administrations. Yet they also gave the Carter administration a difficult time on such issues as requiring the international financial institutions to incorporate human rights considerations, reducing economic assistance to the Philippines because of human rights violations, or pushing for economic sanctions against Uganda because of Amin's atrocities. (The Carter administration was opposed to all of these congressional initiatives, among others.)[10]

Thus, the record shows that many congressmen and some senators used their committee or subcommittee positions to press the executive branch for greater attention to internationally recognized human rights. At this first stage, members of Congress acted for either programmatic or political reasons.[11] They were either genuinely interested in the subject or decided that the subject was good to use in the quest for publicity and power. Congressmen like Fraser and Solarz showed that one could support a human rights ingredient in foreign policy without being hurt politically. Indeed, for some members of Congress human rights action was a path to enhanced visibility in Washington and, perhaps, back home as well. In part, this occurred because human rights was a relatively salient issue with the media and the public, at least on selected issues, and a network of private human rights lobbies existed as well. Hence there were political rewards (i.e., publicity) for congressional action on human rights that made this issue different from some others.

There were, however, limits to the political rewards for activism on human rights. Jerry Patterson was defeated in 1984; his activism on human rights and international banking, especially pertaining to Guatemala, did not enhance his standing among his constituents. The same was true for Clarence Long's activism on human rights in El Salvador. On the Senate side, Charles Percy was also defeated in 1984. (This is not to suggest that members' attention to human rights caused their defeat, only that their activism did not save them from defeat.)

Some have argued that most members of Congress do not oversee administrative action pertaining to defense policy well because they are not interested or there are few political rewards.[12] The same might be said of many members regarding human rights in the period under study. But the members on relevant committees and subcommittees—especially in the House—did vigorously oversee administrative actions, and some legislative follow-up resulted. There were enough interested members and enough political rewards in the period 1973–84 to produce significant congressional initiatives and active review of executive actions.

For whatever combination of reasons, human rights was extensively debated from 1973 to 1984, especially in the House, in the first stage of congressional actions. There were personal and programmatic reasons, as well as institutional ones, at work. The result was a willingness to challenge the executive branch under both parties about human rights in foreign policy. This assertiveness made some difference in policy, but each administration nevertheless put its own stamp on policy. It was still accurate to speak of a Carter policy or a Reagan policy rather than of a congressional policy on human rights because of the nature of the second stage of congressional activity.

The Second Stage.—The second stage of congressional action on human rights shows how difficult it is to get any majority vote or consistent majority votes. However energetic certain members of Congress are at the committee or subcommittee level, they must still get majority support on the floor if they are to push new legislation to a successful conclusion. While some oversight occurs without votes on the floor, it is difficult to bypass a vote in the tough fights on the big issues. One can hold hearings, publicize the embarrassing decisions of an administration, write letters and argue. But if the administration will not yield, a member must have the votes to get a specific law enacted. This is difficult to do in general, and especially difficult on human rights issues.

One of two conditions normally obtains in floor votes on human rights. Either the voting shows no pattern, or it is largely ideological and partisan. On the latter measures Congress is more predictable but so divided as to make the ultimate step in oversight extremely difficult. Two results emerge in the congressional-executive battles over human rights: the executive branch often refuses to compromise, knowing how difficult it is for Congress as a whole to fashion a majority, and when Congress does finally act, it tends to compromise, giving the executive branch at least some of what it wants.

There are exceptions to this larger pattern. Congress can reach a majority or consensus vote rather easily on what have been called motherhood resolutions—those on which almost everyone in Washington agrees. But such resolutions, frequently in the form of nonbinding sense-of-the-Congress resolutions, have little impact on the administration's conduct of foreign policy. At other times Congress can reach general agreement on a more specific policy at odds with the administration's wishes—as it did when recommending a trade embargo on

Uganda under Amin, disassociation from Pinochet's Chile and from Argentina under military rule, no military assistance to Guatemala, and, more recently, economic sanctions on the Republic of South Africa. But no one can reliably predict when Congress will agree on such policies, and no one can explain with any precision why the Congress voted as it did.

Motherhood resolutions aside, Congress usually acts by way of compromise. It does not say "no" to an administration; it says "yes, but." [13] This can be seen especially well on the subject of human rights and El Salvador. The Reagan administration got the better part of the increased economic and security assistance that it wanted, and it got more military advisers and military training for Salvadorans. But it had to certify Salvadoran progress on human rights and report on human rights, and, at one point, it was faced with a withholding of a percentage of authorized funds until certain human rights steps were taken. Hence it got most of what it wanted and could follow the outline of its desired policy, but with conditions and restrictions. Congress could not compel the Reagan administration to change its view of priorities and thereby get tough with the government and military of El Salvador about their human rights violations, but it could keep the human rights issue visible in political discourse and perhaps force the Reagan administration to give more attention than usual to specific human rights violations. Thus there was a Reagan approach to human rights in El Salvador, but it was modified by Congress.

The influence of Congress on U.S. policy toward El Salvador is difficult to pinpoint; but some carefully modulated observations are in order nevertheless.

In my interviews with them, some executive officials argued two different points in suggesting that Congress did not play a very large role in Salvadoran developments: one, that the executive branch was already worried about human rights and was pushing the Salvadoran government about them; the other, that the executive branch made congressional sentiment known to the Salvadoran government but without major results. On occasion, Reagan officials testified in Congress to this effect. Said Assistant Secretary of State Abrams in 1983:

We are well aware that to a very large degree the willingness of the American people and particularly Congress to support America's involvement with the Government of El Salvador depends on their human rights practices. . . .

My sense is that [congressional certification] has helped some and hurt some in El Salvador; helped in that it has given us a lever. There is no question that it has been one of the ways that we in the executive branch have been able to pressure the Government of El Salvador and bring home to them how seriously the Congress feels about human rights.[14]

At least once, Secretary of State George Shultz acknowledged publicly that the threat of major negative pressure was an important element of U.S. policy toward El Salvador. He told the House Foreign Affairs Subcommittee on Western Hemisphere Affairs that if there was no progress on human rights, "as a last resort" the United States must be prepared to "walk away," as required by congressional legislation.[15] But this was theory. When the U.S. ambassador did get tough with the Salvadorans about human rights, he was reprimanded.[16]

The problem was that the administration had made it known by word and deed that, in its view, nothing could be worse than a rebel victory in El Salvador. Thus the executive branch supported the government side no matter what its human rights record was. Abrams had testified in 1981, "So it is my view, again, strongly my own view, to permit a communist victory in El Salvador under the guise of human rights policy is madness."[17] In addition, the administration had certified Salvadoran progress on human rights regardless of the facts.

It was little wonder, then, that the extreme rightists in El Salvador continued with death squads, summary executions, disappeared persons, torture, and mistreatment. They understood that the Reagan administration, unlike the Carter administration, would always provide as much security assistance as possible in the name of anticommunism. The basic problem in Reagan's approach to El Salvador was well summarized by Arthur Schlesinger, Jr.: "The guarantee of military protection means that we renounce the ultimate sanction—the withdrawal of support. Once we declare our commitment to a regime's survival, it becomes increasingly hard to make a beleaguered oligarchy do things it sees, probably correctly, as fatal to its privilege and power. The military shield turns into a blank check."[18]

In this situation, it was exceedingly important that Congress appear to take seriously the option of terminating or reducing significantly

U.S. foreign assistance to El Salvador. It attempted this early on through the certification requirement. Later, it withheld a portion of foreign assistance and did reduce actual levels of foreign assistance for human rights reasons, thereby raising the specter of a U.S. withdrawal if the situation remained atrocious. This congressional action probably made the Reagan administration and moderately conservative elements in El Salvador more diligent about human rights because neither could discount entirely further congressional action.

Congress, against the wishes of the Reagan administration, helped that administration break free of its self-generated limitation in dealing with the extreme right in El Salvador. Insofar as members of Congress seriously considered a change in foreign assistance to that government (and they clearly did so by withholding 30 percent of it), they did influence the other parties involved. It was not only that action was taken in the case of the four American churchwomen; there was also the threat that Congress might act further.

Congress also modified the Reagan approach to other human rights situations. The first Reagan administration could cozy up to the Pinochet government, but it was prohibited by law from resuming economic and security assistance and therefore it could not fully normalize relations. It could rhetorically support a military government in Guatemala, but it could not provide much military assistance—Congress further stipulating that economic assistance was to be provided only through voluntary agencies, not Guatemalan governmental agencies. The administration could harass the Sandinistas in Nicaragua, but Congress took into account human rights abuses by the contras by severely, although inconsistently, restricting U.S. assistance to the rebels. There were many such examples.

Largely because of the difficulty of getting specific or consistent legislation, Congress tended to respond to executive initiatives on human rights by an "approve and attach" pattern. Congress itself did initiate occasionally, as on an early measure restricting U.S. assistance to Chile and through provisions regulating voting by the U.S. delegations to international financial institutions. But the more usual pattern was for the executive branch to initiate and Congress to modify.

Congress played this reactive and modifying role in foreign policy in general. When Congress challenged the president in early 1984 on the use of marines in Lebanon, it invoked the 1973 War Powers Act against the president's wishes; but it then gave the president eighteen months to get the marines out of Lebanon or face an unlikely resolution of non-support. It did not give a firm "no" to the president on the marines, but it sent a clear signal that the president's policy was in deep trouble (and in that election year, Reagan authorized a "redeployment" of the marines from Lebanon to ships, after which they were "redeployed" back home). This same pattern developed in human rights matters. The executive branch proposed and the Congress disposed, usually in the form of modifying attachments.

There is one further point of some importance. A number of observers believe that what can be called the tennis theory of politics also affected congressional form and substance. Snoopy, a beagle starring in a nationally syndicated comic strip, was reported to have said after a doubles tennis match, "It matters not who wins or loses; it's how you lays the blame." [19] Likewise a number of observers remarked in interviews that Congress approved and attached, rather than denying flat out, not only because Congress proceeds by necessary compromise but also because certain members did not want full responsibility for any failure of policy. Some persons critical of Reagan's policy in El Salvador, for example, did not want to ban U.S. assistance to that government. One possible motivation for this posture was that a flat ban would have made the critics responsible for any communist triumph in the civil war. By voting to require certification of human rights improvements as a condition of assistance, they could focus on human rights while leaving the administration responsible for any failures in policy. Such possible motivations are not recorded in any document, and they are not forthcoming in interviews with members of Congress. But there is a strong likelihood that such calculations influenced some members at times.

Summary

In a final summary of the congressional process on human rights, one can see what has been called "subcommittee government" at work in the first stage of congressional action. [20] There has been much action on human rights, especially at the subcommittee level and particularly in the House. This action has been of a combined legislative and oversight nature, and much of it has been serious. Whatever the personal calculations by members of Congress about publicity and power, any number of members have shown an interest in human rights and U.S. foreign policy. In the House some names readily come to mind: Donald Fraser, Tom Harkin (later in the Senate), Stephen Solarz, Ed Koch, Jim Leach, Don Bonker, Howard Wolpe, Gerry Studds, Michael Barnes, Clarence Long, Ted Weiss, Dante Fascell, Jerry Patterson; in the Senate, James Abourezk, Charles Percy, Christopher Dodd, Larry Pressler, Ted Kennedy, Ed Zorinsky, Paul Tsongas, Pat Moynihan, "Scoop" Jackson. This first stage of action was unpredictable, dependent on personal interest by individual members, although House action was more institutionalized than in the Senate. The second stage was, at times, equally unpredictable, since there was a lack of overall consistency in voting for the various human rights measures. The inconsistency also showed up in a list of disparate countries that were targets of country-specific human rights legislation. Yet conservative Republicans tended to vote consistently for legislation that would restrict leftist regimes, and liberal Democrats tended to vote for measures that would restrict rightist regimes. Such splits, and perhaps a desire to avoid responsibility for a clear-cut policy, led to compromise reactions to executive initiatives, which often modified them while permitting the general flow of executive policy.

One might wish for a clearer picture of congressional action on international human rights. But the struggle for control of American foreign policy that the Constitution invites (and that the years from 1973 to 1984 displayed) meant unpredictability so great as to frustrate any neat construct.[21]

Chapter 8

The Wisdom of Congressional Action

> The human rights problem is so complex that mistakes will inevitably be made.
>
> —Elliott Abrams,
> speech, Georgetown University, October 12, 1983

Congress passed three major pieces of general human rights legislation and three lesser general measures. The "big three" linked human rights to security assistance, economic assistance, and U.S. voting in international financial institutions. The other three pertained to refugees, emigration from nonmarket societies, and the Export-Import Bank. While Congress was able to pass all of this general legislation in the 1970s, it lacked the attention span, willpower, and political consensus to oversee effectively the implementation of its original intent in all but one instance: the Jackson-Vanik amendment covering reasonable emigration from communist countries. Congressional attention and consensus focused especially on Romania, initially to stimulate Jewish emigration from that Marxist regime.

Regarding security assistance, many members of Congress may have come to accept the argument of two administrations that publicly naming gross violators of internationally recognized human rights damaged American foreign policy. Yet some in Congress tried to get the Reagan administration to emulate the Carter administration and to invoke the spirit of Section 502B of the Foreign Assistance Act without publicly indicating a gross violator, but they failed. Even when members argued that the original authors of Section 502B never intended a public list of gross violators, Reagan officials were unbending in their opposition to the statute.[1] As noted earlier, Assistant Secretary Abrams testified publicly that the Human Rights Bureau did not try to think about countries in terms of gross violators, which of course would be the first step in implementing this and related statutes. Thus, the Carter policy of linking human rights to security assistance in at least some executive decisions was mostly abandoned from 1981 onward. Congress could not prevent this shift to a policy that effectively ignored the law in question, although several members of House subcommittees kept the issue alive in oversight hearings during the early 1980s. But the votes were not there in floor actions to rewrite the statute in a major way or otherwise pressure the Reagan administration effectively.

Regarding economic assistance, Congress had written Section 116 of the Foreign Assistance Act so that aid could continue even to a gross violator if it was destined for the most needy people in a country. As long as the executive branch tried to comply with this statute, Congress deferred to its judgment. Congress did not oversee this provision extensively. Liberal House Democrats especially were not inclined to spend much time in making the sometimes difficult distinction between development aid and aid to the most needy. There were few members who tracked AID or broader executive decisions under the statute. Congress paid little attention to AID decisions naming countries like Zaire as de facto gross violators eligible for most needy aid only, or other countries as needing special supervisory mechanisms. (There were broader implications to restricting Zaire under Section 116; logically, it should have also been denied security assistance unless the president certified exceptional circumstances, and it should have been targeted for negative U.S. votes in international financial institutions.)

Congress did oversee the Reagan administration's violation of Section 701 of the International Financial Institutions Act linking human rights to U.S. voting in those institutions. When the Reagan team reversed the Carter policy of abstaining on or voting against loan applications in the multilateral banks from regimes engaging in a consistent pattern of gross violations of internationally recognized human rights, members of the House, especially, tried to pressure the administration through the House Subcommittee on International Finance. Eventually, these critics pressed through Congress a slight amendment to Section 701, dropping the word "consistent" so as to signal the administration to stop using any alleged improvement in human rights to justify an affirmative vote for a loan application. But the Reagan administration continued its policy of voting only against leftist regimes in the banks, regardless of human rights violations by rightist regimes.

The many concerned congressional critics were unable to change the obvious violation of U.S. law by an administration sworn to implement it. Congress could not act effectively without cutting off funding to the banks themselves, which liberals, especially, were unwilling to do.

As for refugee affairs, Congress was badly fragmented after 1980 on how to revise the Refugee Act of that year. It was not able to agree on what to do about the Carter and Reagan administrations' distortions of the national and international legal requirement to protect persons who were fleeing because of well-founded fears of persecution. Congress did concern itself with problems, real or imagined, from the Caribbean and Central America. A number of members, again at the subcommittee level, kept up with administration decisions on Haitians, Cubans, Salvadorans, and others including Poles, Afghans, Ethiopians, and Vietnamese. In hearings, vigorous debates raged about naval interdiction of Haitians, the Mariel boatlift from Cuba, and why Poles were presumed to be refugees but Salvadorans were not. But this subcommittee action at the first congressional stage of continuing involvement was effectively negated by a lack of consensus at the second stage. Both the Carter and Reagan teams were able to pursue their policies, since votes were not there to write a new refugee law or effectively pressure the administration through, say, a reduction in funding. During the Reagan administration most of all, refugee policy was controlled by the old cold war bias favoring those fleeing communist totalitarian persecution over those fleeing merely authoritarian persecution. The United States thus violated its own international legal undertakings with its refugee policy, as well as its own national law patterned on international law. Still, there was no congressional consensus on new legislative actions because too many other concerns manifested themselves in U.S. domestic politics.[2]

The Jackson-Vanik amendment on emigration from nonmarket societies deviated from the broader congressional pattern on general human rights legislation. Congress as a whole not only oversaw the measure vigorously through its first stage but also presented the possibility of second-stage consensus voting in support of the original measure. The executive branch therefore had to take into account congressional support of the law in its policy toward these particular states. The process was most easily observed regarding Romania. When Romania introduced a stiff exit tax in the 1980s, Congress reacted swiftly. Congressional personnel went to Romania and met directly with the authorities, indicating that a loss of most-favored-nation status in trade would be forthcoming if the tax were not repealed, which it was. Although interested in a Romanian foreign policy independent of the Soviet Union, the executive branch had no choice but to join in the push for a change in Romanian emigration policy.[3]

The process was not so clear for other countries like the Soviet Union, which did not seek most-favored-nation status after the passage of Jackson-Vanik and which fashioned an emigration policy independently of this legislation. For about a decade after 1974, Soviet emigration figures went up or down depending on other factors; thus, congressional action was much less important when dealing with a superpower concerned about its image of imperviousness.

What made the Jackson-Vanik amendment different as general human rights legislation was that it was not completely general; it pertained only to communist countries restricting international movement. Also, congressional consensus on communist violations of human rights is more easily wrought than on other matters. Second, private groups lobbied diligently, most of all for Jewish emigration from Eastern Europe. The combination of a Congress predisposed to agree on communist violations of rights and interest groups quick to call problems to its attention meant, for example, that Congress would carefully monitor a change in Romanian policy. In this one case, Congress co-determined foreign policy with the executive branch. It established a relatively general but clear rule over the opposition of the executive branch, and it made known to the executive branch that it would have to implement the rule as written. Such a process, however, did not occur so frequently.[4]

Congress expressed no similar interest in using the Export-Import Bank for general human rights purposes except in the case of the Republic of South Africa. Invoking Jackson-Vanik might cost the United States some trade, but Congress was willing to pay this price in defense of emigration rights under communism—and most thought the communist violators would suffer more anyway by being denied access to American markets on most-favored-nation terms. But Congress was not consistently willing to pay an economic price to protect unspecified human rights in other countries. This was shown by the case of Allis-Chalmers and Argentina under military rule: an American company indirectly benefiting from an Export-Import Bank loan mobilized Congress to reverse a Carter administration decision denying the loan for human rights reasons. Congress was sympathetic to the argument that American companies should not lose business because of human rights violations in Argentina.

On the other hand, Congress restricted American companies from doing business in South Africa through an Export-Import Bank loan, and congressional certification requirements effectively achieved this end. Governmental agencies of the Republic of South Africa could not contract with an American company for goods or services under an Export-Import Bank loan, because the executive branch could not certify that the South African agency was committed to the Sullivan principles designed to secure integrated management and an integrated labor force in that country. Halfway through the second Reagan administration, Congress was not willing to make the Sullivan principles mandatory for all American companies in South Africa; they remained a voluntary yardstick of corporate America's commitment to racial justice. Thus, Congress used the Sullivan principles, in a legal sense, only with regard to the Export-Import Bank. While very limited and largely symbolic, this congressional action was at least entirely clear.

At the same time, neither manipulation of the bank nor use of the Sullivan principles more generally is a very powerful tool with which to affect human rights in South Africa. Thus it was more significant that Congress moved toward more general forms of economic sanctions on South Africa in the mid-1980s, forcing the Reagan administration to shift course slightly by its adoption of a form of sanctions. At that point, the use of the Export-Import Bank for human rights purposes became a small measure indeed.

In one sense, general human rights legislation, especially the two statutes trying to link human rights with security and economic assistance, may influence country-specific legislation. The general legislation may set the stage for follow-up congressional action pertaining to specific countries. This may be especially true if an administration refuses to implement the general statute. Rather than proceed under the general legislation, Congress may find it easier to act on particular countries. Though one can seriously question the *direct* importance of a law like Section 502B of the Foreign Assistance Act pertaining to security aid and human rights, especially during the Reagan administration, that legislation may have indirect importance through country-specific legislation. The general legislation becomes a talking point in congressional proceedings. The law legitimizes congressional concern. It socializes persons into thinking about the linkage between human rights and security assistance, and thus it may contribute indirectly to U.S. action on human rights.

This appears to have happened several times from 1973 to 1984, particularly with regard to Latin American countries. The clearest example relates to Guatemala under military rule. The Reagan administration tried to reverse the Carter policy of threatening to deny most military assistance as leverage to stop mass political murder and other gross violations of internationally recognized human rights. Congress blocked this reversal, finding it proper to link U.S. security assistance to the human rights record of the government in question. A more complex example stems from El Salvador, where the Reagan administration wanted to greatly increase military assistance to a regime confronted by an armed insurrection entailing some Marxists—but a regime associated with disappeared persons, summary executions, and a long list of other human rights violations. Again, Congress found it desirable to link U.S. support for the regime with an improvement in human rights. In this example, however, congressional action was less clear-cut, calling for certification or reporting requirements or withholding assistance to press its concern with human rights on an executive branch preoccupied by a perceived struggle with international communism.

Whatever the precise and partially unknowable motivations for specific human rights legislation by members of Congress, the more important country-specific legislation tended to target Latin American countries. The cases of Guatemala and El Salvador showed this in different ways, as did those of Chile and Argentina. In all these cases congressional action on human rights did affect the president's conduct of foreign policy. Security or economic assistance was blocked, limited, or delayed. During the Carter administration, U.S. votes in the international financial institutions were affected. During the Reagan administration, full U.S. normalization of diplomatic relations was prevented.

The case of Nicaragua is different still. Congressional action during the Carter administration and then Reagan policy after 1980 tended to use human rights to oppose Marxists. From 1981 onward, Reagan foreign policy toward Nicaragua was characterized by a shrill and unbalanced emphasis on human rights violations by the Sandinistas, but the primary objective of policy became the removal of that regime from power, not simply the reform of its human rights policies. Congress inexplicably shifted from trying to hamstring Carter's co-optation strategy to trying to hamstring Reagan's confrontation strategy. Having delayed and modified Carter's foreign aid bill for the Sandinistas, Congress did the same with Reagan's measures, even briefly terminating military support for the contras. Human rights issues were an important part of debates about U.S. foreign policy toward Managua, but the overriding issue was the nature of the Sandinista regime and whether it conducted a revolutionary foreign policy that constituted a security threat to the United States. Security concerns in Nicaragua overshadowed country-specific human rights legislation, but then human rights reentered the debates on whether the United States should be supporting the contras—who had violated human rights when part of Somoza's national guard and who after 1980 attacked civilians and mutilated captured or dead combatants.

One more country in this region, Haiti, stimulated country-specific legislation, but its example demonstrates a different point. Generally, the Reagan administration and Congress itself ignored the 1981 certification requirement linking progress on human rights in Haiti to a continuation of U.S. foreign assistance. The administration did certify, perhaps to avoid any implication that Haitians arriving in Miami were refugees from persecution and therefore entitled to remain, thus meeting the procedural requirements of the legislation; but it was a largely bogus certification, as had been the case in El Salvador, even though there was no realistic communist threat to anyone in or from Haiti. Likewise, the members of Congress were generally indifferent to the administration's first certification.

Why Congress renewed the certification requirement in 1983, after barely overseeing the first certification, is inexplicable—aside from the fact that human rights abuses in Haiti were probably the worst in the Western hemisphere. Also inexplicable is why the Reagan administration decided, after two more bogus certifications, to focus seriously on human rights abuses in Haiti, unless it saw irresistible pressures for change in Haiti and wanted to be aligned with the forces for reform. Congress did not force the Reagan team to shift its position, though it may have played some small part in sensitizing the administration to human rights problems in Haiti.

Patterns of congressional action do not hold firmly, but at least some human rights violations in the Western hemisphere seemed more likely to produce country-specific legislation than in the rest of the Third World. Some of this legislation was relatively important on human rights—and other—grounds (El Salvador, Guatemala, Chile, and Argentina), some was relatively important for security debates (Nicaragua), and some was relatively unimportant (Haiti).

On occasion Congress would pass and subsequently pay some attention to specific human rights legislation beyond the Western hemisphere. Several statutes pertained to South Africa, and Congress finally voted general, if weak, economic sanctions in an attack on apartheid, despite the Reagan administration's adoption of token sanctions (to head off the congressional initiative). Why Congress adopted economic sanctions in 1985 and 1986 is largely inexplicable; after all, apartheid and its brutalities were not new. Congress also moved toward measures to combat human rights violations in the Philippines. Through Senators Richard Lugar and Paul Laxalt and Congressman Stephen Solarz and others, it played a role in pressing President Reagan himself to distance the United States from Marcos. Why Congress should act on South Africa and the Philippines but at the same time not on South Korea, Zaire, or Indonesia cannot be explained, save that key members grew interested in South Africa or the Philippines but not in the other countries. Perhaps that interest was stimulated by political instability, as reported by the Western press, which then led to concern with the underlying human rights problems. But this view has not been proven.

With some 160 countries in the world, all with human rights problems, it is unrealistic to expect Congress, in its modern state of disarray, to approach the issue systematically. It proceeds according to the interests of energetic members. This means that Argentina may be targeted but not Bolivia, Haiti but not Paraguay (until 1985), the Philippines but not Indonesia, Liberia (after 1984) but not Zaire. That human rights issues in Panama or Mexico or Paraguay finally get taken up has more to do with the success of individual members or staffers than with any careful judgment as to the most egregious violations, the area of greatest U.S. responsibility, or the most achievable results. The positive side of the situation is that if politics is the art of the possible, then one might as well plunge ahead and do what can be done.[5]

Whatever the reasons for the emphasis in specific congressional action on selected countries in the Western hemisphere, and whatever the debate about this selectivity, most specific human rights legislation beyond that region remained relatively unimportant to U.S. foreign policy. Restrictions on Vietnam, Cambodia, Cuba, and the Soviet Union (the Jackson-Vanik amendment aside) were largely irrelevant since the United States did not provide foreign assistance to any of them. Legislative language pertaining to Pakistan, Mexico, and South Korea was exceedingly soft, indicating little more than lip service to human rights issues.

But such soft congressional action could be the precursor to more demanding legislation and therefore could be important symbolically to an administration, indicating where it should look more closely at human rights problems. But the political process did not always work that way. Language on human rights in Pakistan was not followed by congressional attention to that country, despite prolonged human rights problems there. Large numbers of communist troops in neighboring countries to it and to South Korea inhibited any push for human rights in the anticommunist regime. On the other hand, a sense-of-the-Congress resolution on Liberia passed in 1985 could at least be viewed as a possible forerunner of more congressional action.[6] It was not easy for an administration to determine when Congress was serious in its soft legislative action and when it was not. A given action could indicate more serious things to come, or it could mean simply that a member or coalition had been temporarily successful. Determined administrations tended to believe that Congress did not know what it was doing in foreign policy, so they also had a tendency to assume the latter.

All administrations dislike country-specific legislation, believing that it constrains the executive branch too much in foreign policy. They criticize the rigidity inherent in foreign policy by legislation. On the other hand, Congress frequently believes that the executive branch cannot have it both ways. If Congress legislates generally and then the administration refuses to implement the general guidelines (as the first Reagan administration refused to do on human rights), then it is natural for Congress to turn to more specific legislation. If the Nixon and Reagan administrations had shown more genuine commitment to protecting human rights in Latin America, so the argument runs, they would not have been faced with country-specific legislation in places like Chile, Argentina, El Salvador, and Guatemala. Congress sometimes acts via country-specific legislation where it perceives both a human rights problem and an administration's lack of attention to that problem.

Despite all the discussion in Washington about congressional micromanagement of foreign policy, country-specific legislation on human rights is likely to remain part of the political landscape. No administration since 1973 had established an approach to the issue that commanded bipartisan and bi-branch consensus. The Kissinger years led to the view in Congress that there was too much Machtpolitik and not enough traditional American values in U.S. foreign policy.[7] Congress perceived the Carter administration as highly disorganized and unclear in its human rights (and probably overall) policy.[8] It saw the first Reagan administration as too ideological and too committed to double standards in favor of Third World allies. In this political context, Congress was likely to remain assertive, with its own selectivity in country-specific legislation.

Function-specific rules on human rights eventually turned out to be less controversial than country-specific rules. Two of the most important created the Bureau of Human Rights and Humanitarian Affairs in the Department of State and required the executive branch to report to Congress on the human rights situation in member states of the United Nations. The combined effect of these specific pieces of legislation was to increase the sensitivity of the U.S. foreign policy establishment to the importance of human rights. The process, as usual, did not go smoothly, and, for different reasons, there was much resistance to these congressional actions in the Nixon, Ford, Carter, and Reagan administrations. But by the end of the first Reagan administration, Foreign Service and other State Department personnel had become more accepting of the idea that U.S. foreign policy should have human rights on the agenda as a distinct issue. Debate evolved over the form of the human rights policy and its linkage with other policies, not whether to have such a policy.

This attitude was a clear change from the Kissinger period when human rights was largely regarded as a domestic issue, from the Carter period when many Foreign Service officers and some bureau heads regarded human rights as part of softheaded naïveté in world politics, and from the early Reagan days when high-ranking officials, including the president himself, wanted to substitute simple anticommunism for human rights concerns. Congress must be assigned credit for establishing and maintaining this redefinition of the U.S. foreign policy agenda from about 1973, and the functional legislation discussed here constitutes an important part of that change. The 1981 Lefever hearings in the Senate indicated, among other things, a clear congressional interest in maintaining the Human Rights Bureau and the legislation it was supposed to oversee. This interest was bipartisan and basically non-ideological (only the far right wing, represented by Jesse Helms, supported the Lefever nomination).

The record of the Reagan administration makes clear, however, that one can have reasonably objective reporting on at least some human rights without linking those facts to a widely supported human rights policy. There may be scant correlation between the annual country reports on human rights and overall U.S. foreign policy toward a particular country. As long as this is the case, and as long as an administration does not come up with a persuasive rationale for explaining the discrepancy between reporting and policy, debate will continue about human rights and U.S. foreign policy.

In this regard, we can observe that into the second Reagan administration, U.S. human rights policy resembled somewhat the Carter administration's policy. Against the background of the Kirkpatrick doctrine that had shaped much policy on human rights in the first administration, the president made a speech in March 1985 in which he said, "The American people believe in human rights and oppose tyranny in whatever form, whether of the left or the right." [9] High-ranking Reagan officials also said that human rights in particular countries had to be dealt with on a case-by-case basis. [10] Such statements produced confusion about the second administration's human rights policy. Moreover, the speech calling for a general push for democracy was accompanied by statements of support for repressive regimes in Pakistan, Zaire, and elsewhere. An official of the National Security Council who had a hand in producing the speech (it did not evolve out of the Bureau of Human Rights) said that it indicated no change in overall policy. [11] But Leslie Gelb of the *New York Times* correctly observed that the thrust of the speech implied a shift away from the Kirkpatrick thesis of favorable double standards for anticommunist violators of human rights. [12] Indeed, the situation was as muddled as it had been in the Carter period, if not more so. There was no clear, much less widely supported, rationale for why U.S. reports of gross violations of human rights were not accompanied by certain administration decisions required by law. [13] By 1987 the second Reagan administration was taking strong action against violations of human rights in places like Panama and South Korea but not in Zaire or Pakistan.

While the congressional requirement for annual country reports on human rights had helped make human rights legitimate (even if it caused confusion over U.S. human rights policy), other congressionally required reports did not have the same impact. Indeed, members of Congress on foreign policy subcommittees and their staffers had great difficulty tracking the reports and making them serve useful purposes. In the 1980s Congress—still reacting to the imperial presidency and its bypassing of Congress on many issues—insisted that the executive branch report to it on many foreign policy issues. But if Congress could not oversee the reports effectively, all that transpired was time-wasting exchanges of paper. The Reagan administration was very much in the tradition of the imperial presidency as far as human rights matters were concerned. It was convinced that it possessed the Truth, and it ignored congressional directives when it could. This attitude is reflected in the fate of general human rights legislation as well as its certifications of progress on human rights in places like Haiti. The administration was not going to let congressional statutes interfere with its view of the world if it could avoid doing so. Under these circumstances, many members voted to require reports. But without a better system for tracking and oversight, much power still rested with the executive branch.

By comparison, the congressionally created Commission on Security and Cooperation in Europe came to command bipartisan and bi-branch support. This may have been because it focused on communist implementation of human rights provisions in the Helsinki Accord and, thus, did not have to address questions of U.S. support for repressive but anticommunist regimes in the Third World. The commission's activities also did not deal with the troublesome questions of manipulating foreign assistance or of restricting the American private sector because of human rights violations abroad. It served largely two functions: publicizing situations, directly through reports and indirectly through sense-of-the-Congress resolutions, and dealing with individual cases. It can probably be considered a success in terms of its mandate. It has had some influence on positions taken on human rights within the Western alliance. Its influence on Eastern European states is unfathomable but probably slight.

Moving from function-specific legislation oriented to procedure to that oriented toward programs, one finds three congressional actions of some general importance. The ban on U.S. funding for foreign police training, prisons, and internal surveillance and intelligence did affect overt U.S. foreign policy, although one is never sure what the CIA record might be. The United States was certainly implicated in gross violations of human rights by police and prison personnel in places like South Vietnam. If, from the second Reagan administration onward, renewed U.S. funding for these activities were to include serious controls for past abuses, then Congress would have achieved its objectives. There is not much, if any, evidence that major U.S. interests were hurt by the congressional ban. Rather, the argument for resumed funding is a compelling one if pursued seriously—namely, that foreign officials could profit from U.S. training that encouraged respect for internationally recognized human rights. (In addition to human rights treaties on civil rights including prohibition of torture and mistreatment, there is a United Nations code for prisoners.) Whether Congress can effectively oversee renewed police training in El Salvador and Honduras remains unknown at the time of writing.

Special U.S. funding to counteract apartheid in the Republic of South Africa is a second function-specific program of some importance established by Congress. Funding is slight ($20 million for fiscal year 1986), but, symbolically, an affirmative approach to inducing change in South Africa is arguably important, whatever the fate of economic sanctions. Then, too, particular nonwhite individuals receive assistance in education or training. This human rights program does not substitute for other actions. But during the Reagan administration's policy of constructive engagement—or lack of decisive action against systematic racial discrimination—members of Congress obviously thought it important to make a show of concrete opposition to apartheid. Given the accumulating forces for change in South Africa, it is highly likely that this program will fit well with its times. In retrospect, however, it may appear too small and too late either to influence events in South Africa or to win friends for the United States in the South Africa of the future.

Third, congressional action on UNESCO and freedom of information had some symbolic value. Congressional criticism of attempts within UNESCO to restrict press freedoms indicated support for different administrations' efforts to maintain the principle of a free flow of information. Congressional action thus showed broad support for U.S. policy and sent a strong signal to Paris on the issue. Less positively, the congressional threat to withhold U.S. funding to UNESCO over the issue showed a disregard for international legal obligations.

Less positive still, congressional action in the late 1970s might have been understood by the Reagan administration as permission to withdraw from UNESCO, which it did in 1984. Action by Congress explicitly linked to the Universal Declaration of Human Rights was thus distinctly secondary and largely symbolic, but it did have some importance—positively or negatively or perhaps both.

Other function-specific legislation was important for the particular programs addressed, such as funding for the protection of political prisoners by the International Committee of the Red Cross or funding for the Inter-American Commission on Human Rights.

The Endowment for Democracy is so new that it is difficult to assess beyond the obvious. Reagan appointees had badly damaged the National Endowment for Democracy with an excessively narrow definition of what constituted building democracy. Its right-wing ideological ·approach had aligned the United States with the Nestlé Corporation and against the right to health and nutrition for infants and mothers in the Third World in a well-publicized vote in the World Health Organization; it also had aligned the United States with opposition to democratic socialists in France and with a corrupt military in Panama. Such a policy of covert support for dubious right-wing elements in those two countries made Congress look good as an overseer. If ever a justification for congressional activism in international human rights issues was needed, these events provided it.

But there was a more general point inherent in these events that Congress had not fully addressed. More than its predecessors, the Reagan administration manifested a desire to reinterpret international human rights into the American experience. Simply put, it wanted to transform international human rights into American democracy, conservative style. This was shown in a 1981 internal memo, intentionally leaked to the press, in which human rights was said to mean political freedom and capitalism. The same was also shown in the introduction to the 1982 country reports on human rights practices, in which human rights was said to mean civil and political rights in the Anglo-Saxon tradition. Rather than address human rights as internationally defined, the Reagan team wanted to push for duplication of the American experience and call it international human rights. The two are not the same.

International human rights instruments call for a wide variety of public policies in response to rights of persons or groups. These policies should touch on social, economic, and cultural matters as well as civil and political. Even if one takes just the civil and political matters, they do not collapse simply into a formal democracy. As shown by various authors, a nondemocratic state may do relatively well on a checklist of international human rights, and, conversely, a formal democracy may do very poorly on that same list.[14]

In practical terms, the point is that internationally recognized human rights may be better protected in an authoritarian state like Hungary or Yugoslavia than in "democratic" El Salvador or Guatemala, or even "democratic" Honduras or Paraguay. If one emphasizes respect for the right to life, against which all other rights must necessarily be secondary, and if one accepts socioeconomic rights, then it is easy to understand why many more persons have fled those four Latin American states since about 1960 than the two East European states also named above.

It may be true, and probably is, that international human rights are best protected in the Western democratic states, especially those in Western Europe that have accepted not only the European Convention on Human Rights but also the European Social Charter (the first covers political and civil rights, the other economic and social). But the difficult choices for U.S. foreign policy and human rights are to be found not in Western Europe but in Eastern Europe and the Third World.

In substituting the American political experience for international human rights, the Reagan administration screened out important distinctions. Rather than learn something from international instruments on human rights, the Reagan team pursued its chauvinistic foreign policy in places like Nicaragua. Oblivious to people's concern for better health and housing, it had no satisfactory way to deal with the fact that most Nicaraguans supported the Sandinistas (as shown by the 1985 elections and by popular support for local militia).

The National Endowment for Democracy was, as managed by the Reagan appointees, part of this crusade to duplicate in a formal sense the emphasis by affluent America on property rights as protected by procedural rights. Hence, there was a knee-jerk reaction to democratic socialism in France and to any threats to the status quo in Panama (until U.S. policy shifted in 1987). Such policies helped to isolate the United States from much of the rest of the world, especially from developing nations.

Certainly the United States should promote democratic values and persons around the world, but such support for democracy is not synonymous with defense of international human rights. Much can be done for human rights apart from, or in addition to, promoting democracy; some formal democracies, especially in Latin America but also elsewhere, have a very poor record in implementing international human rights.

Congress did not focus on how democracy related to internationally recognized human rights, perhaps because the subject was too abstract. It certainly reacted strongly to Reagan's handling of the Endowment for Democracy; generally, it had shown considerable interest in a number of civil rights or rights of the integrity of the person apart from political rights, and some of its members also had shown some awareness of how difficult it would prove to work for democracy in the real world of vested authoritarian power and profit. Yet Congress, with its periodic aversion to international organizations and treaties, never pushed the Reagan administration toward fuller U.S. integration with the international framework for human rights.

In summary of democracy and human rights, the Reagan administration might be praised for emphasizing a structural or long-term approach to political rights, however much the idea might be borrowed from congressional Democrats. (It is relevant to note that Congressman Fraser, in the documents on human rights published by his subcommittee in the 1970s, *did* emphasize an international framework for U.S. human rights policy, even though that emphasis was diminished in succeeding years.[15]) Congress might be praised for insisting that the Reagan administration, in its specific policies, not turn its desire for democracy into a right-wing crusade. But both branches might be faulted for a willingness to assume too easily that human rights meant the American experience writ large. Such an assumption only added another dimension to America's increasing estrangement from the rest of the world. As Lincoln Bloomfield wrote, after being in charge of human rights in Carter's White House for two years, "For many non-Americans the most important human rights are not those that Americans regard as paramount."[16]

A few final observations seem to be in order. The first is that international activity on human rights has affected congressional deliberations, even though the United States is not a full party to most of the treaties on human rights. While the executive branch has refused to sign, and the Senate has refused to consent to ratification of, most human rights treaties, Congress as a whole has acted against the background of an international explosion of attention to human rights. Congressional statutes make reference to "internationally recognized human rights." Congressional hearings take into account reports by United Nations rapporteurs, votes in the United Nations Human Rights Commission, resolutions adopted in the General Assembly, and actions by the U.S. delegation to international meetings. Members of Congress or their staffers also meet regularly with private human rights groups, which are also active at the United Nations or in the human rights forums of the Organization of American States. Thus, international human rights activity influences Congress despite the fact that the United States formally holds itself somewhat apart from global action on human rights.[17]

As noted, there is still an American imprint to congressional human rights activity. Congress, after making reference to "internationally recognized human rights," frequently defines them largely in terms of the civil and political rights found in the U.S. Constitution. There still is not much congressional interest in economic, social, and cultural human rights recognized in international law.

Nevertheless, some international human rights activity has entered the political process of making human rights policy indirectly through congressional action. The United States is not as impervious to international action on human rights as a legalist might believe. The Senate's consent to ratification of the Genocide Convention in 1986, after almost forty years of debate, may indicate less formal resistance to international developments as well.

A second final observation is that much congressional legislation on human rights is soft law; it is rarely adjudicated in U.S. courts. Its implementation, or lack thereof, depends on the political rather than the judicial process. Whether a congressional action is technically nonbinding does make some difference, however. The executive branch is freer to resist a nonbinding sense-of-the-Congress resolution than a bill that has become law. Yet, this study has shown clearly that an administration will resist some congressional action even though it is law. One high State Department official even remarked in a 1986 interview that some of these laws were not really laws but "private compacts" between the two branches.

U.S. courts will generally not adjudicate these laws, fearing that they might be caught in the cross fire between the two political branches. Thus, they tend to dismiss any suits brought under contested human rights legislation as political questions—or through some other procedural technicality such as failure to establish standing to sue. The exceptions to this dominant pattern mostly concern refugee and emigration law, where several courts have overturned administration decisions pertaining to what constitutes a well-founded fear of persecution in places like Haiti and El Salvador. A court's willingness to take up the substance of these disputes may arise partially because the subject is intermestic (that is, as much international as domestic). There is also considerable precedent for judicial rulings on such subjects as the applicability of the U.S. Constitution to claimants to political asylum in this country.

The dominant pattern, however, remains unchanged. Much congressional action on human rights may be in the form of law, and this form has psychological and political importance. Congressional action helps turn policy into law, but this does not mean that law is self-executing or that an administration can be easily persuaded to implement it. Obviously, some administrations violate the law more than others, and when this happens Congress ultimately turns to more specific legislation to compel the administration to comply with the original intent. One reason why there is so much "micromanagement" of foreign policy by Congress is because there is so much violation of law by the executive branch. This is certainly true on the human rights issue, and it was certainly true during the first Reagan administration.

Americans are used to thinking of legal enforcement as the power of the state brought to bear against an individual or other private party. This happens, of course. But when a law involves a directive from Congress to the executive branch, the process is different. The executive branch has the power to resist. Organizational disarray and ideological divisions in Congress weaken its ability to enforce its will. The courts seek avoidance. Therefore, Congress attempts to implement its measures by trying to do something further that the executive branch dislikes—private and public discourse, embarrassment, a more specific law, the withholding of funds. The fate of human rights in U.S. foreign policy is essentially a political, not a legal, matter.[18]

A third and last observation concerns the wisdom of congressional legislation on human rights from 1973 to 1984. Observations on this subject depend on a series of prior value judgments having to do with desirability of efficiency in the policymaking process, the extent of a clear and present danger to U.S. security from foreign parties, responsibility of the United States in the world, and the quality of members of Congress, the executive branch, or particular administrations.

It is certainly easy to criticize Congress, in principle or in this one issue area. Congress is not well organized, especially in the present period of decentralization or "subcommittee government." It is probably not helpful to have 535 secretaries of state. On any issue, Congress is likely to be rent by multiple divisions of opinion. On some human rights issues, members of Congress who wish to establish a voting record favoring goodness posture ceaselessly. As on other issues, many Democrats and Republicans are ready to embarrass, or make life difficult for, members of the opposition party. There are members of Congress poorly informed about foreign policy issues, including human rights, and there are those more interested in publicity than programs.[19]

More generally, it has always been difficult to legislate in the American political system, by intention of the Founding Fathers. It is doubly difficult to legislate on foreign policy when there is no congressional or societal consensus on the cornerstone of that policy. Once the foreign policy cornerstone of containment of international communism came under substantial attack in about 1971 (the repeal of the Gulf of Tonkin Resolution is as good a starting point as any), there were few benchmarks for U.S. foreign policy. Moreover, it is extremely difficult to legislate on human rights in foreign policy because the subject is relatively new (although very old in its basic concerns) and there are few established foundations for policy. The explosion of international law on human rights came principally after 1944, and most international agencies concerned with specific human rights violations became active only in the 1960s.

These criticisms and problems can be documented by specifics. Congress should not have passed the Byrd amendment in 1971 defying United Nations sanctions undertaken to end white minority rule and racial discrimination in Rhodesia, not to mention illegal secession from the United Kingdom. The amendment placed narrow American corporate profit (Union Carbide) ahead of concern for human rights in what became Zimbabwe; it also harmed U.S. relations with the government of Zimbabwe, violated international law, and made life difficult for the United States in international forums, especially with black African nations. The Congress should not have threatened to withhold U.S. contributions to UNESCO in the dispute over the Universal Declaration of Human Rights and the free flow of information, for such a threat, if carried out, would have violated the treaty that was the constituent document of UNESCO and would have, thereby, made the United States appear to be trying to dictate to the rest of the international community. In 1979 Congress should not have tried to tie up Carter's first supplemental foreign aid bill to the Sandinista government in Nicaragua with "human rights" attachments. Given the nature of the previous Somoza regime and U.S. implication in its gross violations of human rights, Congress should have recognized the Sandinista front as a relative improvement and given Carter's co-optation strategy a chance to be tested fairly. If found wanting, it could be repealed. Certain members of Congress should not have tried to block implementation of the Panama Canal treaties with "human rights" amendments. One could go on with other specific cases.

Because of all these criticisms and problems, one might conclude that Congress should stay out of the swamp. Yet despite the flaws of the system, Congress has made an important contribution to U.S. foreign policy by putting human rights back on the agenda and by pressuring the executive branch to pay serious attention to human rights, and not just in communist countries.

In the early 1970s, a real and serious problem in U.S. foreign policy arose. The Nixon-Kissinger approach had resulted in the omission of an important factor in U.S. calculations. Their emphasis on stability in East-West relations had led them to ignore forces for change reacting to human rights violations in many countries. Iran and Nicaragua were two cases in which profound forces for change went largely unnoticed in the Kissinger years; the revolutions that exploded during the Carter administration had been fueled during the preceding eight years. One could talk of the same general process in southern Africa and elsewhere. U.S. foreign policy paid little attention to some of the major reasons why people around the world acted politically. In short, human rights matter to many people, and the Nixon-Kissinger approach downplayed the importance of this motivation, with negative consequences for U.S. relations, interests, and standing in the world.

By putting human rights back on the foreign policy agenda, Congress was addressing political reality: the United States should try to deal with one of the major reasons that influences persons to act politically. One should also keep in mind that it was Congress that took human rights off the agenda in the early 1950s by pressuring the Eisenhower administration to back away from international human rights treaties and issues in return for the dropping of the Bricker amendment to the Constitution, which would have reduced the authority of the executive branch to act under treaties.[20] Thus, the interpretation presented here is not that Congress is always more wise than the executive branch but that a fundamental problem that existed by the early 1970s was at least partially corrected, largely by Congress, in the period from 1973 to 1984.

Congress was also saying to the Nixon-Kissinger school of foreign policy that a U.S. approach to the world that emphasized primarily power and order would be difficult to sustain at home. This message, in the view of some, may be unfortunate, but a strong argument can nevertheless be made that it too reflected domestic political reality. Historians have noted, and polls confirm, a moral component in the American political culture.[21] A U.S. foreign policy inattentive to human rights will thus be built on weak foundations domestically, in addition to whatever important factors it screens out internationally. Again, it can reasonably be argued that the congressional push for human rights from 1973 onward reminded the executive branch of important political reality.

If one becomes more specific, one can still argue in support of a number of congressional actions. As for manipulating foreign assistance, bank votes, and trade benefits for human rights reasons, several points can be made. U.S. foreign assistance by itself will rarely be a powerful enough tool to cause a sovereign and nationalistic state to change policy drastically, especially since U.S. foreign economic assistance is declining relative to that provided by other nations. But manipulation of foreign assistance can be symbolically important in two respects. It can show a government that its human rights policies are observed carefully and found wanting, thus maintaining some pressure for beneficial change. It can also disassociate the United States from abuses of human rights, an important point when a regime falls and the United States deals with its successor.

International banks are already political because their decisions are made on the basis of policy choices about society and government as well as economics. Allende in Chile could not get U.S. and international bank support, yet his right-wing successors could—even though many of their economic policies were suspect, to put it mildly. And on what grounds did the international financial community support the likes of Marcos and Somoza with their systems of cronyism and corruption? Could it have been political rather than economic?

Was it because of economics that the Reagan administration blocked a Nicaraguan loan in the Inter-American Development Bank for the construction of rural roads?

Moreover, in principle why should the banks be considered above, or apart from, human rights? If economic development is designed to enhance human dignity, then human rights and economic growth fit together. Congressional legislation linking human rights to the international financial institutions represents an integrated approach to foreign policy, one in keeping with internationally agreed-upon definitions of the purposes of economic growth and development.[22]

The case of the Jackson-Vanik amendment and Romania indicates that sometimes manipulation of economic arrangements can have beneficial results, in that case pertaining to resuming reasonable levels of emigration. There is no moral or political reason not to try the same results-oriented approach in other countries, including noncommunist ones like South Africa. Again, the congressional approach is defensible on both moral and political grounds. Such manipulation does not always work, as the case of Jackson-Vanik and the Soviet Union indicates, but this example also shows, at least, that human rights pressure does not always damage the situation either: Soviet Jewish emigration reached a peak in 1979, five years after Jackson-Vanik became law.

These final observations about congressional wisdom in human rights legislation leave many questions unanswered. There is always the thematic problem of linking different U.S. interests in foreign policy. Should the United States press for human rights changes in Egypt, Saudi Arabia, or Syria, when it also seeks security or economic arrangements with those regimes? How should the U.S. government answer this question, given the cultural and political traditions in those countries? The Islamic world is not known for broad political rights; none of those three countries has a tradition of political freedom or democracy. To try to deal with that level of specificity in human rights policy lies far beyond the scope of this work.

Yet one can note in this regard David Price's argument that Congress is more effective in the early stages of policy making, when its goal is to set the agenda or germinate new ideas. It is also said that Congress is less effective when it comes to more specific fine tuning of policy in the later stages of the policy process.[23] This point of view may have some merit, especially since Price also notes that Congress functions differently in different issue areas. Regarding human rights in foreign policy, Congress has both set the agenda through general and specific legislation and attempted to fine-tune policy. It is difficult to say at which process Congress has proved more efficacious. On the one hand, much of its general and some of its specific legislation has been ignored by the Reagan administration, provoking it to follow up with more precise language. On the other hand, its more precise follow-up legislation has not necessarily damaged U.S. foreign policy. Arguably, Congress has demonstrated sufficient wisdom in adopting precise policies on Chile, Guatemala, South Africa, and some other nations. On balance, then, the distinction between early and late congressional action in the policy process may not be so important for international human rights, whatever the congressional record on other issues. Given the attitudes of the executive branch, Congress has had to act early and late, with general and specific legislation, to affect human rights abroad. If sometimes it has not been wise, sometimes it has been.[24]

Perhaps it would be appropriate to close this study by putting Congress in relative perspective. Foreign policy by Congress, including human rights, presents certain problems. Despite the problems of organization, lack of consensus, and the pull of personal and partisan politics, Congress has made an important contribution to U.S. foreign policy by its insistence that what happens to people matters. Relative to the Nixon-Kissinger administration, Congress correctly noted that the executive branch almost wholly ignored an important motivation for political action abroad. Relative to the Carter administration, it correctly noted that human rights should be integrated with economic policy (via the multilateral banks) and security policy (the Philippines and Uganda, for example). Relative to the first Reagan administration, it correctly noted that human rights violations mattered in friendly dictatorships as well as communist countries. Relative to the other views of human rights that competed in U.S. foreign policy from 1973 to 1984, Congress has not done too badly. The historical total may be better than the simple sum of the parts at any given point. There is nothing in the organization or process of congressional legislation and oversight, however, to guarantee an acceptable amount of wisdom in the future. Making human rights policy is always a difficult task.

Appendix A

Human Rights and Security Assistance

Sec. 502B. Human Rights.—(a) (1) The United States shall, in accordance with its international obligations as set forth in the Charter of the United Nations and in keeping with the constitutional heritage and traditions of the United States, promote and encourage increased respect for human rights and fundamental freedoms throughout the world without distinction as to race, sex, language, or religion. Accordingly, a principal goal of the foreign policy of the United States shall be to promote the increased observance of internationally recognized human rights by all countries.

(2) Except under circumstances specified in this section, no security assistance may be provided to any country the government of which engages in a consistent pattern of gross violations of internationally recognized human rights. Security assistance may not be provided to the police, domestic intelligence, or similar law enforcement forces of a country, and licenses may not be issued under the Export Administration Act of 1979 for the export of crime control and detection instruments and equipment to a country, the government of which engages in a consistent pattern of gross violations of internationally recognized human rights unless the President certifies in writing to the Speaker of the House of Representatives and the chairman of the Committee on Foreign Relations of the Senate and the chairman of the Committee on Banking, Housing and Urban Affairs of the Senate (when licenses are to be issued pursuant to the Export Administration Act of 1979), that extraordinary circumstances exist warranting provision of such assistance and issuance of such licenses. Assistance may not be provided under chapter 5 of this part to a country the government of which engages in a consistent pattern of gross violations of internationally rec-

ognized human rights unless the President certifies in writing to the Speaker of the House of Representatives and the chairman of the Committee on Foreign Relations of the Senate that extraordinary circumstances exist warranting provision of such assistance.

(3) In furtherance of paragraphs (1) and (2), the President is directed to formulate and conduct international security assistance programs of the United States in a manner which will promote and advance human rights and avoid identification of the United States, through such programs, with governments which deny to their people internationally recognized human rights and fundamental freedoms, in violation of international law or in contravention of the policy of the United States as expressed in this section or otherwise.

(b) The Secretary of State shall transmit to the Congress, as part of the presentation materials for security assistance programs proposed each fiscal year, a full and complete report, prepared with the assistance of the Assistant Secretary of State for Human Rights and Humanitarian Affairs, with respect to practices regarding the observance of and respect for internationally recognized human rights in each country proposed as a recipient of security assistance. In determining whether a government falls within the provisions of subsection (a) (3) and in the preparation of any report or statement required under this section, consideration shall be given to—

(1) the relevant findings of appropriate international organizations, including nongovernmental organizations, such as the International Committee of the Red Cross; and

(2) the extent of cooperation by such government in permitting an unimpeded investigation by any such organization of alleged violations of internationally recognized human rights.

(c) (1) Upon the request of the Senate or the House of Representatives by resolution of either such House, or upon the request of the Committee on Foreign Relations of the Senate or the Committee on International Relations of the House of Representatives, the Secretary of State shall, within thirty days after receipt of such request, transmit to both such committees a statement, prepared with the assistance of the Assistant Secretary of State for Human Rights and Humanitarian Affairs, with respect to the country designated in such request, setting forth—

(A) all the available information about observance of and respect for human rights and fundamental freedom in that country, and a detailed description of practices by the recipient government with respect thereto;

(B) the steps the United States has taken to—

(i) promote respect for and observance of human rights in that country and discourage any practices which are inimical to internationally recognized human rights, and

(ii) publicly or privately call attention to, and disassociate the United States and any security assistance provided for such country from, such practices;

(C) whether, in the opinion of the Secretary of State, notwithstanding any such practices—

(i) extraordinary circumstances exist which necessitate a continuation of security assistance for such country, and, if so a description of such circumstances and the extent to which such assistance should be continued (subject to such conditions as Congress may impose under this section), and

(ii) on all the facts it is in the national interest of the United States to provide such assistance; and

(D) such other information as such committee or such House may request.

(2) (A) A resolution of request under paragraph (1) of this subsection shall be considered in the Senate in accordance with the provisions of section 601(b) of the International Security Assistance and Arms Export Control Act of 1976.

(B) The term "certification", as used in section 601 of such Act, means, for the purposes of this subsection, a resolution of request of the Senate under paragraph (1) of this subsection.

(3) In the event a statement with respect to a country is requested pursuant to paragraph (1) of this subsection but is not transmitted in accordance therewith within thirty days after receipt of such request, no security assistance shall be delivered to such country except as may thereafter be specifically authorized by law from such country unless and until such statement is transmitted.

(4) (A) In the event a statement with respect to a country is transmitted under paragraph (1) of this subsection, the Congress may at any time thereafter adopt a joint resolution terminating, restricting, or continuing security assistance for such country. In the event such a joint resolution is adopted, such assistance shall be so terminated, so restricted, or so continued, as the case may be.

(B) Any such resolution shall be considered in the Senate in accordance with the provisions of section 601(b) of the International Security Assistance and Arms Export Control Act of 1976.

(C) The term "certification", as used in section 601 of such Act, means, for the purposes of this paragraph, a statement transmitted under paragraph (1) of this subsection.

(d) For the purpose of this section—

(1) the term "gross violations of internationally recognized human rights" includes torture or cruel, inhumane, or degrading treatment or punishment, prolonged detention without charges and trial, causing the disappearance of persons by the abduction and clandestine detention of those persons, and other flagrant denial of the right to life, liberty, or the security of person; and

(2) the term "security assistance" means—

(A) assistance under chapter 2 (military assistance) or chapter 4 (economic support fund) or chapter 5 (military education and training) or chapter 6 (peacekeeping operations) or chapter 8 (antiterrorism assistance) of this part;

(B) sales of defense articles or services, extensions of credits (including participations in credits), and guaranties of loans under the Arms Export Control Act; or

(C) any license in effect with respect to the export of defense articles or defense services to or for the armed forces, police, intelligence, or other internal security forces of a foreign country under section 38 of the Arms Export Control Act.

(e) Notwithstanding any other provision of law, funds authorized to be appropriated under part I of this Act may be made available for the furnishing of assistance to any country with respect to which the President finds that such a significant improvement in its human rights record has occurred as to warrant lifting the prohibition on furnishing such assistance in the national interest of the United States.

(f) In allowing the funds authorized to be appropriated by this Act and the Arms Export Control Act, the President shall take into account significant improvements in the human rights records of recipient countries, except that such allocations may not contravene any other provision of law.

(g) Whenever the provisions of subsection (e) or (f) of this section are applied, the President shall report to the Congress before making any funds available pursuant to those subsections. The report shall specify the country involved, the amount and kinds of assistance to be provided, and the justification for providing the assistance, including a description of the significant improvements which have occurred in the country's human rights record.

[Footnotes omitted]

Foreign Assistance and Arms Export Act, 22 USC 2304.

Appendix B

Human Rights and Economic Assistance

Sec. 116. Human Rights.—(a) No assistance may be provided under this part to the government of any country which engages in a consistent pattern of gross violations of internationally recognized human rights, including torture or cruel, inhuman, or degrading treatment or punishment, prolonged detention without charges, causing the disappearance of persons, or other flagrant denial of the right to life, liberty, and the security of persons, unless such assistance will directly benefit the needy people in such country.

(b) In determining whether this standard is being met with regard to funds allocated under this part, the Committee on Foreign Relations of the Senate or the Committee on International Relations of the House of Representatives may require the Administrator primarily responsible for administering part I of this Act to submit in writing information demonstrating that such assistance will directly benefit the needy people in such country, together with a detailed explanation of the assistance to be provided (including the dollar amounts of such assistance) and an explanation of how such assistance will directly benefit the needy people in such country. If either committee or either House of Congress disagrees with the Administrator's justification it may initiate action to terminate assistance to any country by a concurrent resolution under section 617 of this Act.

(c) In determining whether or not a government falls within the provisions of subsection (a) and in formulating development assistance programs under this part, the Administrator shall consider, in consultation with the Assistant Secretary for Human Rights and Humanitarian Affairs—

    (1) the extent of cooperation of such government in permitting an unimpeded investigation of alleged violations of inter-

nationally recognized human rights by appropriate international organizations, including the International Committee of the Red Cross, or groups of persons acting under the authority of the United Nations or of the Organization of American states; and

(2) specific actions which have been taken by the President or the Congress relating to multilateral or security assistance to a less developed country because of the human rights practices or policies of such country.

(d) The Secretary of State shall transmit to the Speaker of the House of Representatives and the Committee on Foreign Relations of the Senate, by January 31 of each year, a full and complete report regarding—

(1) the status of internationally recognized human rights, within the meaning of subsection (a)—

(A) in countries that receive assistance under this part, and

(B) in all other foreign countries which are members of the United Nations and which are not otherwise the subject of human rights reports under this Act; and

(2) the steps the Administrator has taken to alter United States programs under this part in any country because of human rights considerations.

(e) (1) The President is authorized and encouraged to use not less than $3,000,000 of the funds made available under this chapter and chapter 4 of part II for each fiscal year for studies to identify, and for openly carrying out, programs and activities which will encourage or promote increased adherence to civil and political rights, as set forth in the Universal Declaration of Human Rights, in countries eligible for assistance under this chapter. None of these funds may be used, directly or indirectly, to influence the outcome of any election in any country.

(2) (A) Of the amounts made available to carry out this subsection, $500,000 for the fiscal year 1984 and $1,000,000 for the fiscal year 1985 shall be used for grants to nongovernmental organizations in South Africa promoting political, economic, social, juridical, and humanitarian efforts to foster a just society and to help victims of apartheid.

(B) In making grants under this paragraph, priority should be given to those organizations or activities which contribute, directly or indirectly, to promoting a just society, to aiding victims of official discrimination, and to the nonviolent elimination of apartheid. Priority should also be given to those organizations whose programs and activities evidence community support. Grants may be made only for organizations whose character and membership reflect the objective of a majority of South Africans for an end to the apartheid system of separate development and for interracial cooperation and justice. Grants may not be made under this paragraph to governmental institutions or organizations or to organizations financed or controlled by the Government of South Africa.

(C) (i) Except as provided in clause (ii), grants under this paragraph may not exceed $10,000.

(ii) Of the amounts allocated to carry out this paragraph, $100,000 shall be available each fiscal year only for grants to organizations which have available for their use resources whose value is at least equal to the amount of the grant under this paragraph. Grants of up to $30,000 may be made to such organizations. For purposes of this clause, the term "resources" includes, in addition to cash assets, in-kind assets and contributions such as equipment, materials, and staff and volunteer time.

(D) Within 9 months after the date of enactment of this paragraph, the Administrator of the Agency for International Development shall prepare, in consultation with the Secretary of State, and shall submit to the Congress a report detailing grants and proposed grants under this paragraph and their conformity with the provisions of this paragraph.

[Footnotes omitted]

Foreign Assistance and Arms Export Act, 22 USC 2151n.

Appendix C

Human Rights and Multilateral Banking

Sec. 701. (1) The United States Government, in connection with its voice and vote in the International Bank for Reconstruction and Development, the International Development Association, the International Finance Corporation, the Inter-American Development Bank, the African Development Fund, the Asian Development Bank, and the African Development Bank, shall advance the cause of human rights, including by seeking to channel assistance toward countries other than those whose governments engage in—

(1) a consistent pattern of gross violations of internationally recognized human rights, such as torture or cruel, inhumane, or degrading treatment or punishment, prolonged detention without charges, or other flagrant denial to life, liberty, and the security of person; or

(2) provide refuge to individuals committing acts of international terrorism by hijacking aircraft.

(b) Further, the Secretary of the Treasury shall instruct each Executive Director of the above institutions to consider in carrying out his duties:

(1) specific actions by either the executive branch or the Congress as a whole on individual bilateral assistance programs because of human rights considerations;

(2) the extent to which the economic assistance provided by the above institutions directly benefits the needy people in the recipient country;

(3) whether the recipient country has detonated a nuclear device or is not a State Party to the Treaty on Non-Proliferation of Nuclear Weapons or both; and

(4) in relation to assistance for the Socialist Republic of Vietnam, the People's Democratic Republic of Laos, and Democratic Kampuchea (Cambodia), the responsiveness of the governments of such countries in providing a more substantial accounting of Americans missing in action.

(c) (1) The Secretaries of State and Treasury shall report annually to the Speaker of the House of Representatives and the President of the Senate on the progress toward achieving the goals of this title, excluding section 704 and including the listing required in subsection (d).

(2) (A) The Secretary of the Treasury will report quarterly on all loans considered by the Boards of Executive Directors of the institutions listed in subsection (a) to the Committee on Banking, Finance and Urban Affairs of the House of Representatives and the Committee on Foreign Relations of the Senate. Each such quarterly report shall include a list of all loans considered by the Boards of Executive Directors of such institutions and shall specify with respect to each such loan—

(i) the institution involved;

(ii) the date of final action;

(iii) the borrower;

(iv) the amount;

(v) the project or program;

(vi) the vote of the United States Government;

(vii) the reason for United States Government opposition, if any;

(viii) the final disposition of the loan; and

(ix) if the United States Government opposed the loan, whether the loan meets basic human needs.

(B) The information required to be reported under subparagraph (A) also shall be included in the annual report to the Congress of the National Advisory Council on International Monetary and Financial Policies.

(d) The United States Government, in connection with its voice and vote in the institutions listed in subsection (a), shall seek to channel assistance to projects which address basic human needs of the people of the recipient country. The annual report required under subsection (c) shall include a listing of categories of such assistance granted, with particular attention to categories that address basic human needs.

(e) In determining whether a country is in gross violation of internationally recognized human rights standards, as defined by the provisions of subsection (a), the United States Government shall give consideration to the extent of cooperation of such country in permitting an unimpeded investigation of alleged violations of internationally recognized human rights by appropriate international organizations including, but not limited to, the International Committee of the Red Cross, Amnesty International, the International Commission of Jurists, and groups or persons acting under the authority of the United Nations or the Organization of American States.

(f) The United States Executive Directors of the institutions listed in subsection (a) are authorized and instructed to oppose any loan, any extension of financial assistance, or any technical assistance to any country described in subsection (a) (1) or (2), unless such assistance is directed specifically to programs which serve the basic human needs of the citizens of such country.

(g) (1) Not later than thirty days after the end of each calendar quarter, the Secretary of the Treasury, in consultation with the Secretary of State, shall report to the chairmen and ranking minority members of the Committee on Banking, Finance and Urban Affairs of the House of Representatives, the Subcommittee on International Development Institutions and Finance of such Committee, and the Committee on Foreign Relations of the Senate, in each instance in which the United States Executive Director of an institution listed in subsection (a) opposes any loan, financial assistance, or technical assistance for reasons regarding human rights. Each such report shall include—

(A) the reasons for such opposition;

(B) all policy considerations taken into account in reaching the decision to oppose such loan, financial assistance, or technical assistance;

(C) a description of the human rights conditions in the country involved;

(D) a record of how the United States Government voted on all other loans, financial assistance, and technical assistance to such country during the preceding two years; and

(E) information as to how the decision to oppose such loan, financial assistance, or technical assistance relates to overall United States Government policy on human rights in such country.

(2) The Secretary of the Treasury or his delegate shall consult frequently and in a timely manner with the chairmen and ranking minority members specified in paragraph (1) to inform them regarding any prospective changes in policy direction toward countries which have or recently have had poor human rights records.

[Footnotes omitted]

International Financial Institutions Act, 22 USC 262g.

☆

Notes

Chapter 1. Congress and Human Rights Legislation: An Overview

1. Congressman Fraser and John Salzberg, his principal assistant at that time, have written extensively about their values and activities. See, for example, Donald M. Fraser, "Freedom and Foreign Policy"; John Salzberg and Donald D. Young, "The Parliamentary Role in Implementing International Human Rights: A U.S. Example"; Donald M. Fraser, "Human Rights and U.S. Foreign Policy: Some Basic Questions Regarding Principles and Practice"; Donald M. Fraser and John Salzberg, "Foreign Policy and Effective Strategies for Human Rights"; Donald M. Fraser, "Congress's Role in the Making of International Human Rights Policy"; Donald M. Fraser, "Human Rights and the United States Foreign Policy: The Congressional Perspective."

2. See especially Cecil V. Crabb, Jr., and Pat M. Holt, *Invitation to Struggle: Congress, the President and Foreign Policy.* For the reasons why Congress, in about 1953, pressured the Eisenhower administration to back away from human rights treaties, in return for which Congress dropped the movement for the Bricker amendment, see Vernon Van Dyke, *Human Rights, the United States, and World Community.*

3. Hugh Arnold traces Kissinger's semantics on human rights, analyzes them, and concludes that they were primarily a facade against criticism; see his "Henry Kissinger and Human Rights." For documentation of the shifting and erratic congressional push for human rights, see Patricia Weiss Fagen, "U.S. Foreign Policy and Human Rights— The Role of Congress." See also David Weissbrodt, "Human Rights Legislation and U.S. Foreign Policy."

4. There are many studies; see, for example, David P. Forsythe, *Human Rights and World Politics,* chap. 3.

5. House Committee on Foreign Affairs, Subcommittee on International Organizations and Movements, *Human Rights in the World Community: A Call for U.S. Leadership,* report, 93d Cong., 2d sess., 1974.

6. This book does not emphasize congressional action pursuant to international treaties on human rights inasmuch as most congressional activity does not *directly* depend on those treaties, and some of the human rights treaties to which the United States is a party are self-executing and do not require congressional action (beyond Senate advice and consent to their ratification). For studies that do emphasize international treaties and the United States, see Richard B. Lillich, "The Contribution of the United States to the Promotion and Protection of International Human Rights," and Lillich, *International Human Rights Instruments.* If there are some thirty-five treaties

on international human rights, and if the United States has become a party to fewer than a dozen, then there are about four whose ratification has been followed by technical implementing legislation, plus military manuals pertaining to human rights in armed conflict. For these legal points I am indebted to Marlene C. McGuirl, chief, American-British Law Division, Law Library, Library of Congress.

7. House Committee on Foreign Affairs, *Human Rights Documents*, 1983, Committee Print. This same document includes congressional action pursuant to the UN Decade for Women. Congressional language, however, deals with this subject in a framework of economic policy, not human rights.

8. 95 Stat. 1547, Sec. 710(c).

9. Foreign Assistance and Arms Export Acts, 22 U.S.C. 2151, sec. 101, reprinted in House and Senate Committees on Foreign Affairs and on Foreign Relations, *Legislation on Foreign Relations through 1983*, 12–13.

10. Cyrus Vance, "Human Rights and Foreign Policy." See also Vance, "The Human Rights Imperative," in which he reiterates priorities.

11. 22 U.S.C. 2304, Sec. 502B(C) (d) (1).

12. 22 U.S.C. 262g, Sec. 701 (a) (1).

13. See Sandy Vogelgesang, *American Dream, Global Nightmare: The Dilemma of U.S. Human Rights Policy.*

14. *Human Rights Documents*, cited in note 7, 34–36.

15. 95 Stat. 1655.

16. 22 U.S.C. 2151, note (1979).

17. 22 U.S.C. 2151, note.

18. See further David P. Forsythe, "Political Prisoners: The Law and Politics of Protection."

19. Even though a law or sense of Congress resolution may not influence public policy in the short run, either type of statement may have profound consequences over time. Repeated congressional endorsement—of the Universal Declaration of Human Rights, for example—may be used as evidence in court that the declaration has acquired the status of customary international law. Repeated congressional endorsement of certain civil and political rights similarly may help such rights acquire a binding force even though the Senate has not ratified the relevant treaties. Congressional statements can also give specific meaning to general or vague international legal provisions.

20. Sec. 502B is reproduced in appendix A.

21. Sec. 116 is reproduced in appendix B.

22. Agricultural Trade Development and Assistance Act of 1954 as amended, 7 U.S.C. 1712, Sec. 112(a).

23. Foreign Assistance Act of 1961 as amended, 22 U.S.C. 2199(L), Sec. 239(1) (1).

24. Sec. 701 is reproduced in appendix C.

25. 94 Stat. 102.

26. 19 U.S.C. 2432, Sec. 402(a).

27. 12 U.S.C. 635 (b) (8), Sec. 2(b) (8). The Sullivan principles comprise "Nonsegregation of the races in all work facilities; equal and fair employment for all employees; equal pay for equal work for all employees; initiation and development of

training programs to prepare nonwhite South Africans for supervisory, administrative, clerical, and technical jobs; increasing the number of nonwhites in management and supervisory positions; a willingness to engage in collective bargaining with labor unions; and improving the quality of life for employees in such areas as housing, transportation, schooling, recreation, and health facilities."

28. Foreign Relations Authorization Act, Fiscal Year 1978, 91 Stat. 844, Sec. 511(b) (b).

29. Foreign Assistance Act of 1973, 22 U.S.C. 2151, note (1976), Sec. 35.

30. International Security and Development Cooperation Act of 1981, 22 U.S.C. 2370, Sec. 726(b) (C).

31. For Haiti see ibid., 22 U.S.C. 2151 note, Sec. 721; for Nicaragua see ibid., Stat. 1552, Sec. 724.

32. 22 U.S.C. 2384, Sec. 624(f).

33. 22 U.S.C. 2151n, Sec. 116(d).

34. See, for example, Department of State, *Country Reports on Human Rights Practices for 1983*, February 1984.

35. See, for example, Raymond D. Gastil, ed., *Freedom in the World: Political Rights and Civil Liberties;* and Amnesty International, *Annual Report.*

36. House Committee of Foreign Affairs, Subcommittee on Human Rights and International Organizations, *Review of State Department Country Reports on Human Rights Practices for 1981.*

37. 22 U.S.C. 2420, Sec. 660 of Foreign Assistance Act.

38. Foreign Assistance Act, Sec. 116, at note 210.

39. 22 U.S.C. 287c note, Sec. 109 of Department of State Authorization Act, Fiscal Years 1982 and 1983, Sec. 109; preceded by Sec. 108. or 96 Stat. 275.

Chapter 2. Congressional Voting on Human Rights Measures

1. William P. Avery and David P. Forsythe, "Human Rights, National Security, and the U.S. Senate: Who Votes for What, and Why," contains a review of literature dealing with Congress's foreign policy voting.

2. The Refugee Protocol has been held to be a self-executing treaty by U.S. courts and thus does not require implementing legislation. Nevertheless, the Refugee Act of 1980 drew from the protocol not only some of its inspiration but also some of its wording.

3. Roll call voting on human rights declined during the Reagan administration. Some Republicans and southern Democrats who had challenged President Carter deferred to the Reagan team. Some Democrats and other liberals concentrated on trying to implement what was already legislated. Measures that were possible candidates for human rights roll call voting were interlaced with security or economic issues to such a degree that efforts to use them led to findings totally inconsistent with other findings.

4. See further Malcolm E. Jewell and Samuel C. Patterson, *The Legislative Process in the United States,* 409; and Herbert Weisbert, "Evaluating Theories of Roll Call Voting."

Chapter 3. The Fate of General Human Rights Legislation

1. Statements of fact in this section not otherwise attributed are drawn from Stephen B. Cohen, "Conditioning U.S. Security Assistance on Human Rights Practices." See also Roberta Cohen, "Human Rights Decision-Making in the Executive Branch."

2. See Jeane Kirkpatrick, "Dictatorships and Double Standards." Her thesis has actually been around for some time. See, for example, Henry Kissinger, "Continuity and Change in American Foreign Policy."

3. Speech to World Jewish Congress, New York City, January 19, 1982. Text furnished by Mr. Abrams.

4. Quoted in Charles Maechling, Jr., "Human Rights Dehumanized."

5. Ibid., 123. Mr. Abrams critiques Mr. Maechling, but does not refer to the statements quoted here, in *Foreign Policy* 53 (Winter 1983–84), 173–74.

6. Department of State, *International Security and Development Cooperation Program*, especially 5, 11. See also John W. Sewell et al., *U.S. Foreign Policy and the Third World: Agenda 1985–86*, chap. 4, especially 98.

7. Interviews, Washington, August 1984.

8. The information from Cohen, "Conditioning U.S. Security Assistance on Human Rights Practices," was supplemented by interviews in Washington.

9. Quoted in David Heaps, *Human Rights and U.S. Foreign Policy: The First Decade 1973–1983*, 43. Also interviews, Washington, August 1984.

10. Interviews, Washington, August 1984. Formally the Reagan administration maintained the InterAgency Coordination Committee; in fact, it atrophied.

11. Prepared statement of M. Peter McPherson, acting director, International Development Corporation Agency, and administrator, Agency for International Development, before Subcommittee on Human Rights and International Organizations of the House Foreign Affairs Committee, March 17, 1982; text furnished by AID.

12. Interviews in AID, Washington, August 1984.

13. Statement cited in note 11 above.

14. House Committee on Foreign Affairs, Subcommittees on Human Rights and International Organizations and on Western Hemisphere Affairs, *Human Rights in Argentina, Chile, Paraguay, and Uruguay*, especially 171–74.

15. AID, *Human Rights*. While Section 116(a) is commonly referred to as the Harkin Amendment, subsection (e) seems to have originated with Don Fraser.

16. Interviews, AID, Washington, August 1984.

17. David Carleton and Michael Stohl, "The Foreign Policy of Human Rights: Rhetoric and Reality from Jimmy Carter to Ronald Reagan." See also David L. Cingranelli and Thomas E. Pasquarello, "Human Rights Practices and the Distribution of U.S. Foreign Aid to Latin American Countries."

18. See, e.g., House Committee on Foreign Affairs, Subcommittee on Human Rights and International Organizations, *Human Rights in Cyprus, Greece, and Turkey*. The hearing turned into one on Turkey, despite its more general title. The chairman's questions were much tougher concerning Turkey than they had been in other hearings held by this subcommittee.

19. Congressional Research Service, *Human Rights and Foreign Assistance: Experiences and Issues in Policy Implementation (1977–1978)*, especially 4.

20. House Committee on Banking, Finance and Urban Affairs, *Report 98–981*, 20.

21. House Committee on Banking, Finance and Urban Affairs, Subcommittee on International Development Institutions and Finance, *Human Rights and U.S. Policy in the Multilateral Development Banks*.

22. Report cited in note 20.

23. Hearings cited in note 21, 79.

24. Ibid., 82.

25. Ibid., 142.

26. House Committee on Banking, Finance and Urban Affairs, Subcommittee on International Development Institutions and Finance, and House Committee on Foreign Affairs, Subcommittee on Africa, *Human Rights Policies at the Multilateral Development Banks*, 21.

27. Ibid., 78.

28. Ibid., 85.

29. House Committee on Banking, Finance and Urban Affairs, *Report 98–178*, 27. See also Leach's comments in House Committee on Foreign Affairs, Subcommittee on Human Rights and International Organizations, *Review of U.S. Human Rights Policy*, 5, 136.

30. *Review of U.S. Human Rights Policy*, 140.

31. *International Herald Tribune*, November 21, 1984, p. 12. For suggestions that the Bureau of Human Rights had been struggling to emphasize the human rights situation in Chile, see hearings cited in note 14, 33.

32. See *Report 98–981*, cited in note 20, 18–19, where the Banking Committee indicated it had considered holding up support for certain IFIs but finally decided that support for the IFIs took precedence over disagreement with Reagan's human rights policies.

33. Interviews, Department of State, Washington, August 1984.

34. See House Committee on Banking, Finance and Urban Affairs, Subcommittee on International Development Institutions and Finance, *Inter-American Development Bank Loans to Guatemala*.

35. Quoted in Americas Watch et al., *Failure: The Reagan Administration's Human Rights Policy in 1983*, 9.

36. Hearing cited in note 29, 82.

37. Interview, Geneva, March 1985.

38. Hearing cited in note 14, 134.

39. David A. Martin, "The Refugee Act of 1980: Its Past and Future." Martin was an official in the Carter administration, responsible for refugee questions.

40. U.S. Public Law 96–212, 94 Stat. 102. Cf. the Refugee Protocol, at 606 UNTS 267, and the basic Refugee Treaty, at 189 UNTS 137.

41. House Judiciary Committee, Subcommittee on Immigration, *Caribbean Migration;* Senate Judiciary Committee, *U.S. Refugee Programs, 1981;* House Judiciary Committee, *Refugee Admissions and Resettlement Program*.

42. Americas Watch et al., *The Reagan Administration's Human Rights Record in 1984*, 120–21.

43. Naomi Flink Zucker, "The Haitians versus the United States: The Courts as Last Resort," 152–53, quoting congressional hearings.

44. House and Senate Committees on the Judiciary, Select Commission on Immigration and Refugee Policy, *U.S. Immigration Policy and the National Interest*.

45. House and Senate Committees on the Judiciary, Subcommittees on Immigration, *Administration's Proposals on Immigration and Refugee Policy*, 2–3.

46. House, Judiciary Committee, Subcommittee on Immigration, *U.S. Refugee Program*, 64.

47. Ibid., 68.

48. Ibid., 63.

49. Ibid., 6.

50. Senate Judiciary Committee, Subcommittee on Immigration, *United States as a Country of Mass First Asylum*, 27.

51. The leading case was *Haitian Refugee Center v. Civiletti*, 503 F. Supp. 442 (S.D. Fla., 1980). See further Senate Judiciary Committee, Subcommittee on Immigration, *Asylum Adjudication*.

52. Arnold H. Leibowitz, "The Refugee Act of 1980: Problems and Congressional Concerns." For a sample of the welter of opinion brought to bear on the early version of the Simpson-Mazzoli bill see House and Senate Judiciary Committees, Subcommittees on Immigration, *Immigration and Reform Act of 1982*.

53. Michael S. McMahon, "Comment: The Jackson-Vanik Amendment to the Trade Act of 1974: An Assessment after Five Years."

54. See Department of State, *Country Reports on Human Rights Practices for 1981–84*.

55. Senate Finance Committee, Subcommittee on International Trade, *Review of the President's Decisions to Renew Most-Favored- Nation Status for Romania, Hungary, and China;* House Ways and Means Committee, *Most-Favored-Nation Status for Romania, Hungary and China*.

56. Senate hearing cited in note 55, 8.

57. Senate Committee on Foreign Relations, *Human Rights Issues in United States Relations with Romania and Czechoslovakia*.

58. Ibid., and Paul Lansing and Eric C. Rose, "The Granting and Suspension of Most-Favored-Nation Status for Nonmarket Economy States: Policy and Consequences."

59. The subject is well treated in Lars Schoultz, *Human Rights and United States Policy toward Latin America*, especially 310–12.

60. Ralph D. Nurnberger, "The United States and Idi Amin: Congress to the Rescue."

61. Vogelgesang, *American Dream, Global Nightmare*, 222.

62. See Schoultz, cited in note 59.

63. See, for example, Senate Banking Committee, Subcommittee on International Finance, *Export-Import Bank Programs and Policies*, and House Banking Committee, Subcommittee on International Trade, *Eximbank Reauthorization*.

64. The Sullivan principles as well as the text of the Evans amendment are con-

tained in Appendix E of Jonathan Leape et al., *Business in the Shadow of Apartheid: U.S. Firms in South Africa,* 217–24.

65. See, e.g., House Foreign Affairs Committee, Subcommittees on International Economic Policy and Trade and on Africa, *Controls on Exports to South Africa;* House Committee on Banking, Finance and Urban Affairs, Subcommittee on Financial Institutions, *South African Restrictions;* House Committee on Foreign Affairs, Subcommittees on International Economic Policy and Trade and on Africa, *U.S. Corporate Activities in South Africa.*

66. Interviewees in the Reagan administration were not forthcoming about the reasons for not contesting or circumventing the Evans amendment.

It may be relevant to observe that when the Reagan team approved a 1982 loan for South Africa in the International Monetary Fund, Congress responded the next year with a law requiring the U.S. delegation to the IMF to vote against drawing rights for any country practicing apartheid. The rationale for such a law was stated in economic, not human rights, terms. Apartheid was said by Congress to impede good capitalism by constraining labor and capital mobility. It is because of this rationale that the IMF is not covered in this book. It is possibly because of a desire to avoid similar legislative restrictions that the Reagan administration did not challenge congressional action regarding the Export-Import Bank and South Africa.

It may also be relevant to observe that signatories to the Sullivan principles affect less than one-half of one percent of the African labor force in South Africa. By extension, any Export-Import loans to American firms would have very slight impact on the situation in South Africa. Thus the entire subject was minor in concrete terms, although perhaps more important in symbolic terms. See Elizabeth Schmidt, "Impose Tough Sanctions on South Africa"; and Schmidt, *Decoding Corporate Camouflage: U.S. Business Support for Apartheid.*

Chapter 4. Country-Specific Legislation: Central America

1. Several U.S. ambassadors, under different administrations, implicated d'Aubuisson in illegal violence by ultrarightists, violence that was well documented by numerous private religious and secular groups.

2. See the statements by Ambassador Robert E. White, in House Committee on Foreign Affairs, Subcommittee on Inter-American Affairs, *U.S. Policy toward El Salvador,"* 100–190. The Carter administration was ambivalent about economic pressure for human rights, holding up an Inter-American Development Bank Loan, then giving the go-ahead. See Sandra Vogelgesang, *American Dream, Global Nightmare,* 174.

3. Kirkpatrick was quoted as saying, "The nuns were not just nuns; they were also political—they were political activists in behalf of the Frente." Secretary Haig also referred to the churchwomen as political activists.

4. These facts are substantiated less by Reagan administration claims than by Ambassador White's testimony cited in note 2. What separates the Reagan administration from its critics on this issue is whether international communist arms were limited primarily to the period 1978–80 and whether that flow of war material continued at the

same level well into the 1980s. For the view of a former CIA official that U.S. claims of communist international intervention were greatly exaggerated, see *New York Times,* June 11, 1984, p. 14.

5. See the testimony of Ambassador White, cited in note 2. His interpretation was that Pentagon officials and Salvadoran rightists, then the Reagan administration, forced the idea of larger military assistance on Duarte and other civilians. Duarte was earlier on record as saying the Salvadoran government needed economic rather than military aid. White pointed out that the rebels' "final offensive" failed before any significant U.S. military aid was delivered. It can also be recalled that Reagan officials suggested military aid to both Costa Rica and democratic Argentina before any such requests were made. Indeed, those two states initially rejected U.S. military assistance as unnecessary.

6. Senate Committee on Foreign Relations, *Nomination of Ernest W. Lefever.*

7. Secretary Haig made these comments to the press, and they were contained as well in a controversial State Department "White Paper" on El Salvador issued during the spring of 1981.

8. John A. Bushnell, acting assistant secretary of state for inter-American affairs, in *U.S. Policy toward El Salvador,* cited in note 2, 19.

9. Haig's position, reported in the press, was confirmed in his memoirs entitled *Caveat: Realism, Reagan, and Foreign Policy.*

10. Quoted in *Foreign Affairs,* "America and the World 1982," 61, 3 (1982), 736.

11. See the statements by Assistant Secretary of State for Inter-American Affairs Thomas Enders, and Assistant Secretary of State for Human Rights Elliott Abrams, issued by the Department of State as *Fourth Certification of Progress in El Salvador.*

12. This argument, put forward vigorously by Secretary Enders, was well received by a number of senators. See, for example, Senate Committee on Foreign Relations, Subcommittee on Western Hemisphere Affairs, *Central America,* 91–92.

13. Senate Committee on Foreign Relations, *The Situation in El Salvador,* 20.

14. Some spokespersons for private human rights groups argued that by taking seriously human rights "strings" on U.S. assistance, the administration could effectively pressure the Salvadoran security forces to clean up their act. See *Central America,* cited in note 12, 113. But the prevalent view, sometimes expressed even by critics of the administration such as Democratic Senator Pell, was that one had to be careful about a communist takeover. See ibid., 116–17.

15. Into the mid-1980s there was continuing right-wing violence. As of 1986 no Salvadoran high official or political figure had been convicted of any violent crime, despite many reports of killers arriving in government vehicles or acting in the presence of military officers.

16. Officially the International Security and Development Cooperation Act of 1981, section 728(d) and (e).

17. The Human Rights Bureau of the Department of State was in favor of certification each time; it did not differ from the Bureau of Inter-American Affairs. Both agreed that progress was being made toward democracy, which constituted progress on human rights, whatever pattern of specific violations might exist. See especially House Committee on Foreign Affairs, Subcommittees on Europe and the Middle East, on Asian and Pacific Affairs, on Human Rights and International Organizations, and

on Africa, *Implementation of Congressionally Mandated Human Rights Provisions*, 200–201. For a detailed review of these events including many references to congressional developments and an extended discussion of the wisdom of the certification requirement, see Richard B. Nash, Jr., "Certifying Human Rights: Military Assistance to El Salvador and the International Security and Development Cooperation Act of 1981."

18. A U.S. appellate court eventually held that the president had acted incorrectly. Secretary of State George Shultz stated publicly that it would have been very difficult for the executive branch to certify a fifth time that human rights progress was being made in El Salvador. It remains unclear why the administration could overlook so many violations of human rights four times but not five, especially when congressional oversight of certification seemed no more attentive than before. There was no increased danger of a congressional rejection of certification or a cutoff of assistance at that time. See further *Congressional Quarterly Almanac* 1983, 111.

19. House Committee on Foreign Affairs, Subcommittees on Human Rights and International Organizations and on Western Hemisphere Affairs, *Human Rights in El Salvador*, 64–65.

20. Raymond Bonner, "Cover-Up Charged in Death of Nuns."

21. See, for example, *Congressional Quarterly Almanac*, 1984, 78.

22. On the continuing linkage of death squads to high military officials, see *New York Times*, March 3, 1984, p. 1. On the collapse of the El Salvador official human rights commission, see *New York Times*, November 23, 1985, p. 5. On governmental crackdown on right-wing violations of human rights, see *New York Times*, April 25, 1986, p. 3. On continuing abuses of human rights, and disinterest in them by the U.S. Embassy, see *New York Times*, June 27, 1986, p. 23.

23. For background see William LeoGrande, "Central America: U.S. Hegemony in Decline."

24. For an overview see *Congressional Quarterly Almanac*, 1979.

25. Ibid., 1980, 332.

26. Ibid., 334.

27. At the end of June 1983, the Reagan administration's veto of a Nicaraguan loan application in the Inter-American Development Bank showed not only the willful politicization of the bank by the United States but also its disregard for the welfare of large sectors of the Nicaraguan population. Manuals provided by the CIA to the contras giving instructions on how to "neutralize" political opponents likewise did not fit well with rhetoric trying to show that the United States was on the side of "the people" who were being brutally exploited by their Sandinista government.

28. See the president's remarks as reported in the *New York Times*, April 14, 1983, p. 1; Assistant Secretary of State Thomas Enders pursued the same line vis-à-vis Congress, as did again the president when he addressed Congress on April 26. See further the *New York Times*, especially December 10, 1983, p. 3.

29. See the op-ed piece by Elliott Abrams, then assistant secretary for inter-American affairs rather than human rights, "Keeping Pressure on the Sandinistas." His argument was that the Marxist Sandinistas were inherently revolutionary as well as violative of human rights. To Abrams and the others of similar view in the administration, all Marxists presented these dual problems. The factual record of Marxist re-

gimes in places like Hungary and Yugoslavia seems never to have affected their views. Such Marxist regimes were neither revolutionary in foreign policy nor violative of all human rights. As for Nicaragua, while there were indeed violations of some human rights, Sandinista cooperation with in-country visits by various private human rights groups was never emphasized by Abrams or other Reagan officials.

30. *New York Times*, July 22, 1983, p. 1.

31. See, e.g., Secretary Shultz's comments reported in the *Washington Post*, October 3, 1985, p. 1. But in March 1986, Donald Regan said on television that the United States was trying to get rid of the Sandinistas. See Elizabeth Drew, "Letter from Washington."

32. *Congressional Quarterly Almanac*, 1980, 334.

33. Agency for International Development (AID), *U.S. Overseas Loans and Grants*, 54.

34. One can see this pattern through a review of the *Congressional Record*, especially during 1983 after *Time Magazine* and *Newsweek* broke the story in early April of extensive CIA involvement in Nicaragua.

35. *New York Times*, June 30, 1984, p. 3.

36. The earlier section on El Salvador noted testimony at the World Court by a former CIA official who argued that the administration lacked the evidence to support its claims in this regard. See further James P. Rawles, "The United States, Nicaragua, and the World Court."

37. Americas Watch, Amnesty International, the Lawyers' Committee for International Human Rights, and other private rights groups all published information on human rights violations in Nicaragua, as did Catholic and secular groups within that country. United Nations reports also existed, as did those from the OAS. See also note 29 above.

38. The ICRC was admitted to the installations of the National Penitentiary Service but generally denied access to police and military installations where security and counterrevolutionary prisoners were first taken. See ICRC, *Annual Reports, 1979–86*.

39. Senate Committee on Foreign Relations, Subcommittee on Western Hemisphere Affairs, *Human Rights in Nicaragua*, passim, especially 13, 43. A previous Senate hearing on Central America during the Reagan administration had not focused much on Nicaragua, much less on human rights there. See Senate Committee on Foreign Relations, Subcommittee on Western Hemisphere Affairs, *Central America*, December 15, 1981, February 1, 1982.

40. House Committee on Foreign Affairs, Subcommittee on Human Rights and International Organizations, *Human Rights in Nicaragua*, 108–9.

41. Ibid., 71; and *Human Rights in Nicaragua*, hearings, cited in note 39, 62–67.

42. See especially Richard Ullman, "At War with Nicaragua." All of the various authors (Alan Riding, Christopher Dickey, and William D. Rogers) writing on Nicaragua for *Foreign Affairs* during 1981–84 were critical of the administration's reliance on the CIA as the chosen instrument of policy.

43. It should be noted that the one time the Senate voted to terminate funding for CIA operations in Nicaragua, in June 1984, it was largely because the issue was linked to a summer job bill in the United States. This was a tactical mistake by the administra-

tion, since the Senate was willing to terminate CIA funds in order to get the more valued jobs bill. Given this congressional attitude toward foreign policy questions, it was perhaps not so surprising that the Congress did not focus on the basic question of whether CIA intervention could be justified.

44. Schoultz, *Human Rights,* 152.

45. House Committee on Foreign Affairs, Subcommittees on Human Rights and International Organizations and on Inter-American Affairs, *Human Rights in Guatemala,* 98.

46. AID, *U.S. Overseas Loans and Grants,* 48.

47. Marlise Simons, "Guatemala: The Coming Danger," 98–99.

48. *Human Rights in Guatemala,* cited in note 45, 28–31 and passim.

49. Ibid., 20.

50. Ibid., 30–31.

51. See further Paul Albert, "The Undermining of the Legal Standards for Human Rights Violations in U.S. Foreign Policy: The Case of 'Improvement' in Guatemala."

52. *Human Rights in Guatemala,* cited in note 45. See also Albert, 249–50, for a discussion of how the Reagan team circumvented human rights restrictions via export licenses to private companies.

53. House Committee on Banking, Finance and Urban Affairs, Subcommittee on International Development Institutions and Finance, *Inter-American Development Bank Loan to Guatemala,* 5.

54. Ibid., passim.

55. Alan Riding, "The Central American Quagmire," 654.

56. Ibid.

57. House Committee on Foreign Affairs and Senate Committee on Foreign Relations, *Legislation on Foreign Relations through 1983,* 1:365.

58. Department of State, *International Security and Development Cooperation Program,* 14.

59. Department of State, *Country Reports on Human Rights Practices for 1984,* 99th Cong., 1st sess., Febuary 1985, 557.

60. The Guatemalan record on human rights was strongly criticized by the Organization of American States. See OAS, *Report on the Situation of Human Rights in the Republic of Guatemala.* There were also critical reports by Amnesty International and Americas Watch. The United Nations Human Rights Commission downplayed the less critical Colville report by its special rapporteur on Guatemala and voted a critical resolution at its 1983 session; it continued to keep the diplomatic pressure on thereafter.

61. Mark O. Hatfield, "Aid Guatemala Doesn't Need." On the prevalence of false democracies in Latin America, bearing out Hatfield's point that "elections in themselves do not usher in democracies," see Tom J. Farer, "Human Rights and Human Welfare in Latin America." This type of situation indicated one problem with the tendency of the Reagan administration to substitute a formal democracy for human rights in its rhetoric and policy. Regimes could be formally a democracy, and thus embraced by the Reagan team, but in fact violative of many internationally recognized human rights.

Chapter 5. Other Country-Specific Legislation

1. See especially Lars Schoultz, *Human Rights and United States Policy toward Latin America*, 176–77. See also Robert C. Johansen, *The National Interest and Human Interest: An Analysis of U.S. Foreign Policy*, chap. 4.

2. Schoultz, 168–77.

3. David P. Forsythe, "American Foreign Policy and Human Rights: Rhetoric and Reality," 51.

4. Schoultz, 202.

5. AID, *U.S. Overseas Loans and Grants*, 41.

6. Ibid., 201.

7. OECD, *External Debt of Developing Countries, 1982 Survey*.

8. Paul E. Sigmund, "Latin America: Change or Continuity," 653.

9. House Committee on Foreign Affairs, Subcommittees on International Economic Policy and Trade and on Inter-American Affairs, *U.S. Economic Sanctions against Chile*.

10. 22 U.S.C. 2370.

11. Executive policy was clearly to declare "progress" on human rights in friendly Latin American authoritarian regimes, whatever the facts. See *Foreign Affairs*, "America and the World 1981," 60, 3 (1982), 751. But the certification requirement for Chile, and in particular its provisions on the murderers of Letelier and Moffitt, could not be dealt with by wishful thinking or double standards in favor of authoritarian regimes.

12. Americas Watch et al., *The Reagan Administration's Human Rights Record in 1984*, 27–30.

13. Once the Reagan administration had indicated a desire for normal relations, Pinochet felt free to take certain steps. In May 1981 Chile indicated it would not cooperate with the Inter-American Commission on Human Rights. Later that year it expelled opposition figures and instituted a new constitution perpetuating authoritarian rule until the late 1980s. In the mid-1980s Pinochet cracked down hard on emerging sentiments for democracy, reinstituting martial law in 1984.

14. House Democrats had tried to get the Kissinger people to deal with the Argentine human rights problems. See House Committee on International Relations, Subcommittee on International Organizations, *Human Rights in Argentina*.

15. See Schoultz, *Human Rights*, and Charles Maechling, Jr., "The Argentina Pariah." The latter makes clear the great difference historically between Argentina and the United States and thus the difficulty of implementing a policy of close relations.

16. Timerman's book, *Prisoner Without a Name, Cell Without a Number*, published in New York by Alfred A. Knopf in 1981, chronicled his "disappearance" and torture. It was widely circulated in Congress and was credited by many with helping to maintain country-specific legislation on Argentina.

17. For a review of these events see the various articles on Latin America in *Foreign Affairs* during the early 1980s.

18. 22 U.S.C. 2370 note.

19. Department of State, *Country Reports on Human Rights Practices for 1982,* 98th Cong., 1st sess., February 1983, Joint Committee Print, 386: "The Argentine government . . . is believed to have provided information to family members on the deaths and in some instances the location of the remains of the disappeared in about 1,450 cases."

20. House Committee on Foreign Affairs, Subcommittee on Human Rights and International Organizations, *Review of State Department Country Reports on Human Rights Practices for 1981,* showed that a network of private groups and members of Congress scrutinized the annual reports under the Reagan administration. The challenge to the 1982 statement on Argentina is found in House Committee on Foreign Affairs, Subcommittees on Human Rights and International Organizations and on Western Hemisphere Affairs, *Human Rights in Argentina, Chile, Paraguay, and Uruguay.*

21. Juan E. Mendez, "Reagan's Argentines."

22. *Human Rights in Argentina,* cited in note 14, 182.

23. Schoultz, *Human Rights,* 355.

24. Ibid., 64–65, and passim. In 1977 a congressional report indicated that the Haitian situation was improved relative to its own past, the structure of repressive government was intact, and U.S. economic assistance should continue given the dire poverty of the country. See Senate Committee on Appropriations, *Factors Affecting U.S. Diplomatic and Assistance Relations with Haiti.*

25. House Committee on Foreign Affairs and Senate Committee on Foreign Relations, *Legislation on Foreign Relations through 1983,* 261.

26. Ibid., 245.

27. Joseph B. Treaster, "Human Rights in Haiti: A Promise Unfulfilled"; Americas Watch et al., *Failure: The Reagan Administration's Human Rights Policy in 1983;* Raymond D. Gastil, ed., *Freedom in the World: Political Rights and Civil Liberties;* Amnesty International *Annual Report.* In addition to these private reports, which were in basic agreement, there were reports by the American Commission on Human Rights within the framework of the Organization of American States. All reports showed both a consistent pattern of gross violations of internationally recognized human rights and a lack of significant steps toward genuine democracy—e.g., a denial of meaningful political participation in the life of the country over many decades. Even the State Department's own country reports indicated no significant movement toward democracy and consistent violations of other rights.

28. A synopsis of events is found in the *New York Times,* February 5, 1984, p. 3.

29. See chap. 3, the section on refugees. At a congressional hearing on Haiti in 1985, two congressmen attended and one other sent a letter. Private human rights groups testified, as did a high-ranking State Department official, but there was little indication of strong congressional concern. See House Committee on Foreign Affairs, Subcommittee on Human Rights and International Organizations, *Human Rights in Haiti.*

30. *Legislation on Foreign Relations through 1983,* cited in note 25, 155.

31. House Committee on Foreign Affairs, Subcommittees on International Organizations and on Asian and Pacific Affairs, *Human Rights in Asia: Non-Communist Countries.*

32. *Legislation on Foreign Relations,* cited in note 25, 321–22.

33. Ibid., 322.

34. See, for example, Sandra Vogelgesang, *American Dream, Global Nightmare,* 128 and passim, and Jerome A. Cohen, "Arms Sales and Human Rights: The Case of South Korea."

35. The Reagan administration, for example, intervened to oppose a death sentence for the leading opposition figure Kim dae-Jung, then later to allow him to emigrate to the U.S. for medical treatment. When he returned to South Korea, the administration, as well as private Americans, tried to protect him from severe actions by the South Korean government.

36. *Legislation on Foreign Relations,* cited in note 25, 690. Congress also instructed the president to take up the subject of free and fair elections with Ugandan authorities and to link that subject to foreign assistance; ibid., 281.

37. Ibid., 281, 304.

38. See, for example, House Foreign Affairs Committee, Subcommittee on Human Rights and International Organizations, *Human Rights in Cuba.* For a change there was not much difference in testimony between the Reagan administration and spokespersons for the private human rights groups. Any difference was one of tone, not substance. But there were few suggestions about how the U.S. government could have an impact on human rights in Cuba. The hearing was largely to document the facts and provide balance in congressional proceedings. One could use the hearing to document also the politics of the process. Important Florida congressmen, like Dante Fascell, chair of the parent Foreign Affairs Committee, participated in this hearing whereas he and others had not attended other hearings by the Human Rights Subcommittee. Expressions of concern for human rights in Cuba are important in Florida's politics.

39. *Legislation on Foreign Relations,* cited in note 25, 652.

40. Ibid., 1118.

Chapter 6. Function-Specific Legislation

1. Before it raised the position to the rank of assistant secretary in charge of the full bureau, Congress first created a coordinator for human rights. I recall discussions with State Department personnel as early as 1971 about the wisdom of reorganizing the department along such lines.

2. Caleb Rossiter has an excellent overview in "Human Rights: The Carter Record, the Reagan Reaction." See also Joshua Muravchik, *The Uncertain Crusade: Jimmy Carter and the Dilemmas of Human Rights Policy,* for a critique of Carter's human rights appointments.

3. See especially Rossiter, cited in note 2, and see also Lincoln P. Bloomfield, "From Ideology to Program to Policy: Tracking the Carter Human Rights Policy."

4. Christopher Madison, "Foreign Policy: Human Rights—Again."

5. Ernest W. Lefever, "The Trivialization of Human Rights."

6. Senate Committee on Foreign Relations, *Nomination of Ernest W. Lefever,* May 18, 19, June 4, 5, 1981.

7. In addition to Madison, see *Washington Times,* April 10, 1986, pp. 1, 2B.

Abrams had some indirect experience in foreign affairs as a staff member for both Senators Jackson and Moynihan. Thus he was not the complete outsider to Washington that Derian had been. He had also worked for two politically oriented Washington law firms.

8. *New York Times*, November 5, 1981, p. 1.

9. House Committee on Foreign Affairs, Subcommittees on Europe and the Middle East, on Asian and Pacific Affairs, on Human Rights and International Organizations, and on Africa, *Implementation of Congressionally Mandated Human Rights Provisions*, 200.

10. Quoted in Madison, "Foreign Policy."

11. In addition to Madison, see Americas Watch et al., *The Reagan Administration's Human Rights Record in 1984*, 28–29. Americas Watch was usually critical of Abrams's HA; its giving credit to Abrams for fighting for human rights in Chile was thus significant.

12. Mary McGrory, "U.S. Stiffens Chile Policy."

13. Madison, "Foreign Policy."

14. McGrory, "U.S. Stiffens Chile Policy."

15. Lewis and Abrams carried on a war of words on the editorial pages of the *New York Times* in the mid–1980s.

16. For a persuasive interpretation along these lines see especially Rossiter, "Human Rights."

17. These were eventually published by Congress as a committee print entitled House Committee on International Relations, *Human Rights Practices in Countries Receiving U.S. Security Assistance*.

18. The process used by the Carter administration is described by Stephen Palmer, Jr. in House Committee on Foreign Affairs, Subcommittee on Human Rights and International Organizations, *Foreign Assistance Legislation for Fiscal Year 1982 (Part 6)*, 232–41.

19. See, for example, Department of State, *Country Reports on Human Rights Practices for 1985*, report, 99th Cong., 2d sess., February 1986.

20. House Committee on Foreign Affairs, Subcommittee on Human Rights and International Organizations, *Review of State Department Country Reports on Human Rights Practices for 1981*.

21. See, for example, House Committee on Foreign Affairs, Subcommittee on Human Rights and International Organizations, *Review of U.S. Human Rights Policy*, starting at 33.

22. Abrams publicly and harshly attacked a number of private human rights groups by name in a speech to a Cuban group in Miami in 1984. He wrote an op-ed piece criticizing some of the same groups for being naive about the politics of Turkey. See Abrams, "The Myopia of Human Rights Advocates," and "U.S. Official Charges 'Apologists' Are Ignoring Cuba's Human Rights Abuses," *Washington Post*, August 24, 1984, p. A–3.

23. See, for example, the op-ed piece by Aryeh Neier, vice chairman of Americas Watch, "Flimflam on Central America," in which he argues persuasively that Amnesty International had important facts about human rights violations in El Salvador which

the U.S. government did not refute; instead, publicly and without foundation, it attacked Amnesty.

24. See *Review of U.S. Human Rights Policy,* hearings, cited in note 21. See also Americas Watch et al., "Critique: Review of the Department of State's Country Reports on Human Rights Practices for 1983."

25. David Carleton and Michael Stohl, "The Foreign Policy of Human Rights: Rhetoric and Reality from Jimmy Carter to Ronald Reagan." See also David L. Cingranelli and Thomas E. Pasquarello, "Human Rights Practices and the Distribution of U.S. Foreign Aid to Latin American Countries." They all conclude about routine (nonsalient) foreign aid decisions that no easy generalizations are possible regarding the effect of human rights. Cingranelli and Pasquarello do find some human rights impact on which countries are considered for aid.

26. Department of State, *Country Reports on Human Rights Practices for 1981,* February 1982, Joint Committee Print, 1–13.

27. See further David P. Forsythe, "Socioeconomic Human Rights: The United Nations, the United States, and Beyond."

28. A good overview of the effect of the reporting requirement has been written by a former member of the HA Bureau. See Judith Innes de Neufville, "Human Rights Reporting as a Policy Tool: An Examination of the State Department Country Reports." In 1984, Congress passed a bill that required U.S. embassies around the world to report back to Washington systematically regarding the practice of torture. The intent was not only to gather information but also to require reporting on U.S. steps to oppose the use of torture so as to increase U.S. opposition to torture via the reports. This requirement became law in 1985.

29. The account here draws heavily on Margaret E. Galey, "Congress, Foreign Policy and Human Rights Ten Years after Helsinki." Galey is on the staff of the House Foreign Affairs Committee and might thus show some favorable bias toward congressional activity and creations. The published essay may indicate more activity than influence. My interviews in Washington in April 1986 confirm the general accuracy of her article.

30. The argument in Galey unfortunately relies heavily on this type of evidence.

31. General Accounting Office, *The Helsinki Commission: The First Eight Years.* See also William Korey, "Human Rights and the Helsinki Accord."

32. For background see Schoultz, *Human Rights and the United States Policy toward Latin America,* 179–83.

33. *New York Times,* November 18, 1983, p. 6.

34. For one overview see Jonathan F. Gunter, "The United States and the Debate on the World 'Information Order'."

35. House Committee on Foreign Affairs, Subcommittees on Human Rights and International Organizations and on International Operations, *U.S. Withdrawal from UNESCO.*

36. Provisions concerning workers' rights can be found in House Committee on Foreign Affairs and Senate Committee on Foreign Relations, *Legislation on Foreign Relations through 1986,* vol. 1, *The Foreign Assistance Act of 1961,* as amended, Title IV (OPIC), sec. 231A, p. 73, and vol. 2, *The Trade Act of 1974,* Title V (GSP), sec. 502(a)(4) and (b)(7), pp. 80–84.

37. See, for example, David P. Forsythe, *Human Rights and World Politics*, 82 and passim.

38. See J. D. Armstrong, "Political Prisoners and the Red Cross." More generally see David P. Forsythe, *Humanitarian Politics: The International Committee of the Red Cross*.

39. House Committee on Foreign Affairs, *U.S. Educational Assistance in South Africa: Critical Policy Issues*.

40. Department of State, *U.S.–Supported Human Rights Program in South Africa*.

41. Ibid.

42. *New York Times*, June 9, 1982, p. 8.

43. A brief review is found in Joshua Muravchik, "Endowing Democracy."

44. See especially Ben A. Franklin, "Democracy Project Facing New Criticisms."

Chapter 7. Conclusions: Congressional Process and Impact

1. Cecil V. Crabb, Jr., and Pat M. Holt, *Invitation to Struggle: Congress, the President and Foreign Policy*, chap. 7, covers human rights. As of the mid-1980s Congress was still fighting the president for the control of both foreign policy in general and human rights policy in particular. See "Hill Fights Reagan for Soul of Foreign Policy," *Washington Post*, September 2, 1984, p. A1–f.

2. Stephen J. Solarz, "The Case for Congressional Activism."

3. See Thomas M. Franck and Edward Weisband, *Foreign Policy by Congress*, for an analysis that uses more, but not necessarily more helpful, categories of analysis.

4. See chap. 6, where it was noted how much Reagan policy in general deviated from campaign slogans. See also chap. 8, where it is noted how much Reagan policy on human rights came to resemble Carter policy in certain respects. One should note also, however, that what came to be called Reagan policy was an eleventh-hour adjustment to reality. Reagan stuck with Marcos in the Philippines and Duvalier in Haiti until opposition forces were on the brink of successful revolution. In these cases there was not so much a shift of policy approach to certain problems (e.g., despotism from a strategic ally) as an acceptance of the demise of old power configurations, while much of the thinking behind foreign policy remained the same.

5. See, for example, Morris S. Ogul, *Congress Oversees the Bureaucracy: Studies in Legislative Supervision*.

6. There was a time in the mid-1970s when a good deal of House action transpired on the floor and bypassed committee and subcommittee chairs. This phenomenon was part of the revolt by the new members of Congress after 1974; it waned somewhat as the new congresspersons became subcommittee chairs themselves.

7. See Franck and Weisband, cited in note 3, for an analysis of the importance of congressional staff in the foreign policy area.

8. "Q & A: Senator Dan Quayle: Turning the Senate Away from Trivial Pursuits."

9. John G. Tower, "The Case against Congressional Activism," 107.

10. For a critique of the Carter administration for not doing enough on human rights and a plea for more congressional activism in this issue area, see Richard B. Lillich, "The Contribution of the United States to the Promotion and Protection of International Human Rights."

11. See especially Lawrence C. Dodd, "Congress and the Quest for Power," for an analysis, based on a literature review, of Congress in terms of programmatic and personal power motivations.

12. See, for example, Robert J. Art, "Congress and the Defense Budget: Enhancing Policy Oversight."

13. For an overview along these lines see I. M. Destler, "Congress as Boss?"

14. "Review of U.S. Human Rights Policy," cited in chap. 6, note 21, 4–5.

15. *New York Times*, March 2, 1984, p. 7.

16. *New York Times*, November 10, 1982, p. 1.

17. House Committee on Foreign Affairs, Subcommittees on Europe and the Middle East, on Asian and Pacific Affairs, on Human Rights and International Organizations, and on Africa, *Implementation of Congressionally Mandated Human Rights Provisions*, 212.

18. The point was well made by Arthur Schlesinger, Jr., in "Failings of the Kissinger Report," 29.

19. Borrowed from Franck, "Constitutional Practice until Vietnam."

20. Dodd, "Congress and the Quest for Power."

21. See further Albert O. Hirschman, "The Search for Paradigms as a Hindrance to Understanding."

Chapter 8. The Wisdom of Congressional Action

1. *Implementation of Congressionally Mandated Human Rights Provisions*, cited in chap. 7, note 17, 190–92.

2. See further Elizabeth G. Ferris, *Refugees and World Politics*,

3. Coverage in the *New York Times* strongly suggested that the Reagan administration might like not to push so hard on Romania about human rights, given its continuing independence from the Soviet Union in foreign policy; see issues of December 4, 1985, pp. 1, 10, and December 16, 1985, pp. 1, 12. "The problems with Romania, which have become acute in recent months as a campaign has built up in Congress, have troubled the Administration because it has long praised Bucharest for a foreign policy that is relatively independent from the Soviet Union."

4. In the mid-1980s there was a movement in Congress to expand the Romanian restrictions beyond emigration to other human rights issues, particularly religious freedom. Senator Symms (R., Idaho) and others were concerned about treatment of Protestant leaders, among others. Once again Congress was taking the initiative and forcing the executive, under threat of legislation that would restrict the executive's freedom to conduct foreign policy, to take up the question with Bucharest. At the time of writing, both houses had passed different measures to deny most-favored-nation status to Romania because of human rights violations beyond emigration, but the measures had not yet gone to conference committee.

5. At one point Congress passed a resolution that authorized creation of an independent Institute for Human Rights, similar to the U.S. Civil Rights Commission. Later it failed to appropriate money for such an institute and eventually killed the idea. Such an institute, if created, could provide Congress with a more systematic approach

to human rights policy. It could at least take a general and coherent view toward priorities in U.S. human rights policy, forcing the executive to address these issues. But its main role could be to encourage Congress to proceed systematically. No part of Congress, and no political party, did this in the 1973–84 period. The closest approximation were documents issued by the Fraser subcommittee in the mid-1970s. See further House Committee on International Relations, Subcommittees on International Operations and on International Organizations, *Institute for Human Rights and Freedom*. Compare House Committee on Foreign Affairs, Subcommittee on International Organizations and Movements, *Human Rights in the World Community: A Call for U.S. Leadership*.

6. See *New York Times*, November 23, 1985, p. 5. The Senate passed a nonbinding resolution focusing on dubious elections and other human rights issues in Liberia. Since the coup in Liberia in 1980, U.S. military assistance had increased by 600 percent. Bipartisan elements in Congress (including Senators Dodd and Kassebaum) grew unhappy with this situation. The focus on human rights in Liberia certainly did not come from the executive, which was interested in certain military arrangements there. That being the case, some members of Congress spoke publicly about the need to reduce economic assistance to that country. Later the House passed a similar resolution. By 1987 the new foreign aid bill contained a provision on human rights and Liberia.

7. This was the central meaning of the documents published by the Fraser subcommittee and implicitly endorsed by the Congress in its subsequent legislation.

8. A report by the Congressional Research Service during the Carter administration noted the basic problems: *Human Rights and Foreign Assistance: Experiences and Issues in Policy Implementation (1977–1978)*. See also Joshua Muravchik, *The Uncertain Crusade: Jimmy Carter and the Dilemmas of Human Rights Policy*.

9. The text was reprinted in *New York Times*, March 15, 1986, pp. 4–5.

10. Ibid., p. 1: " 'The whole point of the President's message today, is that different policies have to be used in different cases,' Admiral Poindexter said."

11. Ibid.

12. Ibid. See also Tamar Jacoby, "Reagan's Turnaround on Human Rights."

13. According to Daniel C. Kramer, "International Human Rights," the Reagan administration was similar to Carter's in that both were inconsistent in practice.

14. See, for example, Jorge I. Dominguez et al., *Enhancing Global Human Rights*, and Tom J. Farer, "Human Rights and Human Welfare in Latin America."

15. See House Committee on International Relations, Subcommittee on International Organizations, prepared by the Congressional Research Service, *Human Rights in the International Community and in U.S. Foreign Policy, 1945–76*.

16. Lincoln P. Bloomfield, "From Ideology to Program to Policy: Tracking the Carter Human Rights Policy," 11.

17. On the influence of international developments on U.S. human rights policy, see David P. Forsythe, "IGOs and U.S. Human Rights Policy," paper prepared for the annual meeting of the American Political Science Association, Chicago, September 1987.

18. See, for example, James C. Tuttle, ed., *International Human Rights Law and Practice*, and Richard B. Lillich, "The Role of Domestic Courts in Promoting International Human Rights Norms."

19. For a readable overview of the problems of Congress see Gregg Easterbrook, "What's Wrong with Congress." For a more positive view of Congress and foreign policy, in addition to Franck and Weisband, *Foreign Policy by Congress*, see Hoyt Purvis and Steven J. Baker, *Legislating Foreign Policy*. It contains no chapter on human rights.

20. For background on Brickerism see Vernon Van Dyke, *Human Rights, the United States, and World Community*.

21. See, for example, Susan Welch, "American Public Opinion: Consensus, Cleavage, and Constraint."

22. For a supporting argument see Stanley Hoffmann, *Duties beyond Borders*, chap. 3. For an opposing view, provocative but unpersuasive, see Richard E. Feinberg, *The Intemperate Zone*.

23. David E. Price, "Congressional Committees in the Policy Process."

24. Ibid., 164.

References

Congressional Committees

House. Committee on Banking, Finance and Urban Affairs. *Report 98–178.* 98th Cong., 1st sess., May 16, 1983.

————. *Report 98–981.* 98th Cong., 2d sess., August 10, 1984.

House. Committee on Banking, Finance and Urban Affairs, Subcommittee on Financial Institutions. *South African Restrictions.* Hearing, 98th Cong., 1st sess., June 8, 1983.

House. Committee on Banking, Finance and Urban Affairs, Subcommittee on International Development Institutions and Finance. *Human Rights and U.S. Policy in the Multilateral Development Banks.* Hearing, 97th Cong., 1st sess., July 21, 23, 1981.

————. *Inter-American Development Bank Loans to Guatemala.* Hearings, 97th Cong., 1st sess., December 8, 1981, August 5, 1982.

————, and Committee on Foreign Affairs, Subcommittee on Africa. *Human Rights Policies at the Multilateral Development Banks.* Hearing, 98th Cong., 1st sess., June 22, 1983.

House. Committee on Banking, Finance, and Urban Affairs, Subcommittee on International Trade. *Eximbank Reauthorization.* Hearings, 98th Cong., 1st sess., April 8, 18, 19, 20, 1983.

House. Committee on Foreign Affairs. *Human Rights Documents.* September 1983. Committee Print.

————. *U.S. Educational Assistance in South Africa: Critical Policy Issues.* Report, Staff Study Mission to South Africa, December 30, 1982.

House. Committee on Foreign Affairs, Subcommittees on Europe and the Middle East, on Asian and Pacific Affairs, on Human Rights and International Organizations, and on Africa. *Implementation of Congressionally Mandated Human Rights Provisions.* Vol.2. Hearings, 97th Cong., 1st sess., November 5, 17, December 10, 1981, February 23, March 9, 17, 1982.

House. Committee on Foreign Affairs, Subcommittee on Human Rights and International Organizations. *Foreign Assistance Legislation for Fiscal Year 1982 (Part 6).* Hearings and markup. 97th Cong., 1st sess., 1981.

————. *Human Rights in Cuba.* Hearings, 98th Cong., 2d sess., June 27, 1984.

————. *Human Rights in Cyprus, Greece, and Turkey.* Hearing, 98th Cong., 1st sess., April 14, 1983.

———. *Human Rights in Haiti*. Hearing, 99th Cong., 1st sess., April 17, 1985.

———. *Human Rights in Nicaragua*. Hearings, 98th Cong., 1st sess., September 15, 1983.

———. *Review of State Department Country Reports on Human Rights Practices for 1981*. Hearing, 97th Cong., 2d sess., April 28, 1982.

———. *Review of U.S. Human Rights Policy*. Hearings, 98th Cong., 1st sess., March 3, June 28, September 21, 1983.

House. Committee on Foreign Affairs, Subcommittees on Human Rights and International Organization and on Inter-American Affairs. *Human Rights in Guatemala*. Hearing, 97th Cong., 1st sess., July 30, 1981.

House. Committee on Foreign Affairs, Subcommittees on Human Rights and International Organization and on International Operations. *U.S. Withdrawal from UNESCO*. Hearings, 98th Cong., 2d sess., April 25, 26, May 2, 1984.

House. Committee on Foreign Affairs, Subcommittees on Human Rights and International Organization and on Western Hemisphere Affairs. *Human Rights in Argentina, Chile, Paraguay, and Uruguay*. Hearings, 98th Cong., 1st sess., October 4, 21, 1983.

———. *Human Rights in El Salvador*. Hearings, 98th Cong., 1st sess., July 26, 1983.

House. Committee on Foreign Affairs, Subcommittee on Inter-American Affairs. *U.S. Policy toward El Salvador*. Hearings, 97th Cong., 1st sess., March 5, 11, 1981.

House. Committee on Foreign Affairs, Subcommittees on International Economic Policy and Trade and on Africa. *Controls on Exports to South Africa*. Hearings, 97th Cong., 2d sess., February 9, December 2, 1982.

———. *U.S. Corporate Activities in South Africa*. Hearings and markup, 97th Cong., September 24, October 15, 22, 1981, May 18, June 10, 1982.

House. Committee on Foreign Affairs, Subcommittees on International Economic Policy and Trade and on Inter-American Affairs. *U.S. Economic Sanctions against Chile*. Hearing, 97th Cong., 1st sess., March 10, 1981.

House. Committee on Foreign Affairs, Subcommittee on International Organizations and Movements. *Human Rights in the World Community: A Call for U.S. Leadership*. Report, 93d Cong., 2d sess., March 27, 1974.

———, and Subcommittee on Asian and Pacific Affairs. *Human Rights in Asia: Non-Communist Countries*. Hearing, 96th Cong., 2d sess., February 4, 6, 7, 1980.

House. Committee on International Relations. *Human Rights Practices in Countries Receiving U.S. Security Assistance*. Report, 95th Cong., 1st sess., April 25, 1977.

——— Subcommittees on International Operations and on International Organizations and Movements. *Institute for Human Rights and Freedom*. Hearings and markup, 95th Cong., 2d sess., 1978.

House. Committee on International Relations, Subcommittee on International Organizations and Movements. *Human Rights in Argentina*. Hearings, 94th Cong., 2d sess., September 28, 29, 1976.

———, prepared by the Congressional Research Service. *Human Rights in the International Community and in U.S. Foreign Policy, 1945–76*. 95th Cong., 1st sess., July 24, 1977. Committee Print.

House. Judiciary Committee. *Refugee Admissions and Resettlement Program*. Hearing, 96th Cong., 2d sess., September 24, 1980, Serial No. 48.

House. Judiciary Committee, Subcommittee on Immigration. *Carribbean Migration.* Hearing, 96th Cong., 2d sess., May, June, 1980, Serial No. 84.

————. *U.S. Refugee Program.* Hearing, 97th Cong., 1st sess., September 16, 17, 23, 1981, Serial No. 23.

House. Ways and Means Committee. *Most-Favored-Nation Status for Romania, Hungary and China.* Hearing, July 12, 1982, Serial No. 97–78.

House and Senate. Committees on Foreign Affairs and on Foreign Relations. *Legislation on Foreign Relations through 1983.* Vol. 1. February 1984. Joint Committee Print.

————. *Legislation on Foreign Relations through 1986.* Vols. 1 and 2. March 1987. Joint Committee Print.

House and Senate. Committees on the Judiciary, Select Commission on Immigration and Refugee Policy. *U.S. Immigration Policy and the National Interest.* Final Report. 97th Cong., 1st sess., August 1981.

House and Senate. Committees on the Judiciary, Subcommittees on Immigration. *Administration's Proposals on Immigration and Refugee Policy.* Joint hearing, 97th Cong., 1st sess., July 30, 1981.

————. *Immigration and Reform Act of 1982.* Joint hearings, 97th Cong., 2d sess., April 1, 20, 1982.

Senate. Committee on Appropriations. *Factors Affecting U.S. Diplomatic and Assistance Relations with Haiti.* Submitted by Sen. Edward D. Brooke. 1977.

Senate. Committee on Banking, Housing and Urban Affairs, Subcommittee on International Finance. *Export-Import Bank Programs and Policies.* Hearings, 97th Cong., 2d sess., September 14, 16, 1982.

Senate. Finance Committee, Subcommittee on International Trade. *Review of the President's Decisions to Renew Most-Favored-Nation Status for Romania, Hungary, and China.* Hearings, 97th Cong., 2d sess., August 10, 1982.

Senate. Committee on Foreign Relations, *Human Rights Issues in United States Relations with Romania and Czechoslovakia.* Staff Report, April 1983.

————. *Nomination of Ernest W. Lefever.* Hearings, 97th Cong., 1st sess., May 18, 19, June 4, 5, 1981.

————. *The Situation in El Salvador.* Hearings, 97th Cong., 1st sess., March 18, April 9, 1981

Senate. Committee on Foreign Relations, Subcommittee on Western Hemisphere Affairs. *Central America.* Hearings, 97th Cong., 1st sess., December 15, 1981, February 1, 1982.

————. *Human Rights in Nicaragua.* Hearings, 97th Cong., 2d sess., February 25, March 1, 1982.

Senate. Judiciary Committee. *U.S. Refugee Programs, 1981.* Hearing, 96th Cong., 2d sess., September 19, 1980.

————, Subcommittee on Immigration. *Asylum Adjudication.* Hearings, 97th Cong., 1st sess., October 14, 16, 1981.

————. *Carribbean Migration.* Hearings, 97th Cong., 1st sess., October 14, 16, 1981.

————. *United States as a Country of Mass First Asylum.* Hearing, 97th Cong., 1st sess., July 1981.

Other Public Agencies

Agency for International Development (AID). *Human Rights.* Policy Determination No. 12. September 26, 1984.

———. *U.S. Overseas Loans and Grants, and Assistance from International Organizations.* CONG-R-0105 [no place or date of publication and no publisher indicated].

Congressional Record, various volumes.

Congressional Research Service. *Human Rights and Foreign Assistance: Experiences and Issues in Policy Implementation (1977–1978).* Report prepared for the Senate Committee on Foreign Relations, November 1979.

Department of State. *Country Reports on Human Rights Practices.* Annual report submitted to the House Committee on Foreign Affairs and the Senate Committee on Foreign Relations. Joint Committee Print.

———. *Current Policy No. 551.* February 22, 1984.

———. *International Security and Development Cooperation Program.* Special Report No. 116, April 1984.

———. *U.S.–Supported Human Rights Program in South Africa. GIST,* February 1986.

———. Bureau of Public Affairs. *Fourth Certification of Progress in El Salvador.* Current Policy No. 501, August 3, 1983.

General Accounting Office. *The Helsinki Commission: The First Eight Years.* Report, Commission on Security and Cooperation in Europe, 99th Cong., 1st sess. 1985.

Haitian Refugee Center v. Civiletti, 503 F. Supp. 442 (S.D. Fla., 1980).

Organization of American States (OAS). *Report on the Situation of Human Rights in the Republic of Guatemala,* October 5, 1983.

Organization for Economic Cooperation and Development (OECD). *External Debt of Developing Countries, 1982 Survey.* Paris: OECD, 1983.

Secondary Sources

Abrams, Elliott. "Keeping Pressure on the Sandinistas." *New York Times,* January 13, 1986, p. 15.

———. "The Myopia of Human Rights Advocates." *New York Times,* August 10, 1984, p. 27.

Albert, Paul. "The Undermining of the Legal Standards for Human Rights Violations in U.S. Foreign Policy: The Case of 'Improvement' in Guatemala." *Columbia Human Rights Law Review* 14, 2 (Fall–Winter 1982–83), 231–74.

Americas Watch, Helsinki Watch, Lawyers' Committee for International Human Rights. *Failure: The Reagan Administration's Human Rights Policy in 1983.* New York: n.p., January 1984.

———. *The Reagan Administration's Human Rights Record in 1984.* New York: January 1985.

Amnesty International. *Annual Report.* London: various dates.

Armstrong, J. D. "Political Prisoners and the Red Cross." *International Organization* 39, 4 (Autumn 1985), 615–42.

Arnold, Hugh. "Henry Kissinger and Human Rights." *Human Rights Quarterly* 2, 4 (Autumn 1980), 51–71.

Art, Robert J. "Congress and the Defense Budget: Enhancing Policy Oversight." *Political Science Quarterly* 100, 2 (Summer 1985), 227–48.

Avery, William P., and Forsythe, David P. "Human Rights, National Security, and the U.S. Senate: Who Votes for What, and Why." *International Studies Quarterly* 23, 2 (June 1979), 303–20.

Bloomfield, Lincoln P. "From Ideology to Program to Policy: Tracking the Carter Human Rights Policy." *Journal of Policy Analysis and Management* 2, 1 (Fall 1982), 1–12.

Bonner, Raymond. "Cover-Up Charged in Death of Nuns." *New York Times,* February 16, 1984, p. 3.

Brown, Peter, and MacLean, Douglas, eds. *Human Rights and U.S. Foreign Policy.* Lexington, MA: Lexington–D.C. Heath, 1979.

Carleton, David, and Stohl, Michael. "The Foreign Policy of Human Rights: Rhetoric and Reality from Jimmy Carter to Ronald Reagan." *Human Rights Quarterly* 7, 2 (May 1985), 205–29.

Cassese, Antonio, ed. *Parliamentary Control over Foreign Policy.* Germantown, MD: Sitjhoff and Noordhoff, 1980.

Cingranelli, David L., and Pasquarello, Thomas E. "Human Rights Practices and the Distribution of U.S. Foreign Aid to Latin American Countries." *American Journal of Political Science* 29, 3 (August 1985), 539–63.

Cohen, Jerome A. "Arms Sales and Human Rights: The Case of South Korea." In Brown and MacLean, eds., q.v., 255–80.

Cohen, Roberta. "Human Rights Decision-Making in the Executive Branch." In Kommers and Loescher, eds., q.v.

Cohen, Stephen B. "Conditioning U.S. Security Assistance on Human Rights Practices." *American Journal of International Law* 76, 2 (April 1982), 246–79.

Congressional Quarterly Almanac. Washington, various years.

Crabb, Cecil V., Jr., and Holt, Pat M. *Invitation to Struggle: Congress, the President and Foreign Policy.* 2d ed. Washington: Congressional Quarterly, 1984.

Destler, I. M. "Congress as Boss?" *Foreign Policy* 42 (Spring 1981), 167–81.

Dodd, Lawrence C. "Congress and the Quest for Power." In Dodd and Oppenheimer, q.v., chap. 14,

Dodd, Lawrence C., and Oppenheimer, Bruce I., eds. *Congress Reconsidered.* 3d ed. New York: Praeger, 1985.

Dominguez, Jorge I., et al. *Enhancing Global Human Rights.* New York: McGraw Hill, for the Council on Foreign Relations, 1979.

Drew, Elizabeth. "Letter from Washington." *New Yorker,* July 7, 1986, 64f.

Easterbrook, Gregg. "What's Wrong with Congress," *Atlantic Monthly,* December 1984, 57f.

Fagen, Patricia Weiss. "U.S. Foreign Policy and Human Rights—The Role of Congress." In Cassese, ed., q.v., 111–36.

Farer, Tom J. "Human Rights and Human Welfare in Latin America." *Daedalus* (Fall 1983), 139–70.

Feinberg, Richard E. *The Intemperate Zone*. New York: Norton, 1983.

Ferris, Elizabeth G. *Refugees and World Politics*. New York: Praeger, 1985.

Foreign Affairs. "America and the World." Annual, various dates.

Forsythe, David P. "American Foreign Policy and Human Rights: Rhetoric and Reality." *Universal Human Rights* 2, 3 (July–September 1980), 35–54.

———. *Humanitarian Politics: The International Committee of the Red Cross*. Baltimore: Johns Hopkins University Press, 1977.

———. *Human Rights and World Politics*. Lincoln: University of Nebraska Press, 1983.

———. "Political Prisoners: The Law and Politics of Protection." *Vanderbilt Journal of Transnational Law* 9, 2 (Spring 1976), 295–322.

———. "Socioeconomic Human Rights: The United Nations, the United States, and Beyond." *Human Rights Quarterly* 4, 4 (Fall 1982), 433–49.

———. ed. *American Foreign Policy in an Uncertain World*. Lincoln: University of Nebraska Press, 1984.

Forsythe, David P., and Welch, Susan. "Human Rights Voting in Congress." *Policy Studies Journal* 15, 1 (September 1986), 173–88.

Franck, Thomas M. "Constitutional Practice until Vietnam." In Soper, q.v., 15–24.

Franck, Thomas M., and Weisband, Edward. *Foreign Policy by Congress*. New York: Oxford University Press, 1979.

Franklin, Ben A. "Democracy Project Facing New Criticisms." *New York Times*, December 4, 1985, p. 28.

Fraser, Donald M. "Congress's Role in the Making of International Human Rights Policy." In Kommers and Loescher, q.v., 247–55.

———. "Freedom and Foreign Policy." *Foreign Policy* 26 (Spring 1977), 140–56.

———. "Human Rights and the United States Foreign Policy: The Congressional Perspective." In Tuttle, ed., q.v. Reprinted in Barry M. Rubin and Elizabeth P. Spiro, eds., q.v., 95–108.

———. "Human Rights and U.S. Foreign Policy: Some Basic Questions Regarding Principles and Practice." *International Studies Quarterly* 23, 3 (1979), 174–85.

Fraser, Donald M., and Salzberg, John. "Foreign Policy and Effective Strategies for Human Rights." *Universal Human Rights* 1, 1 (1979), 11–18.

Galey, Margaret E. "Congress, Foreign Policy and Human Rights Ten Years after Helsinki." *Human Rights Quarterly* 7, 3 (August 1985), 334–72.

Gastil, Raymond D., ed. *Freedom in the World: Political Rights and Civil Liberties*. Westport, CT: Greenwood Press, annual.

Gunter, Jonathan F. "The United States and the Debate on the World 'Information Order'." Report for the Academy for Educational Development, Inc., funded by the U.S. International Communication Agency and the Ford Foundation, Washington: ICA, 1979.

Haig, Alexander. *Caveat: Realism, Reagan, and Foreign Policy*. New York: Macmillan, 1984.

Hatfield, Mark O. "Aid Guatemala Doesn't Need." *New York Times*, January 18, 1986, p. 20.

Heaps, David. *Human Rights and U.S. Foreign Policy: The First Decade 1973–1983.* For the American Association for the International Commission of Jurists, No place or source of publication: 1984.

Hevener, Natalie Kaufman, ed. *The Dynamics of Human Rights in U.S. Foreign Policy.* New Brunswick, NJ: Transaction Books, 1981.

"Hill Fights Reagan for Soul of Foreign Policy." *Washington Post,* September 2, 1984, p. A1–f.

Hirschman, Albert O. "The Search for Paradigms as a Hindrance to Understanding." *World Politics* 22, 3 (April 1970), 329–44.

Hoffmann, Stanley. *Duties beyond Borders.* Syracuse, NY: Syracuse University Press, 1981.

Innes de Neufville, Judith. "Human Rights Reporting as a Policy Tool: An Examination of the State Department Country Reports." Paper prepared for the Human Rights and Statistics Project of the American Association for the Advancement of Science, Philadelphia, May 1986.

International Committee on the Red Cross (ICRC). *Annual Report.* Geneva: ICRC, various years.

Jacoby, Tamar. "Reagan's Turnaround on Human Rights." *Foreign Affairs* 64, 5 (Summer 1986), 1066–86.

Jewell, Malcolm E., and Patterson, Samuel C. *The Legislative Process in the United States.* 3d ed. New York: Random House, 1977.

Johansen, Robert C. *The National Interest and Human Interest: An Analysis of U.S. Foreign Policy.* Princeton: Princeton University Press, 1980.

Kirkpatrick, Jeane. "Dictatorships and Double Standards." *Commentary,* November 1979, 34–45.

Kissinger, Henry. "Continuity and Change in American Foreign Policy." In Said, ed., q.v.

Kommers, Donald P., and Loescher, Gilburt D. *Human Rights and American Foreign Policy.* Notre Dame: University of Notre Dame Press, 1979.

Korey, William. "Human Rights and the Helsinki Accord." *Headline Series.* New York: Foreign Policy Association, 1983.

Kramer, Daniel C. "International Human Rights." In Yarbrough, ed., q.v., 230–55.

Lansing, Paul, and Rose, Eric C. "The Granting and Suspension of Most-Favored-Nation Status for Nonmarket Economy States: Policy and Consequences." *Harvard Journal of International Law* 25, 2 (Spring 1984), 329–54.

Leape, Jonathan, et al., *Business in the Shadow of Apartheid: U.S. Firms in South Africa.* Lexington, MA: Lexington Books, 1985.

Lefever, Ernest W. "The Trivialization of Human Rights." *Policy Review* (Winter 1978), 11–26.

Leibowitz, Arnold H. "The Refugee Act of 1980: Problems and Congressional Concerns." In *The Annals* (May 1983), "The Global Refugee Problem: U.S. and World Response," 163–71.

LeoGrande, William. "Central America: U.S. Hegemony in Decline." In Forsythe, ed., q.v., 369–91.

Lillich, Richard B. "The Contribution of the United States to the Promotion and Protection of International Human Rights." In Hevener, ed., q.v., 291–320.

————. *International Human Rights Instruments*. Buffalo: William S. Hein Co., 1983.

————. "The Role of Domestic Courts in Promoting International Human Rights Norms." *New York Law School Law Review* 24, 1 (1978), 153–77.

McGrory, Mary. "U.S. Stiffens Chile Policy." Syndicated column, March 16, 1986.

McMahon, Michael S. "Comment: The Jackson-Vanik Amendment to the Trade Act of 1974: An Assessment after Five Years." *Columbia Journal of Transnational Law* 18, 3 (1980), 525–56.

Madison, Christopher. "Foreign Policy: Human Rights—Again." *National Journal* 18 (May 1, 1982), 763–66.

Maechling, Charles, Jr. "The Argentina Pariah." *Foreign Policy* 45 (Winter 1981–82), 69–83.

————. "Human Rights Dehumanized." *Foreign Policy* 52 (Fall 1983), 118–35.

Martin, David A. "The Refugee Act of 1980: Its Past and Future." *1982 Michigan Yearbook of International Legal Studies* (Ann Arbor), 91–123.

Mendez, Juan E. "Reagan's Argentines." *New York Times*, December 22, 1982, p. 31.

Muravchik, Joshua. "Endowing Democracy." *New York Times*, June 18, 1984, p. 23.

————. *The Uncertain Crusade: Jimmy Carter and the Dilemmas of Human Rights Policy*. Lanthan, MD: Hamilton Press, 1986.

Nash, Richard B., Jr. "Certifying Human Rights: Military Assistance to El Salvador and the International Security and Development Cooperation Act of 1981." *Columbia Human Rights Law Review* 14, 2 (Fall–Winter 1982–83), 275–310.

Neier, Aryeh. "Flimflam on Central America." *New York Times*, December 14, 1985, 15.

Nurnberger, Ralph D. "The United States and Idi Amin: Congress to the Rescue." *African Studies Review* 25, 1 (March 1982), 49–65.

Ogul, Morris S. *Congress Oversees the Bureaucracy: Studies in Legislative Supervision*. Pittsburgh: University of Pittsburgh Press, 1976.

Price, David E. "Congressional Committees in the Policy Process." In Dodd and Oppenheimer, eds., q.v., 161–88.

Purvis, Hoyt, and Baker, Steven J. *Legislating Foreign Policy*. Boulder, CO: Westview, 1984.

"Q & A: Senator Dan Quayle: Turning the Senate Away from Trivial Pursuits." *New York Times*, September 21, 1984, p. 14.

Rawles, James P. "The United States, Nicaragua, and the World Court." Paper prepared for the annual meeting of the International Studies Association, Anaheim, CA, 1986.

Riding, Alan. "The Central American Quagmire." *Foreign Affairs*, "America and the World 1982," 61, 3 (1983), 641–59.

Rossiter, Caleb. "Human Rights: The Carter Record, the Reagan Reaction." *International Report*. Washington: Center for International Policy, September 1984.

Rubin, Barry M., and Spiro, Elizabeth P., eds. *Human Rights and U.S. Foreign Policy*. Boulder, CO: Westview Press, 1979.

Said, Abduh Aziz, ed. *Human Rights and World Order*. New Brunswick, NJ: Transaction Books, 1978.

Salzberg, John, and Young, Donald D. "The Parliamentary Role in Implementing International Human Rights: A U.S. Example." *Texas International Law Journal* 12, 2–3 (Spring/Summer 1977), 251–78.

Schlesinger, Arthur, Jr. "Failings of the Kissinger Report." *New York Times*, January 17, 1984, p. 19.

Schmidt, Elizabeth. *Decoding Corporate Camouflage: U.S. Business Support for Apartheid*. Washington: Institute for Policy Studies, 1980.

———. "Impose Tough Sanctions on South Africa," *New York Times*, January 17, 1986, p. 23.

Schoultz, Lars. *Human Rights and United States Policy toward Latin America*. Princeton: Princeton University Press, 1981.

Sewell, John W., et al. *U.S. Foreign Policy and the Third World: Agenda 1985–86*. New Brunswick, NJ: Transaction Books, for the Overseas Development Council, 1985.

Sigmund, Paul E. "Latin America: Change or Continuity." *Foreign Affairs, America and the World, 1981*, 60, 3 (1982), 629–58.

Simons, Marlise. "Guatemala: The Coming Danger." *Foreign Policy* 43 (Summer 1981), 93–103.

Solarz, Stephen J. "The Case for Congressional Activism." In Soper, ed., q.v., 37–42.

Soper, Steven P., ed. *Congress, the President, and Foreign Policy*. Washington: ABA, 1984.

Timerman, Jacobo. *Prisoner Without a Name, Cell Without a Number*. New York: Alfred A. Knopf, 1981.

Tower, John G. "The Case against Congressional Activism." In Soper, ed., q.v., 107–12.

Treaster, Joseph B. "Human Rights in Haiti: A Promise Unfulfilled." *New York Times*, September 29, 1984, pp. 1, 5.

Tuttle, James C., ed. *International Human Rights Law and Practice*. Philadelphia: ABA, 1978.

Ullman, Richard. "At War with Nicaragua." *Foreign Affairs* 62, 1 (Fall 1983), 39–58.

"U.S. Official Charges 'Apologists' Are Ignoring Cuba's Human Rights Abuses." *Washington Post*, August 24, 1984, p. A-3.

Vance, Cyrus. "The Human Rights Imperative." *Foreign Policy* 63 (Summer 1986), 3–19.

———. "Human Rights and Foreign Policy." *Georgia Journal of International and Comparative Law* 7, supplement (Summer 1977), 223–29.

Van Dyke, Vernon. *Human Rights, the United States, and World Community*. New York: Oxford University Press, 1970.

Vogelgesang, Sandra. *American Dream, Global Nightmare: The Dilemma of U.S. Human Rights Policy*. New York: Norton, 1980.

Weisbert, Herbert. "Evaluating Theories of Roll Call Voting." *American Journal of Political Science* 22, 3 (August 1978), 554–77.

Weissbrodt, David. "Human Rights Legislation and U.S. Foreign Policy." *Georgia Journal of International and Comparative Law* 7, 2 (Summer 1977): 231–87.

Welch, Susan. "American Public Opinion: Consensus, Cleavage, and Constraint." In Forsythe, ed., q.v., 21–48.

Yarbrough, Tinsley E., ed. *The Reagan Administration and Human Rights*. New York: Praeger, 1985.

Zucker, Naomi Flink. "The Haitians versus the United States: The Courts as Last Resort." In *The Annals* (May 1983), "The Global Refugee Problem: U.S. and World Response," 151–62.

☆

Index